With Best Regards,
George Gist

Federal Justice in Indiana

The History of the United States District Court for the Southern District of Indiana

Federal Justice in Indiana

The History of the United States
District Court for the
Southern District of Indiana

George W. Geib and Donald B. Kite Sr.

Published by the Indiana Historical Society Press in
Cooperation with the District Court Library Fund of the United
States District Court for the Southern District of Indiana

INDIANAPOLIS 2007

© 2007 Indiana Historical Society Press. All rights reserved.

Printed in the United States of America

This book is a publication of the
Indiana Historical Society Press
450 West Ohio Street
Indianapolis, Indiana 46202-3269 USA

www.indianahistory.org

Telephone orders 1-800-447-1830
Fax orders 1-317-234-0562
Ordrs by e-mail shop.indianahistory.org

The paper in this publication meets the minimum requirements of American National Standard for Information Sciences—Permanence of Paper for Printed Library Materials, ANSI Z39.48-1984.

Library of Congress Cataloging-in-Publication Data

Geib, George W.
    Federal justice in Indiana : the history of the United States District Court for the Southern District of Indiana / published by the Indiana Historical Society Press in cooperation with the District Court Library Fund of the United States District Court for the Southern District of Indiana.
    p. cm.
    Includes bibliographical references and index.
    ISBN-13: 978-0-87195-202-8 (cloth) 1. United States. District Court (Indiana : Southern District)—History. 2. District courts—Indiana—History. I. Kite, Donald B. II. Title.
    KF8755.I6G45 2007
    347.73'2209772—dc22

2006038515

No part of this publication may be reproduced, stored in or introduced into a retrieval system, or transmitted, in any form or by any means (electronic, mechanical, photocopying, recording, or otherwise), without the prior written permission of the copyright owner.

*To our wives, Miriam and Grace,
and to our families,
for their support through the years*

CONTENTS

Foreword ix

Preface xv

CHAPTER ONE
The Origins of the Court, 1787–1862 1

CHAPTER TWO
The District Court in Civil War and
Political Conflict, 1862–1902 51

CHAPTER THREE
Creating the Southern District, 1902–1950 107

CHAPTER FOUR
A Multi-Judge Court Develops, 1950–1979 159

CHAPTER FIVE
The Modern Court Develops, 1979–2005 211

Notes 273

Glossary 317

Index 321

Foreword

THIS IS THE FIRST, OFFICIAL COMPILATION OF THE history of the United States District Court for the Southern District of Indiana. Its publication places it among various other, similarly useful, volumes produced by other courts in recent years in an effort to provide a thorough, accurate, interesting, and, in no small way, inspirational account of the jurists into whose hands, for more than two centuries, has been placed the task of delivering on the promise of justice under law in this great, growing, and ever-changing democracy.

For the segment of Americans who call themselves Hoosiers, these pages hold special appeal as a record of many of the remarkably important and far-reaching cases and controversies that have characterized this court's busy docket and the resolutions for which have been meted out by an impressive succession of wise and dedicated judges, assisted by able court staff, in response to the requests of eager, hopeful litigants being served by creative, knowledgeable, and devoted lawyers. This interplay among bench and bar in the ongoing, symbiotic effort to balance the legal interests of business, finance, education, medicine, science, culture, and religion, as well as those between government and its citizens, has shaped, in real and often remarkable ways, the development and progress of our state, indeed, of our country.

The act of preserving and honoring history lies at the very heart of the law and the legal profession. To know, to attempt to understand, and to follow the teachings of history is, in fact, the quintessential task of lawyering. As Indiana's Chief Justice, Randall T. Shepard, has written, "The whole [legal] profession operates in substantial part . . . on the basis of history," by the way in which it approaches modern-day legal problems based on how those issues have been resolved in the past and in applying the rule of precedent. Today's judges and lawyers are well advised first to try to ascertain and then to draw upon the "judgment, wisdom, and experience of those who went before us as leaders in the system of justice."[1] In compiling this particular record, the authors not only marshal such judgment, wisdom, and experience, but they also underscore the important ways in which one, single, but nonetheless significant part of the Third Branch of the federal government has drawn on these values and, in so doing, provide a lens through which the larger story is revealed of how all courts contribute to reinforcing the rule of law and thereby provide for order, stability, and justice for all.

These pages are chock-full of things fun to read and well worth knowing. Starting at the very beginning, for example, is the interesting account of the court's formative years. Born out of the Northwest and Indiana territorial courts that had, by then, been functioning for nearly thirty years, the district of Indiana was brought to life during a "quiet, dignified" session held in the state capitol at Corydon, on May 5, 1817, pursuant to an act of Congress authorizing its creation. President James Monroe appointed Benjamin Parke to serve as the first judge of this district, and Parke took his oath of office that same day. Soon thereafter, five attorneys were admitted to practice before the court. Not until 1837, the authors inform us, did Congress officially separate the Indiana District Court from the United States Circuit Court, which was comprised of the judge of the district court and the member of the United States Supreme Court who was assigned to the Indiana district.

Having read this account in these pages, it was an unexpected pleasure to discover soon thereafter, in the published letters and diaries of one of Indiana's earliest lawyers, Calvin Fletcher, a reference to the newly created circuit court. The following excerpt is Fletcher's account of his interactions as a lawyer and member of the bar with the circuit court during the week beginning Monday, December 4, through Friday, December 8, 1837:[2]

> Monday Decr. 4. This day the Circuit Court of the U. States set for the first time in this state before which we have 23 or 24 cases. Judge McClean [Justice McLean of the U.S. Supreme Court] organized the same with [Judge] Holman the District Judge of the U.S. The court went thro the docket & adopted a rule admitting all the attorneys that practise [sic] in the Sp. [Supreme] Court of this state.

Teusday Decr. 5 1837. Pleasant day. Our court [met]. We went thro'with our cases in C[ircuit] Court U.S. I am asked to spend the eve at Mr. Blakes with Judges McClean Blackford [judge of the Indiana Supreme Court] Porter &c. Where I met them after dark. Judge McClean related some anecdotes as to his first service in Congress. Stated that a well regulated U. States Bank would prove a blessing to the country & if the late U. S. B[ank] had been in existence the late suspension would have not take place &c. Holman was mute on the subject.

Wednesday [Dec.] 6. Pleasant day. Judges McClean Holman Dewey Blackford & Wick & Marshall Taylor dined with us.

Thursday [Dec.] 7. Pleasant. This is our first Thanksgiving ever held by proclamation of the Governor. U. S. Court met read the minutes—adjourned. Divine service at M.E.C. Mr. Edy preached.

Friday [Dec.] 8. Judge McClean left & we finished nearly all our buseness [sic] in U.S. C[ourt]. Pleasant day.

"Pleasant day," indeed, which, in time, turned into "pleasant year," followed by "pleasant decade" and "pleasant century" and finally, now, to "pleasant era," all through the magical re-tellings of history—our history!

The compiling and writing of this particular volume of "our history" has occurred in conjunction with the 2003 centennial observance of the United States District Court courthouse at Indianapolis, in honor of the magnificent edifice that continues to serve as the flagship of the federal judiciary in the southern district of Indiana. The five currently serving federal district court judges, whose privilege it is to call this special place our judicial home and to assume our own places in the long line of our distinguished judicial forebears, are acutely mindful of the legacy entrusted to us and stand firmly committed to fulfilling the obligation that is ours to treasure and to pass on to future generations. Surrounded daily by the grand and beautiful reminders of our historical origins and steeped in the stories and lore of the past, our terms of service as judges—indeed, our very lives—have been enriched beyond measure by the influence of this history.

President Franklin D. Roosevelt stated in remarks made at the dedication of his library on June 30, 1941: "To bring together the records of the past and to house them in buildings where they will be preserved for the use of men and women in the future, a Nation must believe in three things: It must believe in the past. It must believe in the future. It must, above all, believe in the capacity of its own people so to learn from the past that they can gain in judgment in creating their own future."

In overseeing the publication of this volume, those of us who on behalf of our generation have been privileged to serve as judges of the United States District Court for the Southern District of Indiana embrace these noble beliefs as highlighted by Roosevelt—a belief in the past, in the future, and in the capacity of our fellow citizens to build a future on the knowledge of our shared past. We embrace them, we reaffirm them, and we hold them dear, in trust for all those who some day will follow in our paths and in turn assume this august responsibility.

Sarah Evans Barker, Judge
2006

Preface

A STUDY OF A COURT IS OFTEN PRESENTED AS PART of a celebration, and there is much to celebrate in the history of the United States District Court for the Southern District of Indiana. More than two centuries of the rule of law in Indiana, and in the United States, stands in favorable contrast to so many less desirable alternatives that have troubled other lands for shorter or longer periods of time.

This study is not, however, grounded in celebration. Instead, it is based in history: in a desire to describe, explain, and evaluate the work of one of America's busiest federal tribunals (which in 2004 ranked fourth among its counterparts in weighted cases). This history was prepared in cooperation with the Historical Society of the United States District Court for the Southern District of Indiana. It arose from a proposal by the Society's Steering Committee that an effort be made to preserve and document the court's rich history, which proposal also led to the Historical Society's decision to sponsor both a symposium and a gala commemorating the district court's centennial and history. The Southern District of Indiana's Historical Society, which was formed by Judge Sarah Evans Barker in 1994, has accomplished a great deal since it came into existence, and the Society will no doubt accomplish a great deal in the years to come.

Anyone who works with the court quickly discovers that its participants see themselves as members of a "court family." It's a family whose membership extends to include not only judges and magistrate judges but also all of the officers, agents, staff, and attorneys who contribute to its activities and the court's fulfillment of its duties. Each of these individuals, past and present, is an essential part of the court's collective, institutional biography.

Anyone who studies American law equally quickly discovers how wide ranging the study of a court's history can be. Its history surely includes its organizational structure and no doubt the physical structures within which it has functioned. Its history also includes the history of the cases, small as well as great, that have come before the court. These cases, in turn, direct our attention to the constitutional basis of the court's authority and to the contexts of statutes, case law, administration, politics, and public response that have contributed to the dynamism, and sometimes the complexity, of its actions.

The press of cases necessarily imposed the need for selection upon us. Those who desire to find the complete record of the court's decisions will find an outstanding electronic resource in Westlaw. The cases here were chosen for their significance in the development of American law, for their importance in the growth and development of Indiana, for their ability to define the ideas and values of the judges and the court family, and, often, for their interest value.

This book is intended to be an introduction, a description, and an assessment of the court. All of the court's serving judges, and many other members of the court family, have provided interviews, documents, and constructive suggestions. The overall vision is ours, however, and the opinions here are our considered judgment of the court's record.

We are particularly indebted to the late S. Hugh Dillin, senior district judge, and to current district judges Sarah Evans Barker, Larry J. McKinney, John D. Tinder, David F. Hamilton, and Richard L. Young for contributing their time, which is certainly precious given the press of the cases that come before the court on a daily basis, and permitting us access to other resources while we went about the process of attempting to document the court's history. We also thank the court's magistrate judges, particularly magistrate judge V. Sue Shields, for their assistance. We also appreciate the efforts of District Court Clerk of Court Laura Briggs, former District Court (and present Bankruptcy Court) Clerk of Court John O'Neal, and Law Clerk Perry Secrest. Secrest and Briggs deserve our special thanks for their many contributions throughout the process of our working on the history of the court. Briggs's careful supervision of various aspects of the court history project deserves special mention and acknowledgment.

We also wish to thank former United States Congressman Andy Jacobs, Northern District of Indiana District Judge Allen Sharp, Indiana Supreme Court Chief Justice Randall Shepard, Cass County Circuit Judge Julian Ridlin, and attorney Rabb Emison, each for their thoughtful review of the manuscript. We also appreciate Ball State University

Professor Andrew Seager for providing to us his study of divisional courthouses and attorney Sally F. Zweig, of the Indianapolis law firm Katz & Korin, PC, for permitting us access to her collection of articles pertaining to the Cypriot mosaics case.

We would also like to acknowledge our debt to the late William E. Steckler, senior district judge, who during Don Kite's clerkship permitted Kite unlimited access to the archival materials that Steckler had collected and retained during his nearly forty-five years on the bench; Darrol Pierson, Newspaper Section of the Indiana State Library, for his able assistance; the staff of the Indiana Historical Society's William Henry Smith Memorial Library, especially Alexandra Gressitt, former curator of manuscripts and archives; Douglas E. Clanin, former editor at the Indiana Historical Society Press; Saundra Taylor and Heather Munro of Indiana University's Lilly Library (Bloomington); Mary Ellis Medlicott, Franklin College archivist; Johanna Herring, Wabash College archivist; Dennis Covenor, Hanover College archivist; Christine H. Guyonneau, reference librarian at the University of Indianapolis; Barbara Carver, assistant director, Vigo County Historical Society; Martha Murphy, National Archives reference archivist; Fred Bauman, manuscript reference librarian, and Katie McDonough, microfilm reading room, both of the Library of Congress; and Cynthia Harrison, former director; and Peter Wonders, research associate of the Federal Justice History Offices, for their significant assistance. We also wish to express our appreciation to the descendants of many of Indiana's former district judges for their willingness to share letters, photographs, and various other family heirlooms. Finally, we are grateful to have had the experience of working with the Indiana Historical Society Press, especially Thomas A. Mason, vice president; Paula Corpuz, senior editor;

Ray Boomhower, managing editor; Kathy Breen, editor; and Rachel Popma, assistant editor.

The most important years of the district court are, of course, the ones still to come. It is our hope that this study will encourage others to join in researching, reporting, and reflecting upon the history of this important Hoosier institution.

George Geib and Don Kite, July 2006

CHAPTER ONE

The Origins of the Court

1787–1862

IN 1800 THE U.S. CONGRESS DIVIDED THE NORTHWEST Territory into two parts, named the western portion Indiana Territory, and provided it with a separate government. On March 3, 1801, Indiana's new territorial court convened at Vincennes. Entering the courtroom in a simple procession were the territorial governor, William Henry Harrison, and the three territorial judges, William Clark, John Griffin, and Henry Vanderburgh. Joining them in the audience were leading Vincennes citizens, their presence later commemorated in a 1930s mural in the Knox County Courthouse. The court affirmed its authority in federal law and called its first grand jury of nineteen members, with names such as Andrew Montplaiseur, François Turpin, Fr. Languedoc, and Charles Compagnoitte, that affirmed the French colonial origins of the new territorial capital. The first federal court specifically designated for Indiana was now organized.[1]

The Great Charters

The modern U.S. District Court for the Southern District of Indiana thus originated as a territorial court on the frontier rim of the early American republic. Its authority rested upon two fundamental documents, the U.S. Constitution and the Northwest Ordinance, each of which was written in an Atlantic seacoast city in the summer of 1787. The former document was drafted by the Constitutional Convention in Philadelphia, the latter by the Confederation Congress in New York. The Constitution provided the fundamental authority for both territorial and later district courts. The Ordinance contributed the structures and procedures by which the lands north and west of the Ohio River, including Indiana, would proceed to statehood and thus be incorporated in the federal court system.

Legal historians owe a great debt to James Madison, whose detailed notes of the Constitutional Convention's sessions, and whose articulate vision of checks and balances, permeate discourse on the Constitution. His notes reveal that the concepts and language that emerged in article 3, which of course relates to the judiciary, were the product of discussion by several delegates, including James Wilson, Roger Sherman, and Benjamin Franklin. Their words reflected the common acceptance by the Philadelphia delegates of the need for a separate judiciary, a practice well known from English and colonial precedent. Discussed in early June 1787, the notion of a separate judiciary evoked little comment beyond a

Indiana Territory Capitol in Vincennes

discussion of the best appointive process.[2] Article 3, which defined the judicial branch, incorporated judicial tenure and jurisdiction. Section 1 stated:

> The judicial Power of the United States, shall be vested in one supreme Court, and in such inferior Courts as the Congress may from time to time ordain and establish. The Judges, both of the supreme and inferior Courts, shall hold their Offices during good Behaviour, and shall, at stated Times, receive for their Services, a Compensation, which shall not be diminished during their Continuance in Office.

Section 2 added:

> The judicial Power shall extend to all Cases, in Law and Equity, arising under this Constitution, the Laws of the United States, and Treaties made, or which shall be made, under their Authority;—to all Cases affecting Ambassadors, other public Ministers and Consuls;—to all Cases of admiralty and maritime Jurisdiction;—to Controversies to which the United States shall be a Party;—to Controversies between two or more States;—between a State and Citizens of another State;—between Citizens of different States,—between Citizens of the same State claiming Lands under Grants of different States, and between a State, or the Citizens thereof, and foreign States, Citizens or Subjects.... The Trial of all Crimes, except in Cases of Impeachment, shall be by Jury; and such Trial shall be held in the State where the said Crimes shall have been committed; but when not committed within any State, the Trial shall be at such Place or Places as the Congress may by Law have directed.

Where article 3 laid the foundation for the creation of district courts after statehood, article 4, section 3, addressed territorial government. Madison's notes reveal a continuing debate among most of the outspoken delegates at the convention. A substantial number articulated a fear of western growth. They argued that the trans-Appalachian West lacked both social and institutional discipline and posed a threat to public order that had to be restrained by some forms of eastern control. As the West grew in population, these delegates continued, it could overwhelm eastern control by sheer numbers if not by popular violence. A slightly larger number of Philadelphia delegates countered with a vision of American expansion that would enhance American power while avoiding the repressive errors of British colonial rule. They argued that orderly processes of territorial development could provide institutional and social controls while qualifying the West to join the union on a basis of ultimate equality with the East.[3]

The latter group of delegates narrowly won out. The Constitution stated in article 4, section 3:

> New States may be admitted by the Congress into this Union; but no new State shall be formed or erected within the Jurisdiction of any other State; nor any State be formed by the Junction of two or more States, or Parts of States, without the Consent of the Legislatures of the States concerned as well as of the Congress.... The Congress shall have Power to dispose of and make all needful Rules and Regulations respecting the Territory or other Property belonging to the United States.

Interestingly, given the vehemence of the debate, details of territorial jurisdiction in the Constitution are quite sparse. Many commentators have suggested this probably reflected the knowledge on the part of the founders that the Confederation Congress, operating under the authority of the Articles of Confederation, was already crafting a detailed model for phased and orderly western growth.[4]

The Northwest Ordinance, adopted July 13, 1787, and confirmed by the new Congress with minor changes on August 7, 1789,[5] provided for a phased transition from territorial status to statehood. These territories were similar in many ways to colonies, but unlike colonies ruled from England, they could look forward to future statehood on an equal footing with the original thirteen states. In fourteen sections and six articles, the Ordinance provided for the eventual creation of three to five new states, outlined three phases of government that provided progressively greater power to an elected legislature, and offered guarantees of a variety of liberties to present and future settlers of the area bounded by the Ohio River, Pennsylvania, the Great Lakes (except where Connecticut's Western Reserve ran along Lake Erie), and the Mississippi River. These generous boundaries masked the fact that most early settlers, immigrants from Kentucky, New England, and such middle states as Pennsylvania and New Jersey, actually lived along the Ohio River from Marietta to Cincinnati, Ohio.[6]

As part of all phases of territorial government, the Ordinance provided:

> There shall also be appointed a court to consist of three judges any two of whom to form a court, who shall have a common law jurisdiction . . . and their commissions shall continue in force during good behaviour.[7]

The territorial judges' authority showed obvious similarities to earlier English colonial judges. In addition to their judicial functions they enjoyed executive power, as councillors of the governor, and, initially, legislative power as well. Specifically, the Ordinance provided:

> The governor, and judges or a majority of them shall adopt and publish in the district such laws of the original states criminal and civil as may be necessary and best suited to the circumstances of the district . . . which laws shall be in force in the district until the organization of the general assembly therein, unless disapproved by Congress.[8]

These similarities to colonial practice should not, however, blind one to two important differences from the colonial past. First, territorial judges were temporary officers, in the sense that their positions would end with statehood, and they would not remain as permanent officers imposed by a metropolitan, central authority. Second, there were written constraints on their power. Article 2 of the Northwest Ordinance provided specifically that

> The Inhabitants of the said territory shall always be entitled to the benefits of the writ of habeas corpus, and of the trial by Jury ... and of judicial proceedings according to the course of the common law; all Persons shall be bailable unless for capital offences ... all fines shall be moderate, and no cruel or unusual punishments shall be inflicted; no man shall be deprived of his liberty or property but by the judgment of his Peers, or the law of the land.[9]

The Northwest Territorial Court

The original Northwest Territory judges, named by the Confederation Congress on October 16, 1787, were James Mitchell Varnum, Samuel Holden Parsons, and John Armstrong.[10] Armstrong served very briefly and was replaced in 1788 by John Cleves Symmes. Parsons and Symmes were reappointed by President George Washington under the Constitution in 1789. Varnum, who died early in 1789, was initially replaced by William Barton, who declined to serve, and then by George Turner. Parsons died while trying to swim his horse across a flooded river in 1790, and Rufus Putnam served in the position until 1796, when he was replaced by Joseph Gilman. Turner resigned in 1796 in a political quarrel over Indian trade regulation centered in Vincennes and was replaced by Return Jonathan Meigs.[11]

From the start, the territorial judges were politically well connected. The original judges of the Northwest Territory were chosen from the ranks of large landowners and speculators and from those who had given past service in Congress or in the Continental Army. Varnum, Putnam, and Parsons were all tied to the Ohio Company, speculative developer of the Marietta area; Symmes and Turner were similarly involved in the Cincinnati area. Putnam, Parsons, Armstrong, and Varnum were veterans of the Continental Army; Symmes had served in Congress and as a state judge in New Jersey. Meigs later served as governor of Ohio.[12]

The judges' contribution to territorial law took printed form in 1795 when Judges Symmes and Turner met with Governor Arthur St. Clair in Cincinnati and adopted the first legal code for the area. Dubbed Maxwell's Code for the printer who published it, the thirty-seven laws blended eastern practices with the provisions of the Northwest Ordinance. Ostensibly modeled upon laws of the governor's home state, Pennsylvania, the laws were amended to reflect the assumption of the Ordinance that the judges themselves would follow common law practices. "Maxwell's Code" remained in effect until the first territorial legislature met in 1799 and adopted new statutes.[13]

Historians' views of the legal challenges of the frontier have changed over time. It was once common to stress crime and criminal law. The assessment of the territorial judges' task given by Leander Monks, Logan Esarey, and Ernest Shockley in their 1916 centennial history, *Courts and Lawyers of Indiana*, is a colorful example. They noted:

> The West at that time was full of desperate criminals. . . . Every frontier is largely a dumping ground for the social misfits of settled society. In the history of crime there are few

worse criminals to be found than the professional horsethief. The Northwest was full of them. They continued to infest the country until the railroad and telegraph made their business impossible. Counterfeiters rendezvoused in the wilderness and deluged the back country with their spurious products. Less skilled thieves were satisfied with stealing cattle and hogs, which ranged the forest half wild. Another class of criminals frequently in evidence, though rarely convicted, carried on illicit trade with the Indians, using liquor as a means of debauching the Indians and cheating them out of the furs they had collected.[14]

More recent studies have instead emphasized civil issues, often tied to frontier economic enterprise. Disputes over land survey and title, enforcement of contracts, and the collection of debts and taxes—particularly a federal excise tax on whiskey—have commanded most attention.[15]

The attempt to strike a balance between western practice, often innovative, and eastern precedent, often traditional, appears in many early accounts of courtroom practice. Those who favor a western view stress elements of popular participation, particularly the widespread use of juries in both civil and criminal trials, and the presence of colorful legal orators playing to those juries. Those who instead favor an eastern view note that the courts often copied the highly stylized, even ritualized, procedures of English or colonial courts where writs, forms of action, pleadings, and judgments were expressed and even argued in archaic or Latinate language.[16]

A final interpretive problem posed by the territorial courts is the question of whether they were more comparable to state or federal courts. Most of the settled areas of the Northwest Territory in 1803 were incorporated into the new state of Ohio, and the early territorial court became an important basis for the new Ohio state courts. Yet the territorial courts derived their authority from the Constitution and the Congressionally-approved Northwest Ordinance, and the judges were Presidential appointees.[17] The new Indiana Territory raised similar legal topics after its creation in 1800.

Indiana Issues

Only a few of the settlers of the Northwest Territory lived in areas that would ultimately become the state of Indiana. Most of these individuals were French-speaking settlers in towns such as Vincennes, remnants of the French empire that had been conquered by the British in the French and Indian War (1754–63), and subsequently transferred to the United States by the Peace of Paris (1783).[18] Small in number, the French settlers are often contrasted with later English-speaking arrivals. The former are portrayed as traders, whose prosperity rested upon serving as middlemen in the commerce with local Indians; the latter are portrayed as farmers, seeking prosperity through the sale and development of land. Where the French speakers did hold land, they tended to possess long, thin strips extending away from such rivers as the Wabash; later arrivals were more likely to think in geometric plots that reflected the survey practices used under American land ordinances. Most important to early judges may have been different concepts of conflict resolution. Rather than relying upon such Anglo-American traditions as the common law, interpreted by judges, the French settlers acted upon traditional practices, commonly termed the "custom of the country," arbitrated by local leaders. The specific issue that provoked the greatest controversy was the liquor trade with the

Indians, viewed by French settlers as a local customary private right and by American officials as a source of revenues.[19]

Surviving documents, mainly correspondence reporting troubles encountered by Judge Turner on a rare visit in 1794, provide only a sketchy picture of the first legal business in Vincennes. Apparently the territorial judges had hoped to send at least one of their numbers to hold an annual general court there, but the stresses of long distances and poor transportation largely prevented this. Instead, local leaders were issued commissions to serve as justices of the peace and regulate local affairs. Indian liquor sales proved the trigger for Turner's anger but faded from attention with his 1796 resignation, and no doubt with greater respect by subsequent local officers for French practices.[20]

As population growth in the southeastern areas of the Northwest Territory, soon to be joined to the Western Reserve to create Ohio, was supporting the first transition in the region from a territory to a state, the status of the areas to the west and north called for Congressional action. In 1800 the separate Indiana Territory was created. It was a vast area, incorporating almost all of the Northwest Territory except, of course, modern Ohio. Later congressional acts of 1805 and 1809 created the now-familiar borders. A pre-1805 census showed more people living outside than inside modern Indiana's borders, particularly along the Mississippi River in the French Bottom of Kaskaskia and Cahokia and along the northern Great Lakes. French inhabitants initially predominated, but Americans, coming in greatest numbers from Kentucky, would quickly outnumber them.[21]

The New Indiana Territory

The new Indiana Territory came into existence quietly. The May 7, 1800, act presumed the continuity of the Northwest Ordinance and made no

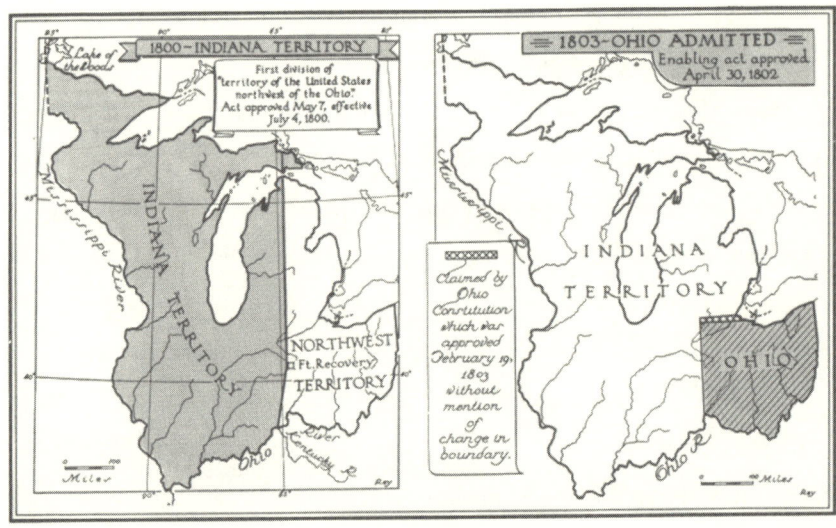

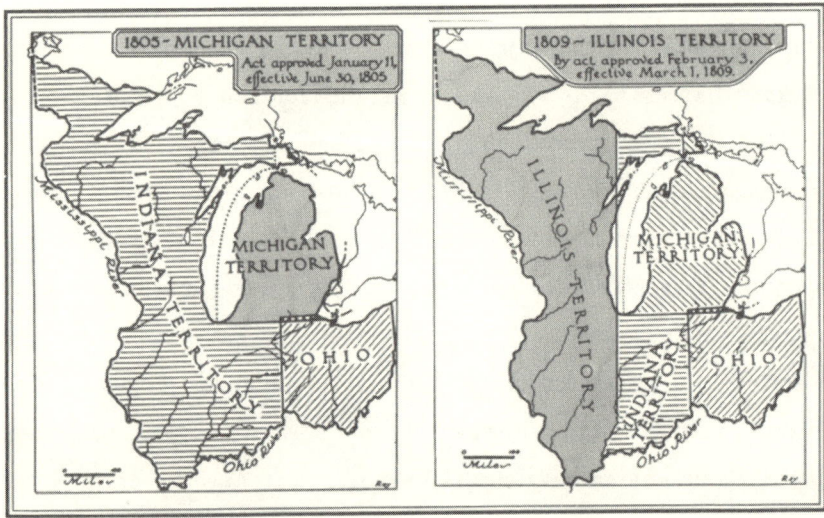

R. Carlyle Buley, *The Old Northwest Pioneer Period, 1815–1840*, 2 vols. (Indianapolis: Indiana Historical Society, 1950), 1:62–63

changes in territorial government structure. The first officers appointed by President John Adams were all individuals familiar with the western scene. Governor Harrison was a younger son of a Virginia signer of the Declaration of Independence. The young man had built a career in the Northwest as an officer under General Anthony Wayne, was a son-in-law of Judge Symmes, and was a territorial delegate responsible for the Congressional Land Law of 1800 that eased purchase requirements for western farmers.[22]

The governor was joined by the three new judges. William Clark was a Kentucky lawyer and Federalist, unrelated to the more famous Clark family. He had gained a reputation in Kentucky as a United States Attorney who vigorously, if often ineptly, sought to enforce the whiskey excise. His appointment in Indiana was apparently an attempt to sooth feelings ruffled by his failed attempts to enforce the law. Clark died of pleurisy in 1802 in Vincennes, leaving no legacy except a young family. He was replaced by Thomas Terry Davis, a spokesman for the Virginia settlers who resided in the George Rogers Clark grant near the modern city of New Albany. The second initial territorial judge was John Griffin, a former Virginian with interests in the Michigan area undoubtedly named to assure representation for the Great Lakes areas. He was appointed by President Thomas Jefferson to the Michigan court when that territory was separated in 1805.[23]

The third, and most important, of the initial territorial judges was Henry Vanderburgh, the justice of the peace who had fenced with Judge Turner in the mid-1790s. Vanderburgh was a significant figure because of his varied connections. A veteran of the Continental Army, he settled in Vincennes after the War for Independence and married into the Racine family, prominent Indian traders. Bilingual, Vanderburgh had assumed a leadership role based upon mediating between French-speaking traders and English-speaking public officers and settlers. Familiar with both American law and French community customs, Vanderburgh was a key figure in the transition to American authority in the 1790s.[24]

Given their authority to write a legal code in advance of the first meeting of the territorial legislature, the governor and judges might have chosen this as an opportunity to deal with French custom and practice. They did not, instead merely allowing the northwestern laws to continue in effect while allowing the courts to wrestle with the ensuing questions, particularly of land title.[25] The most visible changes in the law were gradual responses to the increased presence of Kentuckians in the territory, substituting forms and practices familiar in the South for those earlier adapted from northern precedents. Two examples of these changes that introduced practices familiar to Kentucky immigrants were the reduction in the requirements imposed upon lawyers entering practice before the court and the substitution of a Virginia-based justice of the peace system for its Pennsylvania-based predecessor.[26]

In 1804, however, the Louisiana Purchase created a special situation in which Harrison, Vanderburgh, and the other two judges could express their approaches to French customary law. Upon purchasing Louisiana, Congress divided it into two districts. One became the state of Louisiana. The other portion, sprawling from the Arkansas country north and west to Canada and the Rockies, was first named the District of Louisiana. Most of the settlers in this new upper district lived along rivers, whether the Mississippi, the Missouri, or the Arkansas. Saint Louis was the only town of consequence. As in early Indiana (which stretched to the east bank of the Mississippi until 1809), the majority of the population was Creole, Spanish, or French in ethnic origin. As in the state of Louisiana to this day, there was a preference for the civil law, a formal code of behavior interpreted by judges, over the common law with its unwritten, judge-made character. Harrison and Indiana's territorial judges were charged to perform their functions for this new district until officers could be named from Washington, and for nine months they governed both territories.[27]

In October 1804 the four men met in Vincennes and adopted fifteen fundamental laws for the district. The resulting legal code was an interesting blend. The adoption of a written code obviously spoke to the civil law tradition. But nearly all of the laws themselves, governing such matters as crime, local administration, and legal practice, were simple restatements of Northwest and Indiana territorial laws then in force. The one innovative law, which governed boatmen, was an obvious pragmatic response to the riverine character of the new district.[28]

And then there was the section on slavery. Article 6 of the Northwest Ordinance was clear: "There shall be neither Slavery nor involuntary Servitude in the said territory otherwise than in the punishment of crimes."[29] Article 6 had been popular in Ohio, where both public officials and settlers were disproportionately northern. But the article did not sit as well in the Indiana Territory. Some southern settlers accepted the institution of slavery. Harrison, from a family of the Virginia gentry, considered the plantation model a basis for an orderly society. Vanderburgh knew that many in the French communities owned slaves and that some slave owners had migrated to Louisiana in earlier years to avoid legal complications. It could, in other words, be argued to be the custom of the country. The issue had generally been left alone in Indiana, tolerated or concealed behind spurious labor contracts. But slavery was an institution openly practiced in Louisiana. The 1804 Vincennes meeting considered the options and recognized its legality west of the river.[30]

Ever since these exercises in lawmaking occurred, the issue of slavery has commanded attention among Indiana historians. Slavery continued to be an issue, albeit more political than legal, during the remainder of the territorial period. Eventually it led to a significant shift in power as new migrants, notably future governor Jonathan Jennings, mobilized small farmers against slavery's economic competition and turned Harrison's Vincennes faction out of power.

In the meantime, legal practice in the Indiana Territory continued to develop. Vacancies on the territorial court would lead to three further judicial appointments. Griffin was replaced after 1805 by Waller Taylor, Davis after 1807 by Benjamin Parke, and Vanderburgh after 1812 by James Scott. Taylor was one of Indiana's first two U.S. senators. He was, in Monks's words, "an easy-going old bachelor of Vincennes. He was born in Lunenburg county, Virginia, about 1785 and died there August 26, 1826. He was a friend and comrade-in-arms of Harrison and the other heroes of Tippecanoe. Of his ability at the law no evidence seems to have been preserved."[31]

Scott was an attorney who had practiced in Indiana since 1811, a member of Harrison's proslavery faction, and a prominent figure in the 1816 Indiana Constitutional Convention. He went on to a long career in state legal affairs.[32] Parke, soon to be Indiana's first U.S. District Court Judge, was the most significant of the three later appointees. Born in New Jersey in 1777, he had moved to Kentucky, where he studied law. Moving to Vincennes in 1801, Parke developed a friendship with Harrison. That friendship played a significant role in a quick rise to territorial attorney general, territorial delegate to Congress, and ultimately territorial judge in 1808.[33]

New judges such as Parke moved in a changing world where inherited position or the corporate influence of speculative land companies counted for less than personal reputation and consistency. Referring to criticism of Parke's appointment to a land office position by Jefferson,

Benjamin Parke

historian Andrew Cayton noted, "Men such as Parke jealously guarded their reputation because they had to. If the charge of hypocrisy or deception stuck, their career was over. In a personal political culture, one's honor, the security that one's word was one's bond, was the most important currency of all."[34]

The governor and judges initially proceeded to implement a fairly complicated territorial court system. Its complexity came from two main features. First, the system saw the establishment of a number of separate courts, although not separate judges, to deal with specific subjects. These included an orphans court, a coroners court, and a probate court. Second, the system soon provided separate courts for civil and criminal cases, respectively called common pleas and quarter sessions. The complexity was not lessened by the introduction of justices of the peace in each county, the practice of issuing commissions to private citizens to sit with individual territorial judges if they rode a circuit remote from Vincennes, or a complicated fee structure. This complexity did not survive the first territorial assembly elected in 1805, which began simplifying the system by consolidating the various county courts into a single common pleas court, reducing the number of justices of the peace, substituting salaries for fees, and consolidating record keeping. The number of counties grew in an attempt to keep local government close to a rapidly expanding population.[35]

Such changes suggest a spirit of western innovation and local autonomy. Yet in some ways the courts also showed ties to eastern practice and precedents. Unlike some western areas, the writs of the Indiana General Court ran in the name of the United States.[36] Congress did continue to debate, and sometimes pass, legislation affecting Indiana courts. The right to appeal decisions of the General Court to the United States Supreme Court was approved, when federal questions were involved, in 1805. In the same year Congress also approved the extension of chancery jurisdiction to Indiana. This permitted equity, a branch of law of English origin that sought to correct abuses arising under the common law, to be applied by the courts. A congressional act of March 3, 1805, initially allowed the territorial General Court to exercise such jurisdiction. The new Assembly instead assigned this power to a separate chancery court in an August 22, 1805, law that applied for the rest of the territorial period. Lawyers apparently welcomed the act, the practical effect of which was to give judges the power to convene court between scheduled sessions and to issue writs to prevent defendants from removing property from the area during litigation. Three locally significant individuals served in succession as the single chancery justice. John Badollet, a Swiss-born associate of treasury secretary Albert Gallatin, was appointed in September 1805, to be followed by Thomas Terry Davis and then by future U.S. Senator Taylor.[37]

The three territorial judges themselves were obligated to sit twice a year, in March and September, at Vincennes, in a general, or supreme, court. Here they held both original (limited after 1806 to cases involving more than fifty dollars) and appellate jurisdiction. They conducted oversight of the rest of the court system, issuing a variety of writs including habeas corpus, certiorari, and writs of error, and often remanding cases to lower courts. Individually each judge was also expected to ride circuit, a separate county initially being created to define their jurisdictions. Required to meet once a year, the courts could meet more frequently if the need to try prisoners required a session of trials known in law as jail delivery.[38]

The courts were busy places. In 1808 the General Court, responding to the press of civil business, no longer allowed cases that had been joined in another court to be removed to it. Later anecdotes dwelt upon the rigors of traveling a judicial circuit on bad roads in Hoosier weather. Surviving court records suggest a traditional process rooted in writs, pleadings, and formal language by officials in court proceedings, contrasted with public impatience at the restraints of complex procedures. Legislative initiatives all point to public desire for simplification of court structure and practice. Appeals of court judgments regularly excoriated errors in judges' procedures, and at least one complaint focused upon a grand juror's intoxication. Gubernatorial pardons occasionally responded to publicly unpopular judgments. Enforcement often depended upon harried local officials, and rewards offered for the recovery of escaped criminals or missing property suggest some loose and leaky practices. Diversity, the power of federal courts to rule upon disputes between citizens of different states, laid the foundation for many private actions before the early courts.

Distances did not prevent the judges from striving to enforce the law. As early as August 1803, John Harbin of Knox County was sent to Tennessee to complete the extradition of Robert Slaughter, charged with the murder of Joshua Harbin.[39] Slaughter was apprehended and was tried on September 15, 1804, in the court's earliest recorded murder case. The prisoner's lawyers did not dispute that Slaughter had killed Harbin in order to escape custody after being arrested for horse theft. Instead, there was a spirited dispute over jurisdiction, as Slaughter's defenders argued that he had committed the crime on Indian lands where it was claimed only tribal law applied, that he had not been indicted by the grand jury of the proper county, and that he had been brought before the wrong examining magistrate. The territorial judges debated each point at length before concurring in the jury's guilty verdict and its accompanying death sentence.[40]

Harrison regularly argued that his activities promoted territorial growth. Certainly his attempts to negotiate land purchases from native tribes, such as the controversial Fort Wayne Treaty of 1809, held forth the possibility of ever more available farming land. Similarly, Harrison's military confrontations with the Indian resistance movement led by the Shawnee Prophet and Tecumseh, notably at Tippecanoe in 1811, were designed to quickly advance a settlers' frontier. By 1816 sufficient settlement had occurred that Indiana had the requisite population to qualify for statehood.

What did the territorial period contribute to Indiana legal history? Territorial status was a preparation for statehood, and the territorial courts and laws clearly served as precedent for the Indiana state court system and for much of court practice. The territorial years also provided time for eastern forms of common law and equity to supplant customary practice. By 1816 common law and equity had clearly doomed the "custom of the country" to the status of historical curiosity. Practices might be less formal than on the eastern seaboard, and lawyers less trained, but the courts of the statehood era were enforcing a law recognizably similar to the original states. On balance, the debate in the 1787 Constitutional Convention over the West was being answered in the field of law in favor of those who had argued that an orderly transition would produce a system recognizably similar to, and respectful of, eastern models.

Establishing the District Court in the Statehood Era

The U.S. District Court for the District of Indiana organized on May 5, 1817, in a quiet, dignified session held in the old state Capitol in Corydon. The event was recorded in the elegant copperplate handwriting of the court's first minute book. Benjamin Parke[41] appeared and cited the act of Congress of March 3, 1817, that had created the Indiana district court. He then presented his commission as judge and took the prescribed oath to uphold the Constitution. Henry Hurst was named first clerk of the court, entered a $2,000 security bond, and took his oath. The following day the court adopted its official seal, the arms of the United States surrounded by the words, "The seal of the District Court" along the upper part and "Indiana District" on the lower part."[42]

The transition was quiet and orderly. Thirty years of territorial practice had provided opportunity for attorneys and their clients to become

Old State Capitol in Corydon

accustomed to trial practices. Parke, a familiar figure as territorial judge since 1808, was named to the new district seat by President James Monroe on the president's second day in office, March 5, 1817, and he was confirmed the same day. Gracious in manner, affable in address, and ever alert to the politics of a particular situation, Parke's instinct was to avoid and mediate conflict rather than to seek it out.[43] Described by contemporaries as "nearly six feet, but spare of habit, and of rather delicate frame,"[44] Parke maintained his home in the old territorial capital of Vincennes and commuted to the district court sessions in Corydon and

First page of the Order Book of the U.S. District Court for the District of Indiana

later in Indianapolis and other cities. His friend, Indiana Supreme Court Justice Charles Dewey, later noted that Parke read the great legal writers, Edward Coke and William Blackstone, in preference to novelists such as Henry Fielding and Tobias George Smollett. On the bench, Parke

> listened to argument, whether convincing or otherwise, with a polite and interested attention, which cheered the speaker on in his labors, and satisfied him that he addressed a tribunal desirous to hear, and open to conviction. If, in the progress of a cause, he

sometimes suggested a difficulty, it was kindly done that it might be removed, if possible.... His knowledge was communicated in the form of mild instruction, and not of harsh correction.[45]

No urgent business was before the court. The first case it heard was a land dispute between citizens of different states that, according to the court's docket, led to nothing more dramatic than an order to take depositions in Maryland.[46] Most litigation remained with the state courts and later caused Monks to observe, in comparison to those busy venues, "This court transacted very little business prior to the Civil War."[47]

Nonetheless, four notable areas of activity call for attention in the district court's first forty-five years of existence. One was the creation of an administrative structure of offices and individuals responsible for the enforcement of federal law in Indiana. A second was the conduct of routine matters of federal law, mainly criminal cases. The third was early participation in the changes in business and commercial law that accompanied the economic modernization of transportation, credit, and other entrepreneurial activities in Indiana. The fourth was the court's response to the strong reforming impulses of the antebellum era, chiefly through cases engendered by runaway, or fugitive, slaves.

Court Structure and Personnel

The "court family" as well as the number of practitioners appearing before the court were both initially small. In 1817 only five attorneys were admitted to practice before the court: Henry Cobourn, Charles Dewey, Harbin Moore, William P. Thompson, and Humphrey Webster.[48] A single marshal, John Vawter of Vernon, Indiana, who submitted a bond of $20,000, was the court's only official appointment in that year.[49]

Eventually the court was aided by a set of part-time magistrates, often drawn from the ranks of local judges, who would handle arraignments and petty cases.

Much of the administration and record keeping rested with the clerk of the court, a post held by only two men between statehood and the Civil War. Hurst was clerk under Parke from 1817 until 1835. A member of the Harrison political circle at Vincennes, he served as a militia major at the Battle of Tippecanoe. Hurst brought extensive trial experience that included territorial service as a deputy prosecutor and an attractive penmanship that graces early court records. Replaced at Judge Jesse Lynch Holman's request in 1835, Hurst went on to serve in the state legislature and to accompany Harrison to his presidential inaugural in Washington, D.C., in 1841. Horace Bassett was a Connecticut native who settled in Dearborn County, where he entered the bar and served in the legislature in the 1820s. A friend of Holman, Bassett accepted the clerkship in 1835 and continued to provide quiet and efficient service until his death in 1860.[50]

Criminal cases were brought by a series of U.S. district attorneys, commencing with Thomas Blake (1817–18). From its inception, the position of district attorney was the most coveted position connected with the court. A presidential appointment, the office normally went to an individual in recognition of both proven legal skill and active political involvement. A patronage position in an era of intense political competition,[51] the appointment often changed hands with a new presidential administration or with the support of a new governor in Indianapolis.[52] Of the thirteen men who held the post from 1817 to 1861, in a time of different two-party systems, three were Democratic-Republicans, two were Whigs, and eight were Democrats. Five ultimately served as circuit judges or supreme court justices, and seven served in at least one house of Congress. Three of these, Tilghman Howard, John Pettit, and Daniel Voorhees, became U.S. senators, as did the last territorial attorney general, William Hendricks. Only one U.S. attorney, Benjamin Thomas, who served briefly in the mid-1850s, confined his career to private legal practice and held no other public office.[53]

Where the U.S. attorney's position generally went to a rising political star, the position of U.S. marshal rewarded either an active politician or a senior political figure near the end of a career of noted public service. Thus Jesse Bright, later the dominant figure in state Democratic politics in the 1850s, held the position under President Martin Van Buren in 1840 and 1841, while Robert Hanna, a leading organizer of the Whig movement in the 1830s, held the post under Presidents William Henry Harrison and John Tyler between 1841 and 1845.[54]

Court practice was generally expected to conform to that of other federal courts, particularly to that of Kentucky until 1837. Remote from the eastern seaboard, Kentucky's court in 1789 had initially been allowed to combine the functions of a district and a circuit court, and this latitude was extended to the Indiana court from 1817 to 1837.[55] The normal practice was that district courts would handle lesser criminal cases, involving fines of one hundred dollars or less and jail terms of six months or less, while circuit courts would handle more serious offenses and hear appeals from its district court. When the same judge was charged with both responsibilities, it was the normal practice to convene the court in either its district or circuit authority, conforming as far as possible to local state court practices. Until 1837 appeals were thus only possible to the United States Supreme Court. In 1837 Congress separated Indiana's district court from circuit court, but did so in a manner very different from later practice. A circuit court's judges would be the district judge plus a member of the U.S. Supreme Court assigned to the Indiana district. District decisions could be appealed to the circuit; if the two judges disagreed, the matter would then be forwarded to the Supreme Court. A single Supreme Court justice, John McLean, rode the circuit in Indiana from 1837 until 1861. Actual practice was sometimes less clear than intent. Attorneys were permitted to file cases and appear before either court, and the district judge could sit alone in original jurisdiction on circuit in the absence of the Supreme Court justice assigned to the circuit.[56]

The district court was required to meet twice each year in sessions commencing on the first Mondays in May and November. Holman suggested the contrast with his prior service in the state courts and the consequences of the 1837 changes in circuit jurisdiction in a letter to his son:

> The District Court is left with scarcely any business to do. I have held Court for about an hour today & expect to hold it for about an hour tomorrow and then adjourn until [Circuit] in course. But tho my duties as District Judge are thus diminished I have to hold a Court once a year with the Circuit Judge to [attend to] the business I have heretofore done alone. But altogether I have an easier time than I had here before.[57]

Lacking a separate courthouse, the court occupied offices in post offices and other public buildings. The court often rented and used county or state courtrooms, just as it used county, and later state, prisons to house its accused and convicted criminals. Indiana's district court made extensive use of both grand and petit juries. The former, usually composed of politically influential figures in the community, was clearly intended to legitimize as well as to define the charges brought before the court. The latter, possibly more representative of the community at large, showed a strong preference, common among most western juries, for hard evidence and personal testimony.

Jurors' behavior encouraged pleading skills, or at least served as a justification for them. Consider the lament of District Judge Elisha Mills Huntington in a letter to his sister Louisa Rudd in 1843, in which he described a day on the bench during the trial of a postmaster of Indianapolis:

> one of the three counsel employed by the prisoner is now speaking. For one long hour he has been raving like a Methodist preacher until all the ideas he ever had seem to have escaped. The old clock above my head and the descending sun whose glorious beams now flash from the horizons reddened line through the lofty columns of this beautiful hall, admonish me that night will soon close in and shortly relieved me from this most unconstitutional infliction.[58]

The spirit of improvisation and oratory had its limits. When he looked back over his own experience in the antebellum era, attorney and former U.S. senator Oliver H. Smith offered this summary of Indiana courtroom practice:

> We had the pleasure often, also, of meeting the gentlemanly lawyers from the Kentucky side of the [Ohio] river, in our courts in Dearborn and Switzerland [counties], and of seeing their mode of practice. I found their forte to be in speeches to the jury, and not in watching the evidence in its introduction, as we did on the Indiana side.[59]

Similarly, Smith offered this recollection in 1857 of riding the judicial circuit:

> When I commenced riding the Third Circuit, it was the universal custom of the judges and bar, to meet after supper, in some upper room of the tavern, and play cards and drink, sometimes till near morning.... I set my face, my example, and my kind reproofs of the brethren of the bar, against their practice. I have lived to see it gradually give way, and finally cease—I trust and hope for ever.[60]

Federal Crimes

Federal crimes were much more limited in number in the antebellum era.[61] Most of the individuals who ran afoul of the law did so either because they stole federal property or because they failed to pay federal tax. Theft most commonly was of money stolen from the U.S. mail, or of timber cut on federal lands that had not as yet been sold to private individuals. Tax cases nearly always involved the excise on whiskey, a very common product in a grain-growing state. The first criminal trial on record saw Andrew Hilton acquitted by a jury of a charge of selling twenty gallons or less of whiskey without first paying for a federal license. The next had William Bell acquitted of a charge of possessing 150 gallons of whiskey upon which no excise tax had been paid.[62]

Business Practices

Economically, early Indiana was a land of farmers, in which land ownership was the key legal concern and land speculation a risky but potentially profitable business. Issues of land cessions by Native American tribes, land survey, and land sales to individuals and speculators were central to the federal presence in the state. Most early federal officials, including early judges, engaged in public service that touched upon these topics. Parke had been an Indian agent; Huntington was a former land office commissioner.[63] Once land passed into private hands, it passed under state control, but until that time it could easily become district court business. The first civil cases before the court involved individuals who had failed to complete credit purchases of land on time, just as many early criminal cases included the theft of trees from government land. One of Dewey's notable prosecutions was of Brazil Meek, ultimately acquitted of trespass and tree theft in 1823.[64]

Slowly but surely, however, the new world of transportation and business made itself felt before the district court. Most often this was in the form of cases involving debt and credit. Credit cases became particularly urgent in the aftermath of the periodic depressions that struck the country. Three of these depressions occurred prior to the Civil War, in 1819, 1837, and 1857. Each was a dramatic economic downturn that public opinion often linked to speculation and to the availability of credit from government-chartered banks. Each was accompanied by the strong emotions that caused contemporaries to use the word "panic" to describe them. Each resulted in a spate of litigation, mainly for debt foreclosure. The antebellum district court found itself most directly affected between 1841 and 1843 as the result of a new federal law designed to address one aspect of the problem, the Bankruptcy Act of August 19, 1841. The law sought to serve two somewhat contradictory functions. First, it attempted to help creditors, who could petition for the recovery of debts owed by insolvent commercial businessmen. Second, it attempted to help debtors by allowing them to petition to wipe their financial slate clean by discharging uncollectible debts. Complaints, mainly from creditors annoyed by the second provision, led to a quick repeal by Congress.⁶⁵ Yet in the interim, a few district courts sought to implement the act. Congressman William Taylor Zenor of Indiana, in a later eulogy of the Holman family, recalled that in 1842 Judge Holman presided over the first bankruptcy court held in the western states. Held in the Baptist Church of Aurora, Zenor remembered insolvent debtors coming from all of the "Western country."⁶⁶

Reform Issues
Strong moral beliefs were characteristic of many Hoosier leaders in the nineteenth century and can be heard most often in criminal cases. In November 1840, William Martin, an Indiana mail stage driver, found himself standing in U.S. District Court, convicted of "abstracting a letter from the mail, containing bank notes."⁶⁷ Holman reviewed the evidence that had convinced the jury to return a guilty verdict and then lectured the defendant upon his future prospects:

> The prospect before you is indeed dark and dreary; yet there is a distant ray of hope that may enlighten your path.... You may do much by a patient submission to the law—by a reformation of life and an upright line of conduct ... to some extent, to regain a station among honest men. You may do more than this: By repentance and reformation, you may obtain the approbation of Him, whose favor is better than life or liberty, and far more valuable than an earthly reputation.

The judge then sentenced Martin to the minimum penalty, ten years at hard labor.⁶⁸

Jesse Lynch Holman

Moral conviction, and sometimes an ensuing attempt to improve society by improving the character of its citizens and their institutions, is a favored topic of historians of pre-Civil War America, and Holman's words remind us that judges were among the many who were touched by the moral convictions of that era.

Judge Holman was a native of Kentucky who had read law in Lexington under future presidential contender Henry Clay. Holman had then migrated to the Indiana Territory in 1810, served from 1816 to 1830 on the Indiana Supreme Court, and lost to John Tipton by one vote in the 1831 election for the U.S. Senate. In 1835 Holman pursued the district court seat recently vacated following the death of Parke and received a recess appointment on September 16, 1835. The process to that point was so uneventful that Holman wrote on October 2, "My friends made a quiet but strong effort on my behalf ... but so little was the subject agitated about home, that few of my neighbors, or even my children at home knew anything of my application until my commission arrived."[69]

The nomination process stalled, however, launching Holman on a seven-month political quest that extended from the fall of 1835 to the spring of 1836, took him on journeys across Indiana and to Washington, D.C., included a stagecoach accident on an icy road in the Allegheny Mountains in which he was seriously injured, and concluded with a decisive private interview with President Andrew Jackson. The story is known in considerable detail because Holman kept his family closely posted on the confirmation process, and his family (and later Indiana University and Franklin College) carefully preserved his correspondence.[70]

The lengthy process, Holman suggested, owed more to the emerging two-party factionalism of Democrats and Whigs, and to ensuing rivalries among members of the Indiana delegation to Congress, than it did to him personally. In the process, Holman found it necessary to respond to charges that included purported opposition both to Jackson's administration and the selection of Martin Van Buren as Jackson's successor, and to the claim that Holman lacked sufficient legal qualifications to serve as a federal judge; embarrassing personal behavior; and the belief that Holman was, in words reported to him by Indiana congressman Amos Lane, "a fanatic on the subject of abolition."[71]

Holman eventually satisfied Jackson, and Indiana's two senators, that the first three charges were both politically motivated and factually false. As Holman put it in describing his key interview with the president,

> I was fortunate enough to find him alone. He conversed freely on a great variety of subjects. Talked for some time on the subject of my appointment, & the opposition that was got up against me; seemed to be apprized [sic] that the opposition was not so much against me as against my friends.

On the charge of abolitionism, however, Jackson took the time to ask Holman's detailed views:

> [Jackson] mentioned the charge of abolition . . . which I had answered in several letters, which I had shown him. I satisfied him completely on that subject, & especially by repeating my decision in the first Negro case I acted on a few days after I recv'd my commission, & which I gave a certificate for removal of the slave to Kentucky. I stated the principles upon which I decided. It gave him entire satisfaction & Carr [Holman's political companion at the interview] remarked afterwards that the Gen'l was particularly pleased with my decision.[72]

Holman did not bother in his family letters to include the details of the case involving the Kentucky slave, probably assuming it was well known to his intended audience. In all likelihood, he had been involved in one of the growing number of recaption, or recapture, cases arising under the 1793 Fugitive Slave Act. The act responded to article 4, section 2 of the Constitution, which read,

> No person held to service or labour in one State, under the laws thereof, escaping into another, shall, in consequence of any law or regulation therein, be discharged from such service or labour, but shall be delivered up on claim of the party to whom such service or labour may be due.

The 1793 act made recovery a matter of federal law, creating a process by which slave owners (or their representatives) could, upon oath, recover runaways.[73] Holman's "principles" were undoubtedly those of following the procedures set forth in the act, and Jackson did not press him. Holman's nomination followed on March 21, 1836, and his confirmation and commissioning eight days later.[74]

Had Jackson pursued the matter, he might have been less satisfied. Holman's earlier legal career had dealt with more than recaption cases and illustrated some of the challenges that existed at the intersection between state and federal jurisdiction. Under both the Northwest Ordinance and the 1816 state constitution, slavery was barred from Indiana. Holman had cited the Northwest Ordinance as his reason for freeing slaves owned by his wife when the couple first moved to Indiana in 1810. Yet just across the Ohio River was the slave state of Kentucky, from which some masters sought by legalistic subterfuges to bring and retain their slaves. Slave owners most commonly attempted to thwart the territorial ordinance and the Indiana constitution by claiming that their slaves were simply indentured servants who had signed long-term labor contracts, enforceable as any contract would be in a state court.

One of the most important of these cases, *In re Clark*, had reached Holman fifteen years earlier, in November 1821, while he was serving on the Indiana Supreme Court. The case centered upon Mary Clark, an African American woman (or, in the court's terminology, "a woman of color") who had been purchased by a former slave owner in Kentucky in 1815. The former owner had then brought Clark to Vincennes, where he promptly freed her. At the same time, however, he had contracted with Clark to serve him as an indentured servant for thirty years. A year later he canceled and destroyed her contract. On the same day, General Washington Johnston signed Clark to a twenty-year indenture as a housemaid. Clark subsequently petitioned for a writ of habeas corpus, claiming she was held as a slave. Johnston admitted to the court that he had paid Clark's former owner $350, but argued this was not slavery but merely indentured servitude. A lower court in Knox County agreed with Johnston. The state supreme court, in an opinion written by Holman, disagreed.[75]

The Indiana Supreme Court reasoned that any Indiana resident, including Clark, could enter into a contract for personal services. Contracts would not be specifically enforced, however, because they were indistinguishable from slavery or involuntary servitude, which was banned in the Indiana Constitution. Here are Holman's words:

> Such a performance, if enforced by law, would produce a state of servitude as degrading and demoralizing in its consequences, as a state of absolute slavery; and if enforced under a government like ours, which acknowledges a personal equality, it would be productive of a state of feeling more discordant and irritating than slavery itself.[76]

Neither the issues of the case, nor its decision, should come as a surprise to those familiar with the early factionalism of the Democratic-Republican Party in Indiana. When the state held its first elections in 1816, its dominant political leader, Jonathan Jennings, had campaigned upon a platform that rejected the ideals of the plantation, slavery included. Jennings affirmed instead the primacy of the independent, hard-working citizen—what has often been called the Jeffersonian yeoman farmer. Identifying the center of the old politics with Vincennes and Knox County, Jennings crafted an appeal based upon democratic participation and opportunity that resonated with secure majorities of voters, especially in the Whitewater River valley and other eastern and southern portions of the early state. For a Jennings appointee to Indiana's highest court to overturn a Knox County decision, and thereby reject a form of labor identified with plantation culture, was only to be expected.[77]

The search for the context of Holman's ideas and activities extends beyond politics. Both court history and the legal implications of public morality are established topics within the study of antebellum America. Historians usually treat them in separate chapters, particularly at the state level, saving the intersection of law and morality until discussions of the sectional legislative crises that repeatedly agitated Congress. Yet Holman's responses to the charges of abolitionism show one of the key antebellum moral reform issues, antislavery, rearing its head in the history of the district court independent of any specific national crisis. It can thus serve as an invitation to rethink the manner of interpreting the history of the U.S. District Court for the Southern District of Indiana.

The recent bicentennial of the U.S. Constitution served as the occasion for publishing a number of histories of district courts in other states. The histories are as varied in scope as the states they cover, but in covering the antebellum era they generally include three themes. First, they explore the interaction of law and politics in that exuberantly participatory era. Second, they document that the quest for a federal balance, a definition of the tensions and borders between state and federal authority, was present in the district courts as well as in the Supreme Court. Third, the histories frequently explore landmark district court decisions.[78]

Holman's nomination touches all three themes. He clearly was caught up in current political discourse. It must have been an interesting moment for him, as a lawyer trained by Clay, a prominent Whig, to explain, as Holman did, his support for two of Clay's great Democratic rivals, Jackson and Van Buren. Holman was also clearly expected to have the legal skills to manage the tensions between state and federal authority on issues such as recaption. And he was explicitly asked to explain the "principles" he would use in interpreting federal law and providing legal precedent. Yet what stands out in his tale is the central role that reform, and specifically antislavery sentiment, played in it.

Histories of reform are a staple of antebellum studies, and here again several themes seem to enjoy continued interest. Historians are often asked where in America, when in time, why in motivation, and who in support made the moral impulses of the antebellum years such a force to be reckoned with. Were they broadly national in scope, or more narrowly limited to a particular region such as New England? Were they a continuing feature of several decades, or a force building over time? Were they religious or secular in their underlying spirit? And did they gain or repel adherents as they developed?[79]

Holman is an interesting case study. Born and educated in Kentucky, his relocation to Indiana took him just across the Ohio River to Aurora, where he built his home and career. His best-remembered reform decision, *In re Clark*, came early in his career, and on the surface as much in response to state politics as to any other motive. His motives seem fairly clear until we add one fascinating dimension: his religious beliefs. Holman was a devout Baptist.

His religious training came early. Holman learned his "letters" by reading the Bible in his parents' home in Mercer County, Kentucky. In his adult years he could recollect the contents of the first sermon he heard when he was four years old. He assisted in "gathering" the Aurora church, organized his county's Sunday School Association, went on to become a national vice president of the American Sunday-School Union, and was president at various times of the Western Baptist Publication and Sunday-School Society, the Indiana Baptist Education Society, and the Indiana State [Baptist] Convention.[80] In the admiring words of William Cathcart's 1883 *Baptist Encyclopedia*,

> In 1834 he was ordained, and thus entered upon a work that his soul longed to engage in. So unsullied was his public as well as his private life that men were always glad to hear him preach. While traveling the judicial circuit it was no unusual thing for him to address his fellow-citizens on Bible operations, missions, Sabbath-schools, general education, and temperance. So consistent and earnest was his life that there seemed no incongruity, but rather a singular harmony in his two offices of judge and minister.[81]

Little wonder that, again in Cathcart's words, "He, like his father, was an emancipationist," or that his sentencing of a coach driver for mail theft should have the ring of the pulpit about it. Holman was clearly a nineteenth-century reformer with a powerful moral emphasis.

But was Holman typical of those who sat on the antebellum federal bench in Indiana? He should be compared to his predecessor, Parke.

Since becoming a territorial judge in 1808, Parke continued to be a viable presence, even after the Vincennes/Knox County faction that he was identified with began to lose power to the Whitewater/Jennings faction after 1810. In 1816 Parke was named U.S. District Judge with accompanying circuit authority.[82]

Parke's eulogist, his close friend Charles Dewey, attributed the judge's survival and success to Parke's calm and deferential manner:

> His decisions, though generally the result of correct, and often of profound learning, clear discrimination, and conclusive reasoning, were yet delivered with so much humility—so much diffidence of his own powers—with so evident an anxiety to do right—in fine, so gentle, courteous and kind was his whole intercourse with the bar, that at one and the same moment, we yielded our admiration to the judge and our love to the man.[83]

If one adds his eight years as an article 4 territorial judge to his nineteen of service as an article 3 district judge, it makes Parke the longest-serving federal judge of the nineteenth century in Indiana. It certainly gave him time to define his approach to the bench and community.

In many ways, Parke is a contrast to Holman. Where Holman was a man of organized publicly proclaimed faith, Parke has the look of a privately motivated seeker. Dewey, Parke's frequent traveling companion, put it this way:

> he made no public profession of his faith, and entertained towards the intolerance of sectarian feeling an utter abhorrence. ... Uninfluenced by human authority and the dogmas of teachers, he held himself responsible to his God alone for the exercise

of those powers and faculties which he had bestowed upon him, and left others to account for themselves.[84]

William Woollen quoted Parke's friend Barnabas Hobbs, who phrased it thus:

> Benjamin Parke was a Christian in the true acception of the term, though he identified himself with no religious denomination.... He very often rode out three miles into the country to sit in silence with the Friends at their midweek meetings.[85]

Where Holman was a man of morality, Parke was a man of mentality. Parke's community interests were centered upon secular education and access to the printed word. He was a founder of the Salem Academy for young men, an organizer of the first law library in the state, and a founding member of the Indiana Historical Society. Similar to the patrician leaders of Knox County with whom he started his career, Parke sought to train and shape leaders for an emerging polity.[86]

Parke and Holman had differing voices on slavery. Where Holman is known for *In re Clark*, Parke left us his 1818 opinion *In re Susan*, which involved a Kentucky slave owner's attempt to recover Susan, "a fugitive from labour [sic]."[87] The case had already been heard in the state courts, which had followed the more complicated procedures for recovery under state law rather than those of its federal counterpart, the 1793 Fugitive Slave Act. When the case came before Parke, Susan's attorney argued those state laws took precedence over federal statute. Parke rejected the argument, after noting it was "the first occasion on which the validity of this law [the Fugitive Slave Act] has been questioned." State recovery laws, he suggested, were an artifact of an era before the Constitution gave power on the issue to Congress:

In the formation of the constitution of the United States, the state parted with this authority, and devolved it upon the general government, and it is a privilege secured to the people of the states, respectively, to seek redress before the tribunals, in the mode designated by congress.

That standard having been met, Susan was returned to Kentucky.

If one wants to be technical about appointments, one could argue that Dewey followed Holman. President Tyler had first offered the position to Huntington, a former state circuit court judge who was serving as commissioner of the General Land Office. Huntington, however, initially declined to accept the judicial offer, instead recommending Dewey. The president, who may have assumed that Huntington had discussed the matter with the nominee, subsequently nominated Dewey. In any event, the Senate confirmed Dewey early in 1842. But he promptly declined the appointment—perhaps because he preferred the higher $1,500 salary he earned as a justice of the Indiana Supreme Court to the mere $1,000 salary of a federal district judge.[88] Huntington[89] was again offered the appointment and this time accepted. Tyler officially nominated him on April 26, 1842. The delays in communication with Dewey and Huntington were sufficient to permit a flurry of opposition to develop. Two of Indiana's congressmen, Joseph L. White of Madison and James Harrison Cravens of Marion, wrote in opposition. They noted the presence of other strong candidates and stressed the failure of the president to consult with members of the House delegation. Tyler had, however, secured the support of the state's two senators, and Senate confirmation followed a week later on May 2, 1842.[90]

Judge Huntington did not leave an extensive record of his private thoughts and feelings on moral and intellectual topics. Because he so sel-

Elisha Mills Huntington

dom spoke on such questions, contemporaries often looked to his family for clues, noting, for example, that Huntington's wife was a champion of genteel feminism who led a women's campaign to thank Robert Dale Owen for his actions advocating women's independent right to property in the 1850 Indiana State Constitutional Convention. Instead, the judge was usually interpreted through his political stances and was normally assigned to the northern wing of the Democratic Party. On some issues, such as support for the California Compromise of 1850, this approach had merit. The judge proved to be a Unionist who sought sectional reconciliation and often praised Illinois senator Stephen A. Douglas, the individual most responsible for the passage of the compromise measures. After hearing Douglas speak in Terre Haute in 1858, Huntington enthused, "I never heard so fine a speech before. He is the greatest I know by all odds."[91] Huntington eventually became very unhappy with the newly formed, and Northern-focused, Republican Party. By 1858 he privately fulminated against the content of "Black Republican [news] papers" and in 1862 criticized Abraham Lincoln for "his foolish twaddle about Emancipation."[92]

But it should be remembered that the president who appointed Huntington had been chosen to run for vice president with Harrison on the 1840 Whig ticket. Upon Harrison's death and Tyler's accession to the presidency, the latter had quickly proven to be a maverick independent on many issues—often in disagreement with his cabinet, sometimes seeking advice outside the formal channels of power, and periodically interested in building an independent power base. It is not impossible that Tyler, however limited their contact, sensed these characteristics in Huntington—or that Huntington may have interpreted his unsolicited appointment as a liberation from party discipline. The judge's views in an 1847 letter take on special meaning in this context:

> This being my unfortunate state, I have if C[...] to look around me and see if can what I am and what I am to be. I find myself with the most independent position of any man in the west—a life office and dignity[,] some $2000 in debt, and with some $10,000 worth of property.[93]

It is also worthy of note that, whatever his opinions during the sectional crisis of the 1850s, Huntington's appointment was initially interpreted as a Whig victory. The *Indianapolis Sentinel* editorialized, "no doubt something must have been done to have caused [Terre Haute's] citizens to receive so many favors at the hands of a whig administration, *besides begging for office*; for we don't believe the whigs of Terre Haute can beg harder than others we are wot of."[94]

Huntington clearly enjoyed serving on the bench. His private journal and letters often speak of his focus upon court business, and, especially, of his desire to be both physically and intellectually prepared for court sessions. He regularly wrote of his experiences in the courtroom, often in colorful idiom. In 1843, for example, the judge presided at the trial of Postmaster John Cain, who had been indicted for opening, or attempting to open, private letters addressed to his predecessor, Joseph M. Moore. Moore and several postal clerks testified for the government, but failed to convince the jury—which returned an immediate verdict of not guilty. In a letter to his sister written during the trial, Huntington revealed both his judicial mindset and his humorous literary style:

> For you know the constitution says that "cruel and unusual punishments shall not be inflicted"—Oh, it is horrifying to be compelled to sit for hours and listen to such rant.[95]

In a similar vein he later observed, "But I am writing this during the trial of an old Sarcall [sic] for counterfeiting.... The lawyers have gotten into a snarl."[96] On another occasion, he commented,

> I have been in Court every hour since I came setting generally until after we lighted the gas in the Senate Chambers where I

hold my sessions. . . . There is an unusual amount of criminal business. I begin to fear that I may be kept here over Christmas. I hope not however.[97]

He regularly sought cooperation with the state courts, especially over jury selection and courtroom practice. U.S. Supreme Court Justice David Davis described Huntington's demeanor on the bench in a funeral address:

> Judge Huntington's perceptions were quick, and his judgment was practical and accurate. Whenever a difficult question was presented to him for decision, he endeavored to subject it to the test of common sense; and if it was of such a nature that he could bring it to a moral solution, and could feel satisfied where the justice of it lay, there he rested. In such a case, even contrary adjudications had a slow and difficult impression on his mind. . . . He was eminently genial and social in his nature, and in his personal address was uncommonly endowed.[98]

The sectional divisions of his time eventually attracted Huntington's greatest attention. In 1850 these divisions became the subject of federal law through several of the laws that were included in the compromise measures that admitted California as a free state in exchange for various concessions to the Southern states—including a new, and tougher, law for recovering fugitive slaves. Although passed by narrow majorities in Congress and signed by President Millard Fillmore, the new laws angered many in the Northern states and led to vocal criticism by abolitionists and other moral reform groups. Huntington's subsequent opinions toward reform issues appear mainly in his vigorous criticism of abolitionism, which he evinced in one of his 1850 grand jury charges regarding enforcement of the 1850 Fugitive Slave Act:

> Evil passions seem to have been let loose, and madness, in some sections of the country, seems to rule the hour . . . the raising a body of men to obtain by intimidation the repeal of a law, or to oppose and prevent, by terror, its execution, is levying war against the Government. . . . We must stand by the rights of others as we stand by our own. We must observe the laws and we must enforce their observance where they are resisted—we must keep faith not only with each other, but with the citizens of other States.[99]

The 1850 law led to two types of cases. One was for the recovery of black slaves. The other was for damages against whites accused of improper involvement, be they abolitionists accused of hiding runaways or slave takers accused of false accusations against free blacks. One would have expected Huntington, with his strong attachment to maintaining the political balance within the Union, to have played a central role in these matters. Actually, few fugitive slave cases came before him. Partly this was because those seeking to impede slave taking preferred to take their cases to state courts where damages were thought to be easier to collect from whites who tried to catch runaways, and habeas corpus thought to be easier to obtain for the runaways themselves. Partly, also, this was because federal commissioners (provided in the 1850 law) and local magistrates, rather than the judge himself, initially heard most cases and often disposed of them before they arrived at Huntington's bench.[100]

An important exception was the Benjamin Waterhouse case of November 1854. Waterhouse was a resident of Lagrange County, near the Michigan border. Strong religious convictions caused him to oppose slavery and eventually to harbor runaway slaves on their journey north to freedom. Such assistance was a crime under the 1850 act, and Waterhouse was arrested and transported to Indianapolis for trial in Huntington's circuit court. Critics, almost certainly exaggerating from the five or six individuals named in the indictment, claimed Waterhouse had helped a hundred or more runaways. Supporters, a small but vocal group of abolitionists and other reformers led by attorney and Free-Soil politician George Julian, sought to use the trial to publicize the unfairness they perceived in the act. In his trial defense, Julian singled out the tactics of the U.S. marshal, John Robinson, comparing them to the brutal and perjured tactics of slave takers. A local jury sought compromise, convicting the defendant but accepting the prosecutor's promise of a light sentence.[101]

The case served notice upon Huntington, if any was needed, of the emotional intensity that accompanied such recovery cases. The judge subsequently found himself attacked in the press by one of Waterhouse's attorneys, charging a "want of fairness on the trial." Angered, Huntington fired off an official letter to the local press:

> as pains seem to have been taken by an artful blending of fact and falsehood to wholly misrepresent the ruling of the Court, and as my silence might be taken as admitting the truth of that part of the pretended report, I feel it due to myself to state briefly what was said by the Court.[102]

He then went on to paint his actions as a strict reading of the 1850 law, to cite the jury's guilty verdict, and to stress that he "assessed an almost nominal punishment."[103] It is one of the few instances of an Indiana federal judge debating in the press a case that was before his court and a further proof of the contentiousness of the reform spirit of the age.

It would thus be possible to read into Huntington's public and private positions a continuing hostility to reform issues. But it is also important to read a deep commitment to the enforcement of federal law. Most modern historians' opinions reflect the Northern criticism of the 1850 Fugitive Slave Act. But that law was a federal statute enforceable in federal court—and Huntington enforced it. His stress upon the power of federal courts to enforce federal law, moreover, was not limited to this one highly visible area. To see Huntington's consistency, it is useful to look at his role in defining the power of mandamus—the ability of a court to issue a writ to compel compliance with its decisions. Prior to the Civil War, federal courts had been reluctant to impose such orders upon other branches and levels of government. But in 1861, sitting in his circuit capacity, Huntington ruled in the case of *Aspinwall v. County Commissioners*. Aspinwall held bonds issued by the county, but the county commissioners had refused to pay interest to him on the grounds that the sums they raised through taxation were insufficient to meet their obligation. The judge found for Aspinwall and issued a writ of mandamus ordering the county to raise the funds. The commissioners appealed to the U.S. Supreme Court, which ruled in support of Huntington's position and held the writ necessary to exercise jurisdiction and thus federal law.[104]

Federal law did not offer provisions for disability at the time, and Huntington served his last two or three years suffering from a severe respiratory disease. Illinois district judge Samuel Treat presided over at least one session of Huntington's court. At various times Huntington traveled as far as Havana, Cuba, and later Saint Paul, Minnesota, in search of relief. He died in the latter city on October 26, 1862, and was later buried in the Saint Joseph cemetery (then known as the Catholic burying ground) in Terre Haute.[105]

Three conclusions seem warranted. First, the U.S. District Court made an orderly and effective transition from territorial to national (and hence from article 4 to article 3) jurisdiction prior to the Civil War. Second, each of its first three judges was a clearly different individual, in both their opinions and in the sources of their values and beliefs. Third, the economic changes and moral reform sentiments that transformed antebellum America were central to many of the cases heard by those judges, placing the court in the mainstream of American federal law from its earliest decades.

CHAPTER TWO

The District Court in Civil War and Political Conflict

1862–1902

THE U.S. DISTRICT COURT FOR INDIANA WAS INFLUenced by three major factors between 1862 and 1902. First, the court ruled upon legal issues that surrounded the American Civil War, and Judge David McDonald ultimately played a central role in defining the role of military tribunals in wartime. Second, the court was drawn into the intense political partisanship that followed on the heels of the Civil War and handed down several key decisions that addressed the issue of ballot integrity. Third, the court became intimately involved in new directions of business law and legal professionalism, playing a major role in shaping the use of injunctions in labor disputes. As Indiana aggressively participated in the Industrial Revolution, the quiet antebellum court became a busier and more varied venue.

The Civil War: Unprecedented Judicial Turnover

The decade of the 1860s was a period of unusual events in the history of Indiana's district court. One such set of events was the unexpected turnover of judges. Following the death of Judge Elisha Mills Huntington in 1862, four other individuals were appointed in succession as judge in a

David McDonald

de in the court's history has seen such
Superimposed upon the turnover in
issues related to the Civil War. Most
the attempt by military tribunals to
by federal court—attempts that cul-
rt's significant *Ex parte Milligan* deci-

were not the only consideration in the
olved in Huntington's replacement. In 1862

President Abraham Lincoln was seeking a gracious way for Secretary of the Interior Caleb Blood Smith to exit the cabinet. Smith, as head of the Indiana delegation to the 1860 Republican National Convention, had been instrumental in securing Lincoln's nomination.[1] But, as David Davis later noted, Smith had been less successful in his managerial style as secretary of the interior and was probably perceived as a liability in the forthcoming off-year elections.[2] Smith, for his part, was pleading ill health, a claim given substance by his death two years later.[3] He left the cabinet in 1862 after writing a letter to Lincoln stating that he had developed a "functional derangement of the heart." He simultaneously sought the vacant judgeship because "the duties of the position are adapted to my tastes and habits and are sufficiently light to be performed without inconvenience."[4]

Smith was followed in his judicial service by two other Lincoln appointees, Albert Smith White, who served for only a few months in 1864, and David McDonald, who served from 1864 to 1869. Together their appointments tell something of Lincoln's approach to judicial appointment. All three judges were supporters of Lincoln's war effort and had made that support known to the president. Smith did so in the cabinet, White did so on the floor of Congress, and MacDonald did so in personal meetings with Lincoln in both 1862 and 1864.

Smith's career combined law, politics, and economic enterprise. He was born in Boston, Massachusetts, in 1808, raised in the Cincinnati area, and attended Miami University before entering the law in Ohio in the 1820s. He worked ceaselessly to overcome a pronounced lisp, eventually developing a powerful oratorical style that many compared to enthusiastic religious preaching. Moving easily between Cincinnati and Indianapolis, Smith entered Indiana politics in the 1830s as a Whig and eventually served three terms from 1843 to 1849 in the U.S. House of Representatives.[5]

After completing his service as a congressman, Smith turned his hand to business, becoming in succession president of two financially troubled railroads designed to connect Cincinnati with Indiana. In the process he also gained a reputation as a specialist in early corporate law. A man who believed that government should be enlisted as a partner to private enterprise, particularly in supporting banking and in funding internal improvements, Smith made an easy transition to the new Republican Party and an easy return to Indiana by 1860. But the canny negotiating style that had served him well in the Ohio valley served him less well in Washington. In particular, Smith was perceived by some contemporaries to be uncomfortable with the Emancipation Proclamation. Indiana Congressman George W. Julian, an early Free-Soiler, recalled a Smith speech that proclaimed "this is not a war upon the institution of slavery, but a war for the restoration of the Union." Both Smith and Lincoln probably saw his district court appointment as a form of semiretirement. Smith was nominated on December 16, 1862, and confirmed and commissioned six days later.[6]

Albert Smith White was born in Blooming Grove, Orange County, New York, in 1803 and moved to Lafayette, Indiana, in 1829, soon after the city was founded. An early and active Whig, he served in the U.S. House of Representatives from 1837 to 1839 and in the U.S. Senate from 1839 to 1845, where he opposed the annexation of Texas and the extension of slavery into the new western territories. Like Smith, White was a friend of internal improvements. He returned to become a founding settler of Stockwell, south of Lafayette, and to serve as president of two early local railroad lines, including the Indianapolis and Lafayette. His speeches were considered scholarly and admired for their rich use of classical allusions.[7] William Woollen described him in those years: "Physically he was weak; intellectually he was strong."[8]

Albert Smith White

White returned to Congress as a Republican during Lincoln's first term, championing many of the president's early plans and chairing a committee exploring gradual emancipation and subsequent colonization of freed slaves.[9] He then served on a three-man commission that adjudicated claims in Minnesota and Dakota after the 1862 Indian uprising.

White was nominated on January 14, 1864, and confirmed and commissioned four days later. Ill health denied him any real chance to speak out during his brief eight-month tenure on the bench, and he left most of his cases on the docket for his successor.[10] Senator David Turpie, a personal friend and admirer of White's skills and character, reflected on White's brief service on the court:

> I have since deeply regretted that Mr. White did not live some years to preside in the federal courts of our state. He would have brought to the duties of the bench a great store of legal learning and acumen, the most patient diligence in all his work, accompanied by an inborn courtesy, an urbane suavity of manner, which much becomes those who sit in these high tribunals. [11]

McDonald's modern reputation rests primarily on his legal scholarship, which included serving as a founding professor at the Indiana University Bloomington law school and writing a text instructing justices of the peace in their duties and procedures.[12] He was born in central Kentucky in 1803. Largely self-taught, McDonald showed a lifelong preference for English poets and essayists—and an independence of judgment that manifested itself in scorching private criticism of many of his contemporaries. McDonald moved to Indiana in 1817 and progressed from farm laborer to schoolteacher to politician and lawyer. He was a state legislator in the 1833–34 session and an elected judge of the Tenth Indiana Circuit Court from 1838 to 1852. McDonald settled in Bloomington in 1841 and began offering a three-month law course each year at the university, continuing until he moved to Indianapolis to enter private practice in 1853.[13]

McDonald sought the district court appointment when it became vacant in both 1862 and 1864, finally succeeding on his third attempt.

He kept a candid and detailed diary recording his path to appointment, ranging from his personal worries to his interviews with Lincoln—and left little doubt how personal and political he found the process. He described an era when the president himself, not a senior figure of the president's party, made the final decision on appointment:

> Friday, 9 Sept. 1864. . . . Lincoln was not in; but entered shortly, and seemed to receive me very cordially. We had met before. He recognized me and began to talk of old times in Indiana. . . . Finally I mentioned my business, made him a poor stump speech, and told him all I could. He heard me patiently, and I think encouraged me to expect success. But he told me that, as several had telegraphed him not to make a sudden appointment, he would have to delay until he heard from all applicants.

> Tues. Dec. 6, 1864. . . . Then I was called in. The President said he had thought of making me judge in [recently deceased Supreme Court Justice John] McLean's place. . . . Afterwards he said he thought seriously of me when he appointed Smith, and so also when he appointed White. He said he cared nothing about recommendations. He said, in fine, everything from which I might infer that he would appoint me without promising it directly. I feel sure he will do it. Yet the doubt and the uncertainty are painful.[14]

McDonald was nominated on December 12, 1864, and confirmed and commissioned the next day. In contrast to his earlier worries, this was McDonald's description of his first day on the bench:

> Thurs. [Dec.] 15. . . . To day I took possession in the U.S[.] States Judges rooms in the P. O. building. Every thing nice here—an Irish man to make fires—nice carpets—rich furniture—Elegant stationary [sic]—all free of expense to me—and all this for life. . . . It is like some of the fond creations in the Arabian Nights' Entertainment.[15]

Ill health, including a partial paralytic stroke, plagued McDonald after 1868, and he also left a crowded docket for his successor.[16]

War Issues and Reform Concerns
Moral reform cases faded from the wartime court's agenda. There is little evidence that any of the three Civil War judges offered strong expressions about reform issues while on the bench. It could, of course, be argued that by striving to maintain the rule of law in wartime the three Indiana district court judges were forwarding the reform agenda of the Union government. The attitudes of these three judges toward the sources of inspiration and morality that had been so important in the antebellum era also varied. Smith and White, when evaluated by their contemporaries, were often described as orators and former railroad presidents—suggesting, perhaps, a greater respect for enterprise than for inspiration. Smith's oratory was clearly influenced by Baptist preachers, including the Reverend Caleb Blood, for whom the judge was named. One observer noted of Caleb Smith:

> he had neither rival nor superior. His voice, singularly clear, sonorous and penetrating, rarely encountered a crowd that could exhaust its power. . . . He possessed the ability to argue a

proposition convincingly, while covering it with apt and pleasant "hits," and could, when it served a purpose, say as bitter things as John Randolph himself.[17]

Under the pressures of the war, however, Smith's oratorical powers did not serve him well on all occasions. Shortly after his appointment, Smith chose to speak at a rally in Indianapolis. On a flight of rhetoric he spoke "illustrating a point by a comparison between the former and present condition of Rome." A young Roman Catholic attendee took offense and began to hiss—leading to the attendee's arrest and the levy of a heavy fine by the mayor. Smith generally avoided public presentations thereafter.[18]

McDonald had been a "new light" preacher in the 1820s and showed a lifetime interest in matters of faith.[19] Late in his career he sought the most unusual extralegal source of inspiration of any jurist who has sat on the Indiana district court. His obituary in the *Richmond Palladium* noted:

> In his later years he gave much thought to the subject of "Spiritualism," and was a complete convert to the doctrine of the presence and action of the spirits of the departed in our present visible life. He . . . expressed his entire faith in the spiritual origin of certain phenomena exhibited by the mediums, thus affording another illustration of the truth that the extreme of infidelity is far more apt to change to the extreme of credulity, when it changes at all, than it is to the moderate convictions of a judgment that has never been shaken.[20]

One may judge whether to credit a report in the *Indianapolis Journal* that McDonald even communicated with six persons in full daylight the day after his death by writing a message in his handwriting on a slate.[21]

Ill health cut short each of these three judges' terms, but did not prevent them from ruling on cases related to the Civil War. Smith was notable for his actions in 1863 at the trial of six alleged rioters from Morgan County, who were accused of membership in a secret antiwar society allied to the Knights of the Golden Circle and indicted for encouraging Union soldiers to desert and for firing on troops sent to recover the deserters. The prosecution painted a vivid picture of armed civilians firing on soldiers and presented a witness who admitted to membership in a secret society complete with passwords. The defendants based their response on confused testimony that cast doubt as to whether they had actually fired their pistols. Significantly, Smith instructed the jurors to treat the issue as a conspiracy and to convict if they were convinced the defendants intended to resist the soldiers. All six were found guilty. Satisfied with a conviction, Smith imposed a fairly lenient five hundred dollar fine against each defendant, using the occasion as an opportunity to speak out in support of legal authority and the war effort.[22]

White made his views about the rebellion clear in an elaborate dedicatory address for Crown Hill Cemetery in Indianapolis in June 1864, where he proclaimed, "The blood of the brave and the wisdom of the wise are invoked to save a mighty commonwealth torn by civil strife."[23] However, he seldom took advantage of opportunities to express himself in the courtroom. Partly this was a matter of White's judicial temperament, which was noted in the *Indianapolis Journal*:

> His extraordinary and I had almost said *excessive* conscientiousness, caused him while on the bench to hesitate in some instances in giving a decision lest he might be guilty of the

slightest partiality, and many matters which the majority of the courts would have decided without a thought were held in reserve by Judge White, for careful and critical examination, to the no small annoyance of attorneys who could see but one side of the case.[24]

War-related cases on White's docket included criminal actions relating to the obstruction of the enrollment of soldiers, assault upon an enrollment officer, and counterfeiting of the new paper currency (with its distinctive colored greenbacks).[25] The judge's most widely reported cases were a series of confiscation suits in which the U.S. attorney had pursued the forfeiture of property owned by individuals who had served the Confederate government or in the Confederate army. Most federal judges appear to have avoided confiscation cases because the most important item to be confiscated, slaves, were being dealt with by the Emancipation Proclamation and later by Constitutional amendments that affirmed them to be persons and not property, and because there was a serious question of whether other forfeitures for treasonous actions was covered by the Constitutional provision regarding "corruption of blood." This would have limited property forfeitures to the life of the individual and then allowed their return to his heirs. But White himself, while a Congressman, had voted for the Confiscation Acts of 1861 and 1862, which he now helped to enforce vigorously. The judge did not speak to his underlying motives, but others in Congressional debates in 1861 and 1862 had stressed the need to punish Confederate behavior, to reward loyalty (or at least neutrality) in border states, and to affirm the war powers of the government. The issues in White's cases, such as the applicability of confiscation laws to slain rebel soldiers, allowed Smith to affirm such war powers, while voicing strong Unionist sentiments.[26] A good example was the case of John King, whose Confederate enlistment made his real property a target for confiscation. King, through his counsel, satisfied White that he had met the terms of a presidential amnesty proclamation. But King also argued that his amnesty entitled him to have his legal costs paid by the government. Called to decide upon the issue, White ruled,

> it certainly was not the intention of the President that suits of this character should be discontinued at the cost of the Government, that such was not the legal effect of the proclamation when the rules of law were applied to it; and that such discontinuance should therefore be at the cost of the claimant who had been at war with his government.[27]

Ex parte Milligan

Although the civil courts were open, they were not dealing with one important set of cases by 1864: trials for alleged disloyalty. Instead, a new military tribunal had emerged in Indiana that was trying the more serious issues of resistance to the war. Its most important case, which eventually reached the Supreme Court in 1866, was *Ex parte Milligan*. In the process, the *Milligan* case involved a key appeal to McDonald and produced the best-known decision of his tenure.

American wars have often seen citizens or politicians express fear that the country's enemies enjoy support, open or secret, among some portions of the civilian population. Indiana Unionists, including many Republican officials, abounded in the expression of such fears during the Civil War. When asked for evidence, some Republicans pointed to opposition by Democratic speakers and legislators to wartime finance measures, particularly after the Democrats won majorities in the Indiana General Assembly in 1862. Other Republicans placed emphasis upon opposition to Union army recruiting or to the 1863 draft laws, particularly in several heavily Democratic counties in southern Indiana. Some Republicans gave credence to reports that secret societies were directing antiwar efforts such as stockpiling weapons or planning to liberate Confederate prisoners from Indiana prison camps. Many supporters of the war demanded firm enforcement of the wartime legal measures of the Lincoln administration, and some supporters expressed willingness to suspend peacetime civil liberties during the emergency of the Civil War.[28]

In the fall of 1862 Lincoln had granted military tribunals the power to try civilians charged with disloyalty. Congress confirmed that power in March 1863. Such military courts were boards of senior army officers who heard evidence, made a determination of guilt or innocence, and then passed sentence. Prosecutions were conducted by a judge advocate with broad powers to introduce evidence. Defendants were entitled to legal counsel. But with no citizen jury and little control over the admission of evidence, the defense was at a far greater disadvantage than it would have been in civil court.[29]

Starting in September 1864, such a military tribunal sat in Indianapolis and heard the cases of several prominent members of the Democratic Party who were accused of treason. As presented by Major Henry Burnett, the judge advocate, the government's case rested upon allegations of conspiracy. The defendants were accused of being members of secret societies, particularly the Knights of the Golden Circle, who had met to oppose the war effort and to plan armed resistance to the Lincoln administration. A parade of witnesses, including paid government informers, detailed a series of meetings—the most serious of which was claimed to have been held in Chicago with Confederate officials on July 20, 1864.[30] Former Chief Justice William Rehnquist offered this useful summary of the prosecution's legal position:

> As understood in the federal courts in the mid-nineteenth century, conspiracy consisted of an agreement among two or more persons to commit an offense forbidden by the criminal law, together with an overt act by one or more of those persons in furtherance of the conspiracy. The conspiracy need not have been successful, and indeed need not ever have come to fruition.[31]

Defense attorneys countered at two levels. First, they pictured the defendant's actions as legitimate political opposition, arguing that attending meetings did not meet the constitutional definition of treason. Article 3, section 3, clause 1 of the Constitution states:

> Treason against the United States, shall consist only in levying War against them, or in adhering to their Enemies, giving them Aid and Comfort. No Person shall be convicted of Treason unless on the Testimony of two Witnesses to the same overt Act, or on Confession in open Court.

Second, they called the evidence into question, challenging the integrity of paid informants and showing that particular defendants could not even have been present at the times and the places the prosecution alleged. But the defense case suffered a blow when the principal defendant, Harrison Dodd, fled to safety in Canada. Several of the remaining accused, including Lambdin P. Milligan, were convicted and sentenced to death.[32]

The motives of the prosecution remain debatable to this day. A trial conducted while wartime passions were high could certainly validate the fears of those politicians and voters who looked for conspiratorial behavior in political opponents. A trial designed to prove a secessionist conspiracy during the 1864 election canvass certainly could contribute to a unionist victory, if only by helping to blur the distinction between disloyalty and simple political opposition. At the very least, the trial raised partisan questions of timing.[33]

From the standpoint of the federal court, another interesting question of timing existed. The Supreme Court ultimately ruled in the *Milligan* case that the military commission lacked jurisdiction because the civil courts were open. But it is also true that the court was adjourned in September when the treason trials began and would remain so until Lincoln filled the vacancy created by Judge White's death on September 4, 1864. Contemporaries certainly took this into account. This is reflected in the revealing comments in McDonald's diary describing both his opinion of the military tribunal's authority and the role of Democratic senator Thomas Hendricks in the appointment process:

> Mon. 26 to Frid. 30 [September 1864] The trial of H. H. Dodd before a Military Commission is in progress here. The disclosures in this case make the "Sons of Liberty" a most treasonable association.[34]

> Wed. 23 [November 1864] Hendricks came [to my office] to talk about the District Judgeship. It is strange that always when I have sought office, Democrats have helped me more than my own party. I do not now know a Democrat of any consequence in the State that does not wish to see me get this office. This is

Lambdin P. Milligan

not because I am inclined to their political faith, but because they believe I would try them fairly in Court.³⁵

The *Milligan* case quickly tested McDonald's fairness because Milligan promptly filed a petition seeking a writ of habeas corpus. Because of the severity of the charges, such cases were filed under the circuit court jurisdiction that the Indiana district court had exercised since 1837. Had the *Milligan* case first been tried in civil court, it would have been tried by Judge McDonald. Now that it was being appealed, the case involved both McDonald and the Supreme Court justice assigned to the Indiana circuit. Since 1861 this had been John McLean's successor, Justice David Davis. Davis was one of Lincoln's close associates, having been the judge of the Illinois state circuit court before whom the future president tried so many of his cases. Davis studied at Kenyon College and Yale Univer-

David Davis

sity and had amassed a fortune in Illinois real estate. In 1860 Davis managed Lincoln's nomination in Chicago and after McLean's death in 1861 was appointed to the Supreme Court. Davis was a huge man physically, six feet tall and more than three hundred pounds. One wit commented that Davis was not measured for a suit of clothes, he was surveyed. Davis carried a reputation for honesty, directness, and very detailed legal opinions. His access to the president caused most observers to assume that his political judgments reflected conversations that had been, or would be, held with Lincoln. Davis had firm opinions on resistance to the war. Addressing a grand jury in Indianapolis, he said,

> It is charged that there are secret organizations . . . with "grips, signs and passwords" having for their objects—resistance to Law, and the overthrow of the Government. . . . If anywhere in this State bad men have combined together for such wicked purposes, I pray you, bring them to light and let them receive the punishment due to their crime.[36]

With the war ending, Milligan might have hoped for postwar leniency. But the assassination of Lincoln, by another group of conspirators, triggered an intense burst of Northern political anger against the South and its friends—and probably doomed any chances of pardon or amnesty that Milligan might have enjoyed. His only hope lay in the federal courts.

McDonald and Davis both knew this and wanted to find a solution to the case in law. The approach eventually taken by the two judges was to agree to disagree on Milligan's request for a writ and thus cause the matter to be forwarded to the Supreme Court. The key features are described in McDonald's diary:

Tues. 9 [May 1865] ... the authorities have fixed on Friday the 19th instant for hanging ... the "Sons of Liberty", tried last Fall. I am sorry to hear it, not that they are not traitors, but that there is too much doubt of their having been convicted by a Court of competent jurisdiction. Judge Davis has the same fears I have on this topic. We will try to induce the President to delay the execution till the Supreme Court shall pass on the question.[37]

Thurs. 11. The application ... was made for a writ of habeas corpus to be delivered from military custody under sentence of death. On a certificate of division of opinion [it] was sent to the Supreme Court of the United States.[38]

During its December 1866 term, the nine justices of the Supreme Court decided that Milligan should be released. The majority further ruled, in a decision written by Justice Davis, that Milligan and his co-defendants should not have been tried by a military tribunal when Indiana's civilian courts were open. It is upon that affirmation of the authority of the civil courts that the fame of the *Milligan* case rests. Thus, by availing themselves of the procedural vehicle that required a division of opinion in the circuit court be forwarded to the Supreme Court, McDonald and Davis played a significant role in the most important federal court action in nineteenth-century Indiana legal history.

Walter Q. Gresham in a Changing Postwar World

McDonald's death on August 25, 1869, allowed President Ulysses S. Grant to make one of the early judicial appointments of his administration. Grant's choice became one of the best-known judges of the district court and the first who did not complete his public service with the court.

Walter Q. Gresham brought many "firsts" to the court. He was the first district judge born in Indiana (Lanesville in 1832). He was the first to attend law school at Indiana University, although he also apprenticed in a Corydon law office before gaining admission to the bar in 1853. He was the first, and ultimately the only, district judge who served in the

Walter Q. Gresham

Civil War, enlisting in the Union army in 1861. In the course of that war he rose to colonel of the Fifty-third Indiana Regiment and achieved the brevet rank of major general. He was the first judge since Jesse Lynch Holman to enjoy a recess appointment, on September 2, 1869, prior to his formal nomination to the district court on December 6 of that year. He received both Senate confirmation and his commission on December 21, 1869.[39]

The short week between McDonald's death and Gresham's recess appointment allowed critics of both Grant and Gresham to question the process of selection. The *New Albany Commercial*, for example, clearly had both men in mind when it praised Lincoln's earlier appointments and warned that "[m]eanness and mediocrity can not hide behind the judge's robes."[40] It was an unexpected appointment for two reasons. First, some had thought the more obvious candidate was John D. Howland, clerk of the court and master in chancery. Second, apart from his military service, Gresham had a relatively short résumé that included only one term in the state legislature and a brief tenure as Indiana's financial agent in New York in 1867–68. But Howland's greater age and lack of military service probably counted against him, and Gresham's military service had gained him the personal friendship of Grant.[41]

Marion County Superior Court Judge Pliny Webster Bartholomew, in an 1895 memorial address, recalled an 1870 conversation with Gresham:

> He spoke about his appointment as District Judge by General Grant. And as he grew more confidential and friendly in our talk, he said to me that came to him wholly unexpected. That he had returned from the war not expecting to occupy any judicial position, but to practice law among his old neighbors and

friends in the southern part of the State, and he said when that appointment came (I think these are the words he used), "I was worse frightened than I ever was in battle." . . . But he said that General Grant urged him to accept it, and he finally did so.[42]

Gresham suffered from ill health during his early years as judge. A broken hip aggravated his wartime injuries and kept him away from the bench on long trips to spas and warm climates. Others, often circuit court judge William Drummond, sat in his absence.[43] When he did return to the bench, Gresham soon evoked strong responses. His demeanor on the bench evoked this characterization:

> His favorite attitude in court was with one foot up on the corner of his desk, his body swung back in a chair, his eyes half closed, and the thumb and forefinger of his right hand toying with his knife. He would sit for hours and open and snap the blade, and never move another muscle. Lawyers might talk . . . the Judge's eyes were closed and his knife went on with its click. Presently: "What was that authority?" So and so, would say the attorney, surprised that he had even been heard. "Thanks! Go on, sir." And then the eyes closed again and the penknife clicked on the measure of time as before.[44]

Gresham evinced opinions quite different from his predecessor on the subject of spiritualism. In early 1883 George Thompson of New Albany appeared in court to protest his disinheritance, documenting the manner in which a local spiritualist had gained such influence over Thompson's father that the elderly gentleman had changed his will to benefit the medium. Gresham heard witnesses that convinced him of the father's diminished capacity and overturned the will. The judge then added a lengthy section to his decision under the heading of "Religious Delusions—Spiritualism." "A belief in spiritual communication," he noted, "is not ipso factor an insane delusion, rendering the believer incapable of making a valid will." But when the spirit medium was a beneficiary of largesse in a will, the burden to disprove undue dominion and influence rested with the medium and not the family.[45]

Jacob Piatt Dunn, the most influential historian of Indianapolis in Gresham's era, described the judge this way:

> He was not considered a profound lawyer at the time of his appointment, but he was a man of ability. . . . He developed as a judge, his chief failing being an impetuous nature, which caused him to administer what he considered justice like a roadroller when he once got his head set.[46]

Gresham first showed these tendencies when he confronted one of the messy scandals of the Grant administration, the Whiskey Ring. The Ring, a pejorative term applied by its critics, was a group of whiskey distillers and sellers who conspired to evade the payment of federal excise tax and various licensing fees.[47] Although centered in Saint Louis, the group's activities extended up the Ohio River valley into Evansville, Indiana. There, in June 1875, in the first prosecution of the group, Gordon and John Bingham were convicted in Gresham's court of the administrative offense of distilling without the presence of a government monitor, or "storekeeper." More important, Gresham induced them to reveal the names of others in the ring, ultimately naming twenty-five individuals, who were indicted in December 1875 and tried in Gresham's Indianapolis court in January 1876. Twenty-four were convicted, including several government excise collectors—although one agent obtained acquittal as a result of the skillful pleading of his counsel Benjamin Harrison.[48] Harrison's cross-examination of the key government witness, which exposed inconsistencies in the witness's description of the defendant's attire at a formal wedding, helped earn Harrison the epithet "kid-glove lawyer."[49]

The Whiskey Ring case attracted national attention to Gresham. He held discussions with treasury secretary Benjamin Bristow as early as 1874 urging the secretary to pursue the case, and Gresham used his opinions to affirm a position of strong civic morality that would characterize his later opinions. Gresham's later disputes with Harrison may have originated in their mutual displeasure with one another's behavior in such cases.[50] A later anecdote captures Harrison's sentiments. Approached, while president, and asked by a group of Indianapolis lawyers to appoint Gresham to a vacant seat on the court of appeals,

> Harrison with a twinkle in his eye remarked: "Gentlemen, you are well aware of the fact that I have practiced law before Judge Gresham for many years, just as you have done. I know that you will believe me when I say that I can well understand how any lawyer whose clients' business takes him in Judge Gresham's court can be perfectly willing to see Judge Gresham assigned to any other court."[51]

Gresham also played a central judicial role during the great railroad strike of 1877. The strike came after another of the periodic depressions, or panics, of the nineteenth century had gripped America in 1873. The railroads, by now the dominant form of both passenger and freight transport, were especially hard hit as receipts plummeted. Many rail companies were soon resorting to emergency measures, such as failing to pay debts or past wages. To do this legally, many lines sought the protection of bankruptcy receivership. Such measures were sure to be felt in Indianapolis, which had become, as W. R. Holloway termed it, a "Railroad City," where many rail lines met and where much local manufacturing was tied to producing railway cars and parts.[52]

The issue came to a head in the summer of 1877, when a number of the lines announced a 10 percent cut in wages. This sparked a series of strikes that started in Martinsburg, West Virginia, and spread across much of the country from Maryland to Colorado. At its height the work stoppage was probably as close to a national strike as America has ever experienced. Initially most strikers expressed a desire for a nonviolent work stoppage that would lead to the restoration of recent wage cuts. But in some areas, most notably Pittsburgh, events spiraled out of control. Indianapolis, where workers struck on Monday, July 23, never experienced violence. William Sayre, secretary of the Brotherhood of Locomotive Engineers, speaking for the strikers, promised to avoid violence. But many civic leaders were sufficiently concerned that they began proposing a variety of different measures, from conciliation to coercion, to deal with the strikers. Indianapolis mayor John Caven, for example, swore in two hundred strikers as special city deputies with the understanding they would help him keep the peace. Such responses seemed to quiet the situation, and later interpreters have argued that the strike had largely run its course by the time Indianapolis became involved.[53]

But Judge Gresham was clearly among those who were still alarmed, and his preferred method of dealing with the strikers ran toward coercion. In a telegram to President Rutherford B. Hayes on Wednesday, July 25, Gresham opined, the mob is the only supreme authority in the state at present. They commit no other violence but to interrupt railroads, but they sheep together, stop all business, & by the suspension of business large numbers of men will soon be out of employment, upon the streets, and swelling the mob. . . . There may be an outbreak at any moment and the consequences will be most disastrous.[54]

When Hayes did not immediately respond, Gresham next took the lead in creating a committee of public safety, whose purpose was immediately to recruit a local militia. The judge even made his courtroom a barracks for the members of the company that he raised.

The threat of force would be necessary, Gresham felt, if he was to enforce the injunctions he planned to issue against the strikers. The issue could have involved his court in one of two ways. Interference with the U.S. mail, which could occur if a mail car was stopped, was a federal crime. Issues of railroad bankruptcy could fall under jurisdiction of the 1867 Bankruptcy Act.[55] Several such bankruptcies, of lines that ran to or through Indianapolis, were already supervised by court-appointed receivers. Of the two approaches, the first was more problematic because the strikers avoided stopping the passenger trains upon which most mail traveled.[56] So Gresham concentrated on the latter. The judge was encouraged in his approach by representatives of the affected railroads, who were advocating the use of injunctions. It was an approach previously seldom used in labor disputes. Judge Gresham acted specifically on a request from the receiver of the Indianapolis, Bloomington, and Western Railroad, issuing a writ for the arrest of any persons interfering with the receiver's operations. Gresham also ordered U.S. marshal Benjamin Spooner to assist in enforcing the writ. But a cautious U.S. attorney,

Charles Devens, approved this approach only for "processes issued" by the court for individual cases. Fearing delay, Gresham secured the support of the circuit judge, Thomas Drummond, for a blanket writ banning any unlawful interference with "any property in the custody of any receiver in this court." Drummond, who became a champion of the use of the injunction in such receivership cases, also approved the creation of adequate forces to enforce the writ.[57]

The strong show of force worked, and the strike collapsed by Friday, July 27, even before the arrival of two hundred federal troops. But to make the point very clear, a number of strikers were arrested over the weekend, brought before Gresham, and tried the following week for contempt. Because Gresham had organized the citizen militia, he recused himself from the decision—while continuing to make comments from the bench. Drummond came down from Chicago to run the proceedings under circuit court jurisdiction, which jailed all but two of the defendants for three months. The case became one of the most important precedents to arise from a federal court in Indiana, and it was broadened within a few years in other courts to permit contempt proceedings without a jury trial to be used to enforce injunctions in labor disputes. As Lawrence Friedman has observed, "The injunction was an ancient, powerful, and honorable tool of courts of chancery. It had infinite possibilities and uses. Its suppleness and power made it an especially deadly threat to labor."[58]

Intellectual Property

Another area where Gresham used the district court as a forum to establish precedent for legal changes was in the field of patent law, or "intellectual property" law as it has come to be called. His son, Otto, summarized the family's perception of Gresham's role:

My father's work on the Bench was harder than it ever had been at the Bar. Instead of the work being light, it was heavy, especially on the mechanical side. . . . The patent branch of the law is a matter of technicalities and machinery. . . . The District and Circuit judges, all past middle age before appointed, could not or would not master it. . . . My father turned to his mechanics and so far mastered that branch of the profession that until the time he left the Federal Bench his court was crowded with patent litigation.[59]

Gresham's opinions, especially in the 1880s, reflect this judgment. In *Streit v. Lauter*, Gresham, exercising circuit court jurisdiction, presided over a matter that involved the allegation that the defendant had infringed the plaintiff's patent regarding an improvement to rocking chairs. In a detailed opinion that focused on the technical aspects of the patent in question, Gresham concluded that the holder of the patent "was not entitled to a reissue embracing what he had discarded as faulty, even if he was the first to discover the rigid connection." Ultimately, the judge concluded that the suit must be dismissed because the holder of the patent had lost his right to a reissuance of the patent as a result of his unreasonable delay.[60]

Another interesting patent case to come before Gresham was *Gottfried v. Crescent Brewing Co.* In *Gottfried*, Gresham presided over a suit that alleged patent infringement and sought an injunction and an accounting. The invention that was at issue "consist[ed] in preparing casks for receiving pitch or other melted substance, which will render them impervious, by introducing into the casks a blast of highly-heated air." The defendants argued that the patentees who had filed the suit were not the original and first inventors of the alleged improvement and that the alleged improvement had been the subject of "certain English letters patent and foreign printed publications." After analyzing the workings of the invention, Gresham concluded, "I think from the evidence a skillful mechanic, familiar with the art, and this publication before him [an 1861 German publication entitled 'Newest Discoveries'], could readily have constructed this model." In dismissing the plaintiff's lawsuit "for warrant of equity," Gresham observed that

> The patentees took old and well-known mechanical contrivances for accomplishing useful results, and applied them to a new purpose. In this there was nothing to support a claim for a patentable invention or process.
>
> The plaintiff's patent was not for the application of an old machine to a new use. The interior of moulds and other receptacles had been previously heated by a hot blast, and the patentees used a blast of the same character to heat the interior of beer casks. No new application of a natural force or element in nature was pointed out or described in the patent.[61]

On September 21, 1882, after his initial written opinion was issued, Gresham granted the patentees' motion for a rehearing and reached the opposite conclusion. Specifically, Gresham concluded that the device that was at issue "was the first and the proof shows that it is to-day the only, means by which brewers are enabled to pitch barrels and kegs without removing the heads." The judge explained,

> Compared with other means for heating the interior of casks and receptacles, the complainants produced a new mechanism

or thing which enabled them to pitch casks and kegs more rapidly and economically than they had ever been pitched before. I think the complainants were entitled to a patent, not for the improved or better result of effect, but for the mechanism or means by which the result was accomplished.

Lest there be any question, Gresham's decision was grounded in policy:

> It is the policy of the law to encourage useful improvements, and I am unwilling to hold that the complainant's device, consisting of old elements, combined and operated as stated in the specification, practically superseding, as it does, all other known means of pitching kegs and other small receptacles, and greatly superior, as it confessedly is, to Siebel's machine for pitching large casks, is the mere mechanical equivalent of the latter, or of any other device.[62]

On November 5, 1888, the *Gottfried* decision was reversed by the U.S. Supreme Court. Writing for the Court, Justice Samuel Blatchford described the procedural history of the case, including Gresham's original opinion and his opinion on rehearing, and observed that there had been "a great deal of litigation as to this patent" in other courts. The Supreme Court, in what appears to have been a unanimous decision, concluded that "the process of flowing melted pitch on the inside into the pores and joints of casks which were to be filled with spirituous or volatile liquids, such flowing taking place while the casks were in a heated state, was not new," that "the apparatus used for applying the heated blast to the interior of the cask" existed before, and that the patent was invalid because "the defendant's apparatus is, to all intents and purposes, a faithful copy of 'Pewterer's Blast' apparatus."[63]

The same year that his decision on rehearing in the *Gottfried* case was reversed by the Supreme Court, Gresham issued his decision in a case that involved an alleged improvement in threshing machines. Gresham's opinion, which was announced orally, concluded that alleged improvements in threshing machines and separators did not involve invention. Gresham described the basis for his decision:

> A skilled mechanic, with the Westinghouse machine and these patents before him, could have made the improvement which is described in the Blinn patent.... Neither the slight change that Blinn made in the incline of the grate, nor in the location near it in the cylinder of the beater, involved invention. Indeed, Blinn did little more than take the beater as he found it in a Throp machine, and put it in the Royer machine.

Gresham's decision resolved the case, as the parties had stipulated that the court's decision would be final and binding and that neither party would appeal Gresham's decision.[64]

Judge Gresham and Politics

Gresham occupied the bench during a time of intense political competition, both between and within the major political parties, and the press paid particular attention to cases that reached his court involving contested federal elections. Most important was a June 1879 criminal trial of thirteen Jennings County Democrats, who were accused of "conspiracy in importing voters from Jackson into Jennings County in the State and Congressional election of 1878."[65] According to one account of the trial, most of the defendants were prominent men in that southern Indiana county. The defendants' counsel included former Indiana governors Thomas Hendricks and Conrad Baker. The government was represented by U.S. Attorney Nelson Trusler and by Benjamin Harrison, who had been appointed by the Department of Justice on Trusler's recommendation.[66]

A dispute quickly arose over jury selection. Colonel William W. Dudley, U.S. marshal for the district of Indiana at the time, was responsible for summoning prospective jurors. The modern practice of drawing names blindly and randomly from the voter registration rolls was not yet in effect, permitting the marshal more discretion. Thus, the original pool of twenty-four prospective jurors was determined to contain twenty-one Republicans, two Democrats, and one Greenbacker (a supporter of a third party advocating expansion of the paper money supply). The Republicans included deputy postmasters, revenue collectors, and county committeemen. After the jury selection process was completed, the jury itself was comprised of eleven Republicans and the Greenbacker. This compelled Hendricks to make what he described as "the most extraordinary motion addressed to the sound discretion of the Court that has ever been made in a legal proceeding."[67] He urged Gresham to discharge the jury and pick another. Gresham agreed, saying to the original panel as he discharged them:

> All the Democrats on this panel have been excused, the jury left is made up of ardent political partisans. It is unreasonable to suppose this could have happened from chance alone. The Court believes it is the result of design. . . . The circumstances of your selection cast a suspicion over your organization, and the Court believes from the circumstances that it would be dangerous for these defendants to submit their cause to you.[68]

A new jury was picked from a list that had been composed by the judge himself and included an equal number of Democrats and Republicans. Gresham further indicated that if a member of the new pool was struck, he would be replaced with another individual of the same party. Gresham also reportedly warned Dudley that if he ever again attempted to pack a jury, Gresham would send him to jail. The decision is often cited as a cause of Gresham's long political feud with Harrison. Harrison "vehemently" objected to the discharge of the jury and was warned by Gresham to take his seat. When he failed to do so, Harrison was further admonished to sit down or Gresham would instruct Dudley to arrest him. Only three of the defendants were ultimately convicted.[69]

As his health recovered in the late 1870s, Gresham's own interests in politics grew. Not only did he show this in his decisions and in the communications that surrounded them, but he also became a player in state and national politics. Although he sought to conceal his role at the time, his modern biographers identify him as the source who revealed the Mulligan letters detailing apparent personal corruption by Republican presidential aspirant James G. Blaine of Maine. By 1883 this political involvement, combined with financial challenge, caused Gresham to become the first Indiana district judge to resign his appointment. The *Indianapolis News* asserted that John Foster, a Hoosier Republican serving as minister to Spain, informed President Chester Arthur that Gresham would soon resign to accept a partnership promising $10,000 per year at the firm of McDonald & Butler. Foster asked Arthur if he would agree to find a new judicial appointment for Gresham if the return to private practice did not work out. The president, the paper continued, responded, "How would Gresham do for postmaster general?" Foster, the article concluded, made the arrangements.[70] Gresham went on to replace Thomas Drummond on the circuit court, to challenge

Harrison for the 1888 Republican presidential nomination, to change political parties, and to conclude his public service as President Grover Cleveland's secretary of state between 1893 and 1895.

A Changing Court

The rapid changes in practices and precedents that marked Gresham's fourteen years on the bench were accompanied by changes in court organization, legal codes, the court family, and the Indiana legal profession. The district court's relationship to the circuit court was redefined by statute in 1869. At that time Congress reduced the responsibility of Supreme Court justices to ride circuit, requiring the justices to hold only one circuit term every two years. Instead, the president was empowered to appoint separate circuit court judges. Indiana was assigned, as it would remain, to the seventh circuit. Thomas Drummond, previously an Illinois district judge, held the new post from 1869 to 1884. He was succeeded by Walter Gresham, who was appointed by President Arthur in 1884, and Gresham was replaced by Wisconsin District Court Judge James Jenkins in 1893.[71] In the midst of those changes, in 1874 Congress issued a set of revised statutes that furthered the creation of a uniform national code of law and that sought to define more clearly the lines between state and federal jurisdiction in ways that expanded federal jurisdiction.[72]

Congress added a separate U.S. Court of Appeals in 1891. However, the existing circuit courts maintained a separate existence until 1911 when an act of Congress abolished the courts and assigned cases to the respective district courts. These changes were of particular importance to judicial selection in Indiana because each of Gresham's two successors resigned their district court appointment in connection with U.S.

William Allen Woods

Court of Appeals vacancies—one to assume an appellate seat, the other to allow a relative to do so.[73]

A second change was the political status of the U.S. District Attorney. Although the office continued to be political and in fact to change in even closer conformity to changes in the national executive, it became less of a stepping-stone to higher office. Twelve men held the post between 1861 and 1901, but only David Turpie (1886–87) went on to the U.S. Senate, and only Thomas Browne (1869–76) entered the U.S. House of Representatives. More commonly the office now was the province of future state legislators, circuit court judges, and county prosecutors.[74]

Third was the introduction of the new U.S. Commissioners in 1874. Given responsibility for such matters as arraignment and bail, these commissioners served renewable four-year terms. Technically allowed jurisdiction throughout the state, they were in practice assigned areas roughly coterminous with congressional districts.[75] The new commissioners were an obvious response to increased court business, as were increased court staffs. Gresham's successor, Judge William Allen Woods, helped to define the legal status of commissioners in 1886 during an election fraud case. The judge upheld a contempt citation issued by a commissioner against a defendant who had refused to be examined upon state election matters at his arraignment. Woods then reviewed the statutory history of the office, noted it was now an essential feature of the federal criminal justice system, and contended a commissioner had the full powers of an examining magistrate. While the circuit court agreed to the importance of the office, they refused to sustain Woods on an issue that involved questions related only to state law.[76]

The district court sat most frequently in Indianapolis, where it occupied offices and a courtroom in the old U.S. Federal Building. The economic growth of the Hoosier capital, particularly tied to railroads, manufacturing, and food processing, assured an increasing flow of cases as the century progressed. But the court remained responsible for the entire state of Indiana, and each district court judge traveled a circuit that took them regularly to other cities, including Evansville, New Albany, Terre Haute, and Hammond. Court offices were also maintained in those cities, usually with a small permanent staff and a commissioner to conduct routine business between sessions of the court.

The U.S. Courthouse at the southeast corner of Market and Pennsylvania streets, erected in 1860, now demolished.

A government building program in the 1870s and 1880s added new federal buildings in several cities, including Evansville, New Albany, and Terre Haute. Following a pattern that prevailed for many years, these new structures offered accommodation to a number of government agencies, including the district court. The Evansville post office, courthouse, and custom house on Second Street between Sycamore and Vine was designed by William Potter and built between 1875 and 1879. The Terre Haute U.S. Courthouse and post office at the corner of North Seventh and Cherry was designed by Mifflin Bell and built between 1884 and 1887. The New Albany U.S. Courthouse and post office was also designed by Mifflin Bell and built between 1886 and 1889.[77]

The records of the construction of a new federal post office and courthouse in New Albany in 1887 give a sense of the district court's

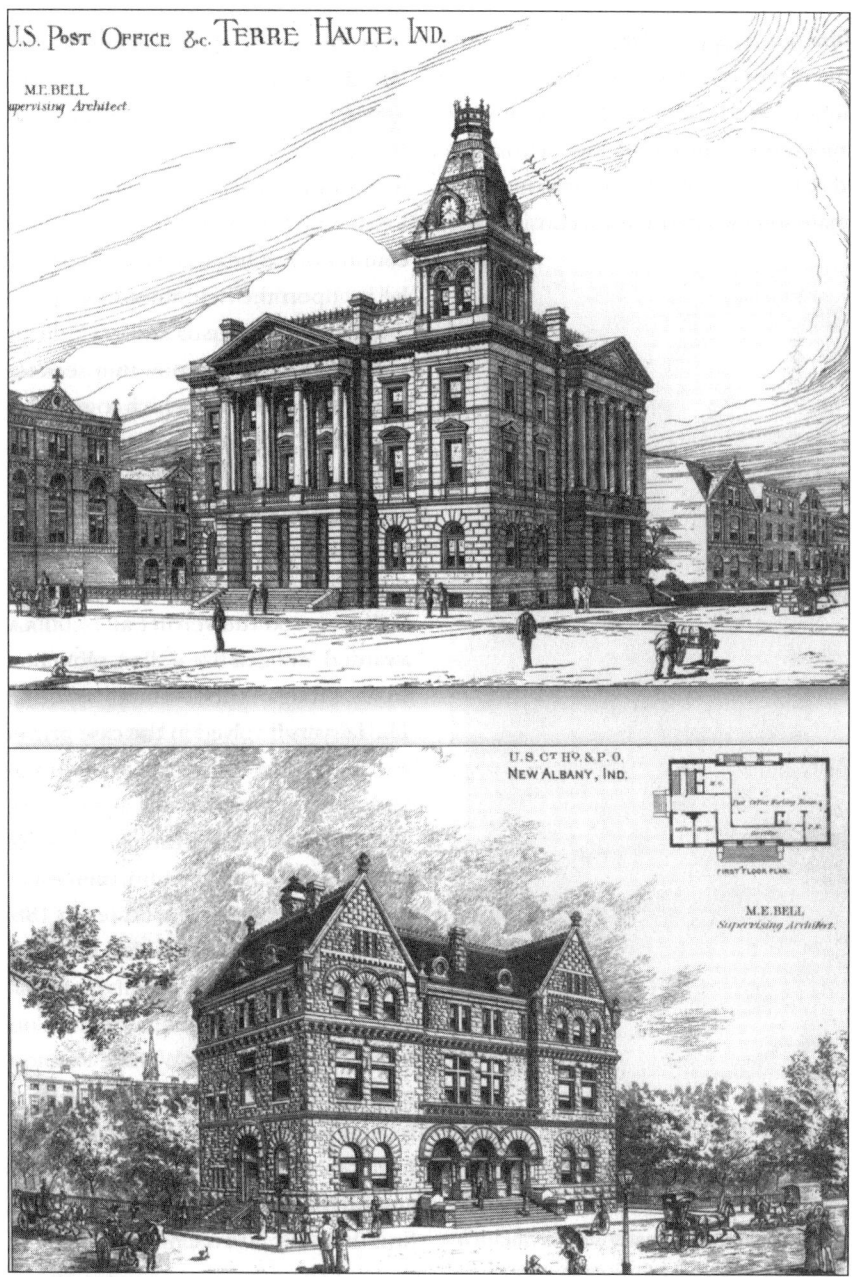

The September 18, 1886, issue of the American Architect and Building News *featured drawings of the new federal buildings in Terre Haute and New Albany. Both of the structures were designed by Mifflin E. Bell.*

presence in that Ohio River city. The contract for the building was advertised for bids not to exceed $100,000. The building was to consist of two stories, post office below and district court above, and the number of upstairs rooms and their functions were specified by court officers, but the room dimensions were left to the contractor to propose within the cost limit. The contract required a courtroom (eventually 20' by 40'), and eleven other rooms (each 20' by 16') for the judge, the clerk, the deputy clerk and assistants, the grand jury, the petit jury, the court library, "lady witnesses," "gentlemen witnesses," the district attorney, the marshal, and the janitor. With a vault for records, an elevator, wide stairs and hall, and lavatories, it would house the court for many decades.[78]

Court functions continued to be supervised by the clerk of the court in Indianapolis, who usually also held the title of master in chancery, and the clerkship continued to be a post with very little turnover. Two men, John Rea and Watt Smith, served short terms during the Civil War. Thereafter, only three individuals held the post between 1865 and 1922. John Howland served from 1865 until 1877, William Pinkney Fishback from 1877 to 1879, and Nobel Chase Butler from 1879 until 1922. All were respected attorneys; Howland and Butler were each considered at one point for elevation to the district judgeship. Howland enjoyed special respect for his literary interests. The organizer of the Indianapolis Literary Club in January 1877,[79] he was later memorialized as "a quiet man of forceful character, a lover of good books, fond of the society of cultured men."[80] Charles Evans, a local attorney, recalled this anecdote in 1927:

> The Supreme Justice of the Court at this time was David Davis, who made the Howland residence, from choice, his home while on the circuit. Justice Davis was very corpulent, weighty in both

person and decisions. His departure and arrival at the Court was always a matter of some ceremony.... On the entrance of the Justice all would stand until he had heavily seated himself ... leaving to the capable hands of Mr. Howland, and the bailiffs, the further decorum and procedure of the Court.[81]

The post of U.S. marshal continued to be a four-year presidential political appointment, held by nine individuals between 1860 and 1901. It could change with a national political administration, as it did in 1861 when David Rose replaced Elisha English and in 1889 when William Dunlap replaced Edward Hawkins. It could also change in response to political pressure within the district court, as it did in 1879 when William Dudley resigned in the aftermath of the selection of jurors for the Jennings County vote fraud cases. Most commonly, however, the marshals simply served their terms and returned to private life.[82]

A Modern Legal Profession
The legal profession itself was also growing and changing, reflecting a series of changes that one historian has dubbed a "culture of professionalism."[83] At its heart, the new professionalism was the result of an attempt to provide and enforce standards of conduct that would assure high levels of performance by participants in a given field. Medical doctors, public accountants, university professors, and a variety of similar professional groups were seeing their expertise subjected to new standards of training and performance. The changes were clearly felt in the practice of law.[84] The Indiana State Bar Association, organized on June 23, 1896, committed itself in this spirit to "advance the science of jurisprudence, promote the administration of justice, uphold the honor of the profes-

sion of the law, and encourage social intercourse among the members of the Bar of the State of Indiana."[85] The association soon involved itself in defining the conditions of admission to the bar and in suggesting criteria of judicial selection.[86]

Many of these professional initiatives drew upon a growing number of law schools within the state. Indiana University at Bloomington, which the state legislature had closed in an economy move in 1876, reopened in 1889. It joined DePauw (Greencastle), Tri-State College (Angola), Indiana Law School (Indianapolis), Benjamin Harrison Law School (Indianapolis), and Central Normal College School of Law (Danville) among state institutions that, for some period of time after the Civil War, offered a structured curricular alternative to training within a law firm.[87]

The new profession was also aided by the expansion of the state law library. The library had actually been founded early in the century when District Court Judge Benjamin Parke donated a portion of his personal library to the state. Those books, together with later donations, were shelved with the rest of the state library—stored until 1835 in the governor's mansion, and then in the old state capitol building. In 1852 the state legislature required the state librarian to keep the books in a separate place in the library, and then in 1867 required separate rooms for them. Initially the separate space was less than ideal: "according to the old lawyers who frequented the rooms, it was an extremely hazardous place to reach [at the top of] a narrow and steep stairway."[88] A new state capitol building finally provided larger quarters to house a collection that required 725 pages to list in the 1898 catalog prepared by librarian John McNutt.[89] At least two members of the district court family contributed to the collection through their own writings. Court clerk John Howland coauthored *A Manual for Executors, Administrators, and*

Guardians, with Forms Adapted to the Statutes of Indiana in 1862.[90] U.S. attorney David Turpie coauthored an edition of *The Revised Statutes of Indiana* in 1881.[91] Their efforts are a forceful reminder that although the district court enforced federal law, it did so in the presence of a legal community trained in, and comfortable with, Indiana laws and courtroom practices—an enduring federal balance.

These changes were accompanied by growth in the size of some law firms in major cities such as Indianapolis and Evansville. Most early firms in Indiana were small partnerships in which one of the partners commonly attended to such local activities as debt collection and the other traveled the circuit of the state or federal district courts. Now the expansion of legal business, often a reflection of commercial expansion of the state, began to produce firms of larger size and longer tenure than just the life of a partner. Baker & Daniels, initially a partnership of the 1880s, and Krieg DeVault LLP, originally a two-lawyer practice led by Acquilla Q. Jones in the 1870s, are examples.[92]

Court Appointments and Republican Factionalism

The struggle during the 1870s between Gresham and Harrison, on and off the bench, set an acrimonious tone that marked the appointment of the next two judges to Indiana's district court—William Allen Woods in 1883 and John Harris Baker in 1892. Each was selected from among a crowded field in which legal competence vied with political service and personal associations in determining support and endorsement. Factional divisions within a divided Indiana Republican Party often dominated the discourse.[93]

The 1883 appointment process was set in motion by President Chester Arthur's appointment of Gresham to the cabinet as postmaster

John Harris Baker

general. A crowded list of potential district court successors initially appeared. They included U.S. attorney Charles Holstein, former governor Conrad Baker, and district court clerk Noble Butler. But the choice quickly narrowed to two men. Harrison, now U.S. Senator, championed one of his law partners, Cyrus Hines. Gresham proposed Justice William Allen Woods[94] of the Indiana Supreme Court. Eventually, Arthur chose Woods. Woods received a recess appointment on May 2, 1883, and was confirmed and commissioned on January 7, 1884, to the delight of Harrison's critics who crowed:

> It is enough to make one weep to think of the despair of Senator Benny Harrison. He remained here [in Washington, D.C.] for long weeks to straighten out Hoosier patronage. His short, stumpy figure, pale face, shadowed by an awful dignity of backwoods commonplaceness, and lengthened out by a gray goat's beard, were seen in the lobbies of hotels for weeks. . . . Nearly every day he went up to the White House to see a great-bored but much-enduring President.[95]

The same paper later added that just as Gresham's appointment had been "a stinging rap between Senator Ben Harrison's eyes," the Woods appointment was "another heavy blow."[96]

It certainly appeared more a struggle among Washington figures than a battle in Indiana. Woods's daughter, the noted author and artist Alice Woods Ullman, in an affectionate unpublished memoir, provided a picture of much more limited involvement by her father:

> "Well, Mama, here it is!" He handed [his wife] a telegram that she'd been watching him read.
> "It's hard to believe, isn't it?" She laid down her gloves that she always pulled on when working, even with her fuchsias indoors. "Now children," She looked at us, "we'll be moving at last, out of this one-horse town."
> . . . We stood against the arms of his chair and he let us read the telegram. It told him that President Arthur had appointed him to be federal judge for the District of Indiana.

... Said [Woods's son] Floyd, out of the blue, "What I can't understand, Papa, is how a man like the President ever heard of you."

... [Woods] told us all that he knew about his appointment and how he came to get it. "You see, Floyd, I rolled up a pretty good vote when I ran here—these things get around in the party."[97]

John Harris Baker's[98] appointment nine years later to replace Woods again involved a crowded field of possible nominees, including two members of the Indiana Supreme Court, three state trial judges, U.S. attorney Smiley Chambers, and several practicing attorneys. With Harrison now president, it could be assumed different factional considerations would prevail. The *Indianapolis News* offered the following assessment:

> As President Harrison has the reputation of using his own counsels in selecting his own appointees, no one ventures very positively to utter a prediction in this case, and probably no great surprise will be experienced if Judge Woods's successor be some man not heretofore mentioned in connection with the appointment.[99]

The surprise came when Harrison named another member of the Goshen bar, Baker. The two Goshen attorneys had often faced one another in the county seat's courtroom. The *Goshen News* recalled one episode:

> Woods was an arrogant man before the bar. He asserted his claims in a loud and positive voice, and a lock of his auburn hair used to hang down over his Jove like front that he shook as the lion

shakes his mane to emphasize his language, which was at times quite deeply tinged with personality, and grew stronger with the increasing heat of the contest. Baker was always smooth, polished and deliberate, self-possessed and exceedingly courteous, but one day Woods went a little too far by something more than insinuating that Baker had lied. The latter, livid with rage, sprang to his feet, and seizing a chair, rushed upon his burly antagonist. What might have happened is hard to calculate, but members of the bar and court officers interfered and but little damage was done. Subsequently the gentlemen met, explanations followed and their usual friendly relations were resumed.[100]

Baker received his nomination on March 24, 1892, and was confirmed and commissioned five days later. Baker received the news of his appointment in his Goshen office and received a recognition unique among Indiana district judges when "After Supper Rogers' Goshen Band tendered Mr. Baker a delightful serenade at his office."[101]

The two successive judges from Elkhart County shared many outward similarities in their biographies.[102] Both had been born in the 1830s in another state: Woods in 1837 near Farmington, Tennessee, and Baker in 1832 in Monroe County, New York. Both were college graduates: Woods at Wabash College, Baker at Ohio Wesleyan. Both were admitted to the Indiana Bar shortly before the Civil War, but neither served in the army. Both were Republicans who served a single term in the Indiana legislature in the 1860s, Woods in the house, Baker in the senate. After the war Woods chose a judicial career, serving as a judge of the circuit and the supreme courts of Indiana. Baker stayed more active in partisan politics, winning three terms in the U.S. House of Representatives in the 1870s.[103]

Each man brought a distinctive temperament to the bench. Woods was described by a Hoosier friend, former vice president Charles Warren Fairbanks: "He was tenacious of his opinions; but in no merely dogmatic way. He was willing to recede from them if convinced that they were founded in error."[104] Tom Ochiltree, an attorney who became involved in a fee dispute in Woods's court, had different memories. As the *Indianapolis News* told the story,

> When a Federal officer went to Rushville to make the arrest of [his clients], Ochiltree made him the unwilling witness of an injudicious criticism of Judge Woods. "If my clients were Democrats," said Ochiltree, "they could not get justice before Judge Woods."

The attorney was discomfited when Woods learned of the matter, made the Federal officer a witness in court, and required Ochiltree to confirm or deny the charge.[105] Ochiltree refused, left the courtroom, and later claimed the deputy marshal attempted to throw him over a balustrade. Ochiltree further contended that when the incident was brought to Woods's attention, the judge's only comment was that he was late catching his streetcar. Woods denied the story.[106]

Labor issues continued to occupy the court. In one of his last cases, Baker heard a dispute from Hammond involving a strike against a printing company, W. B. Conkey Co. The strike had many of the familiar elements of labor disputes at the time, including threatened violence against strikebreakers. It also had an unusual political dimension produced by the presidential election of 1896 because the printers had produced a number of copies of an unflattering biography of the Democratic candidate, William Jennings Bryan, causing Judge Baker to comment, in the negative: "the question as to whether or not the 20,000 men who are said to have voted against Mr. Bryan because a history of his life prepared by somebody was printed at the Conkey establishment,—all that is matter that is foreign to any issue that we have here." But the actual legal issue, as the judge saw it, was whether an agent of the Typographical Union of Chicago, if not named in a previous injunction against the strikers, could be punished for encouraging the strike. The judge thought he could and fined the offender $250.[107]

Extralegal community coercion or violence, sometimes called vigilantism, has long been an undercurrent in America's legal history. Claiming to speak for the popular will, yet often shrouded by nighttime darkness or fear-evoking costumes, this distinctive attempt to impose a group's values or behavior patterns on unwilling citizens has periodically agitated Indiana. The most famous example is the Ku Klux Klan in the 1920s, but the Klan had several precursors, such as the Horse Thieves Protective Association. Most groups were challenged and eventually suppressed by state authorities. Yet on at least one occasion a masked rural crowd, the Whitecaps, reached Baker's court.

The case proved to be the last one tried in district court by the judge, and the length of the case delayed by a week his retirement and transfer of power to Judge Albert Anderson. Local newspapers described the case as an act of violence triggered by a family's social behavior. As sometimes happens, the issues that perplexed the court were not necessarily those that had attracted the press. The defining legal issue proved to be the prosecution's power to summon a witness in a criminal proceeding. While the Fifth Amendment makes it clear that defendants may summon witnesses in their defense, the issue was less clear when opposing counsel battled over the technical issue of the distance a prosecution witness could be required to travel to attend the court.[108]

Baker's service on the bench subsequently inspired colorful recollections. His work could inspire affectionate recollection:

> [S]itting in [his] chair [in the old federal building] listening to an argument in chambers—he arises from his chair without interrupting the speaker, walks to the book shelves, removes a volume of the United States supreme court reports or of the reports of the opinion of inferior federal courts, turns to a page always remembered, returns to his chair and then interrupts the speaker to call attention to some pertinent decision which he thinks of persuasive or perhaps controlling influence on the question under discussion.[109]

Late in his service on the bench, the judge also was the subject of one of the few accounts that survive describing the day-to-day operation of the district court. The *Indianapolis News* offered this description of a day in November 1899.

> The wheels of justice would not turn in the Federal Court this morning. Judge Baker started the machinery at 9 o'clock, but something was wrong with the lubricants and the cogs just would not go. United States Marshal Kercheval, three men from the district attorney's office, post office inspectors and court bailiffs were there to give their help or their hindrance, but every few minutes there was a general tie up. The judge, usually in good humour, had his temper ruffled, the marshal grew red in the face because things were not going his way and District Attorney Wishard yawned as if he wished he were out of it all. [With one side or the other announcing each time a case

was called that they were not ready to proceed, Judge Baker had reached his limit. The judge joked with the jurymen about the delay, and announced that they should return in the afternoon.] Then the Court took his gray hat from its nail, stopped at the silver pitcher to get a drink of ice water, and went down to his study, on the floor below, without waiting for the crier to declare that court had adjourned.[110]

New Business Before the Court

Each of the new judges participated in the change and development of American law that accompanied the economic and social development that so transformed the later nineteenth century. Viewed from a later century, the cumulative effect of such change is great. Viewed from the perspective of individual cases, it emerges as a slow, cumulative process. Examples abound of the varied cases that came before the court, including the following:

- In 1866 McDonald found that the *Morning Star*, a passenger steamer, was at fault (in a collision with a towboat) under admiralty law for entering a fog bank south of Evansville at twelve miles per hour without a lookout. The judge rejected claims that a single unpaid passenger on the towboat (*Crescent City*) required it to violate common practice and post a lookout on the stern where it was rammed.[111]
- In 1868 McDonald found that a vessel itself, rather than its owner, was in violation of admiralty law by failing to have its name, *Lewellen*, painted conspicuously on its wheelhouse.[112]
- In 1879 Gresham found that the state of Indiana was responsible for the discipline of convicts that it leased by contract as unskilled

laborers, and that it had failed to hire sufficient guards to control "their turbulent and vicious propensities." The judge therefore substantially reduced a bankruptcy judgment against the contractor, the Southwestern Car Company, who had been unable to use such laborers effectively in producing its product.[113]

- In 1886 Woods found that the 1787 Northwest Ordinance continued to provide rights to the Miami Indians of Indiana and accordingly voided a sale of Indian land for delinquent taxes that had been improperly assessed.[114]
- In 1901 Baker found that alimony payments awarded in a state court could not be discharged under federal bankruptcy law. The court "will not release a bankrupt from his obligation of support ... [because] the duty of marital support springs out of the contract of marriage, and continues until dissolved by death or the judgment of a competent court."[115]

Political Cases and Positions

As district judges, both Woods and Baker were watched for their political positions, and each ultimately involved himself in ways that contributed to earning presidential favor. Woods first attracted attention by his intervention in the Tally Sheet Forgery Cases of 1886. Although the 1886 election resulted in a Democratic victory for most Marion County offices, it left two offices in doubt when the canvassing board met on the Thursday after the election. As the tally sheets were counted, however, angry Republicans—who had obtained copies of the original returns in six precincts—alleged that erasures had been made to increase the Democrat vote. Over a year of litigation followed, with Woods intervening twice in the process. The first intervention came in the initial week of the vote count, when Woods convened a grand jury and ordered it to investigate the voting because the federal office of U.S. Representative was on the ballot. Records were impounded, but after a three-week review the grand jury reported insufficient evidence for an indictment, and the judge reprimanded and dismissed the jury.[116] Testimony continued to be taken by a new grand jury, however, and Woods soon jailed one of the election officers—who refused to testify—for contempt, at least until Gresham, on the court of appeals, ruled federal jurisdiction was lacking.[117]

The case then moved for a time to state court. But Woods received a "second opinion" from Justice John Marshall Harlan, another seventh circuit jurist, that the district court did have jurisdiction. A new grand jury was promptly convened, the key witness induced to testify with a grant of partial immunity, and several leading Democrats were indicted—including County Chairman Simeon Coy. Two rounds of trials followed. In the first, the jury divided: eight for conviction and four for acquittal. In the second, the key figures were convicted by a new jury that finally accepted the testimony of the government's chief witness.[118]

Woods's next involvement on the bench was in a case close to the heart of President Harrison: the "block of five" case. The case had arisen in the heat of the presidential election of 1888 in Indiana, as always a closely contested state. A postal worker, probably illegally, had obtained a copy of a letter written on stationery of the Republican National Committee. The letter contained a set of instructions to local Republicans to raise money to pay for the votes of "floaters" in the upcoming election. Given to the Democrats, the letter sparked a wave of partisan complaint, and led to the impanelment of a grand jury shortly after Harrison's victory in the state and nation. Woods initially instructed the grand jury that federal law made it a crime for an individual to advise others to bribe voters, and the grand jury reportedly stood ready to indict one or more Republican operatives. But informal contact from Harrison supporters caused Woods to rephrase his instructions to require actual bribery before a federal crime had occurred. Dudley was never indicted, and Woods subsequently quashed actions against local Republican recipients of the letter.[119]

Baker also became involved in partisan politics, but did so through actions taken outside the courtroom. He was actively involved in a factional struggle for one of Indiana's U.S. Senate seats. The root of the struggle was a split in the state Republican Party. Its older leadership, including Benjamin Harrison and Charles Fairbanks, had formed an alliance with President William McKinley and Ohio senator Mark Hanna. An insurgent group had formed around Albert Beveridge, and against the odds elected him to the Senate. Beveridge credited his success in part to the letters and conversations of support made by Baker, who had admired Beveridge ever since the young lawyer in his first outing had bested Harrison in a jury trial.[120] In Beveridge's words,

> [W]hen my race for the Senate seemed hopeless, judge John H. Baker and his son [Francis] . . . voluntarily came to my aid with their great influence. He wrote letters for me all over the state— two hundred of them. He adjourned court and personally saw members of the Legislature in my behalf. His son threw several northern members to me without reward or hope of it.[121]

In December 1891 Woods was elevated to the new court of appeals by President Harrison. In 1901 Baker resigned to allow his son, Francis, to be appointed by Beveridge's ally, President Theodore Roosevelt, to the vacancy created by Woods's death.[122] Having reached seventy years of age and served for ten years, Baker was the first Indiana district judge to retire with full salary. He was also the first to be the recipient of a commemorative dinner. "Judge Baker was a general favorite, and on his retirement he was given a banquet by the bar, on December 30, 1902, the first occurrence of the kind in the history of the court since its organization in 1817."[123] Baker left a district court that had changed significantly in the previous forty years. It was about to change even more in the context of a new century.

CHAPTER THREE

Creating the Southern District

1902–1950

New currents in both political and legal thought appeared with the new century and helped to reshape the district court. Politically, a desire for progressive improvement in both government and society led to a number of new approaches to moral reform and economic regulation. Legally, a significant expansion of federal criminal and civil jurisdiction, new rules of procedure and practices of administration, and national concerns tied to depression and war commanded the attention of both bench and bar. Caseloads continued to grow at a faster rate than population and, combined with political considerations in the 1920s, produced the separation of the Indiana court into its modern northern and southern districts. Labor leaders, baked-bean canners, politicians, gangsters, and a fascist leader all contributed to the mix of parties who appeared before the court.

Albert Anderson Takes Charge

Judge John Harris Baker's resignation in 1902 presented President Theodore Roosevelt with the opportunity to make one of his early judicial appointments. Roosevelt was a careful politician who considered the political implications of each appointment. In the case of the Indiana vacancy, he was presented with several qualified candidates, including attorneys Cassius Clay Shirley of Kokomo and E. G. Hogate of Danville. But James Noel was probably correct when he noted in a later memorial address for Shirley that aspirants with fewer friends were not appointed.[1] Eventually the weight of recommendations leaned strongly toward Albert Barnes Anderson, a Wabash College graduate whose only previous office had been one term as Montgomery County Prosecutor. Anderson had been politically active, however, and had won the enthusiastic support of his Congressman, Charles B. Landis.[2] Both men were also political allies of U.S. Senator Albert Beveridge, whose endorsements within the shifting world of Republican factional politics carried great weight with Roosevelt.[3]

The influential position of Anderson's legal friends was also vital in the appointive decision. He enjoyed the strong support of Albert Baker and Edward Daniels, partners in one of Indianapolis's leading law firms,[4] and through their numerous professional and political associations a statewide network of support. In his letter of support to Roosevelt, Daniels spoke of a friendship dating back to college and noted that he and Anderson were roommates while serving as law clerks.[5] Baker was

Albert Barnes Anderson

equally straightforward in his comments to the president, noting his support for

> Mr. Albert B. Anderson of Crawfordsville, Indiana, my brother-in-law, in case there should be a vacancy in the judgeship of the District Court of the United States. . . . Mr. Anderson and I have been intimately acquainted for about twenty-five years. He

is ruggedly honest. He could not be swayed by unworthy influences and he has the acumen that would not admit of his being swayed, without his knowledge, by considerations of friendship. From the moral standpoint, I know of no better man for this place.[6]

Others seconded the call. Indiana Supreme Court Justice James Jordan spoke of Anderson's briefs before the court, which caused the justice to have "been very favorably impressed with his ability as a lawyer."[7] A. A. Hargrave of the *Rockville Republican* spoke of Anderson's "high standing as a fearless attorney whose opponents dread to meet him in trials."[8] Roosevelt was clearly impressed, and he sent Anderson's name forward in November 1902 to a rapid confirmation.

Anderson on the Bench: Political Trials

During his twenty-three years on the district court bench, Anderson sought to project an austere, no-nonsense style. He quickly established a reputation for keeping the docket clear and for handing down tough sentences in criminal cases. Albert L. Rabb presented this characterization in later memorial remarks:

> Judge Anderson was a kindly man and his severity was brought to bear only on those defendants who he thought were trying to put something over on him or on those attorneys who he thought were lazy, unprepared or too garrulous. The Judge disliked arguments that apparently were leading to nothing and often interposed questions designed to bring matters to the point. He liked to decide questions immediately, if possible, and his mind was as

brilliant as any in his court. Judge Anderson never liked to work at night and when he left his chambers in the Federal building it may have been late but he never returned until the next day.... His manner was abrupt and his words sharp and cutting when he showed disapproval. Defendants often were heard to say that they would rather be sentenced than lectured by him.[9]

As with his predecessors, Anderson was watched closely when he presided over cases that carried strong political implications. The Panama Canal libel suit, decided in 1909, is a good example. The case arose from an *Indianapolis News* article reviewing the acquisition of the Panama Canal during the Roosevelt administration. The article suggested that the acquisition of the canal properties had been accompanied by corrupt dealings severe enough to warrant the words "thieving" and "swindling" in connection with the government's role. Angered, the new administration of President William Howard Taft filed an indictment charging criminal libel against the newspaper's publishers. The charges were filed in Washington, D.C., based on the argument that copies of the paper had been sold in that city. The government then asked Anderson for a warrant of commitment that would permit the defendants to be removed to the national capital for trial.[10]

Anderson refused. In an oral ruling, he rejected the government's claim that Washington was the proper trial site. The Sixth Amendment, he reminded the prosecution, provided "In all criminal prosecutions the accused shall enjoy the right to a speedy and public trial by an impartial jury of the state or district wherein the crime shall have been committed, which district shall have been previously ascertained by law." The *News*, he concluded, was an Indiana paper; only about fifty of its ninety thousand copies were sent by mail to Washington. Anderson ruled that if a crime had occurred, it could only have occurred in Indiana. The defendants were discharged.[11] Anderson forcefully observed,

> If the history of liberty means anything, if constitutional guarantees are worth anything, this proceeding must fail. If the prosecuting officers have the authority to select the tribunal, if there be more than one tribunal to select from, if the government has that power, and can drag citizens from distant states to the capital of the nation, there to be tried, then, as Judge Cooley says, this a strange result of a revolution where one of the grievances complained of was the assertion of the right to send parties abroad for trial.[12]

The decision infuriated Roosevelt and led him to a rare display of public criticism for Anderson. As president, Roosevelt had been outspoken in his desire for a bench of high quality. As he then described his views on judicial appointment:

> There is no body of appointments over which I exercise greater care. . . . My first consideration has in every case been to get a man of the high character, the good sense, the trained legal ability, and the necessary broadmindedness of spirit, all of which are essential to a good judge.[13]

But in 1910 the former president visited Indianapolis and stopped at the Columbia Club, which had been a center of Republican politics since being founded as the Harrison Marching Society in the 1888 election. While there, Roosevelt was drawn by future U.S. Senator Henry New into a discussion of Anderson's performance on the bench. Speaking as if in a private conversation, but accompanying his remarks with flamboyant hand gestures and clearly intending to be heard by others in the room, Roosevelt barked, "That was the decision of a damned jackass and a crook. Yes, he is a crook and a jackass and I said it. This is not confidential."[14] Anderson made no public response.

Partisan politics again reached Anderson's courtroom in the aftermath of a major election case from the 1914 elections in Terre Haute. The city and Vigo County Democratic leaders were charged, and ultimately convicted, of an elaborate conspiracy to fraudulently elect a ticket that included their candidate, Eli Redman, for Vigo County Circuit Court Judge. To achieve their ends, the conspirators solicited campaign funds from a number of operators of "saloons and gaming houses." Each operator was promised they would receive

> immunity from prosecution and arrest for all violations of the law that they should commit, and would be permitted to conduct gaming devices and gaming houses without hindrance or interference, and would be permitted to keep open their saloons and sell intoxicating liquors when prohibited by law, and to sell intoxicating liquors to persons to whom the law forbade them to sell, and to conduct dance halls, wine rooms, music, and restaurants in connection with their saloons, in contravention of law, and would keep Terre Haute a wide-open town.[15]

With these funds, the conspirators then proceeded to recruit a number of nonresidents and "floaters" who would cast ballots under fraudulent names. Several election workers were trained to manipulate lever voting machines and cause votes intended for Redman's Republican opponent to be recorded for Redman. In addition, members of the

Terre Haute police department were recruited by its chief to appear at voting places to conduct "fraudulent manipulation of voting machines" accompanied "by force, threats, intimidation, and by the use of pistols and other firearms." Then, to complete the fraud, corrupt police officers arrested several uncooperative Republican election board members and watchers, confining them in detention cells in the city and county jails until the vote was counted.[16]

When the defendants appeared in Anderson's court, their defense hinged upon the assertion that the federal courts lacked jurisdiction because the object of the fraud was to capture a state judicial office. Anderson rejected the argument, pointing out that the conspirators had used the U.S. mail to send reminder notices to a number of their paid workers, and that the offices of U.S. senator and representative were on the ballot. In the process, the judge was among the first to make judicial use of the recently approved Seventeenth Amendment, which provided for direct election of senators, as a basis for a voting rights decision.[17] A number of conspirators were eventually convicted and jailed, and Redman was removed as Vigo County circuit judge.[18] The defendants' appeal to the Seventh Circuit, based upon the argument that the fraudulent voters had not actually been registered at the time the fraud was planned in September, was rejected early in 1916.[19]

Almost a decade would pass before Anderson heard his last major political case in April 1924, the trial of Indiana governor Warren T. McCray for mail fraud. John Niblack, later a Marion County judge but then a young newspaper reporter, kept notes that blended partisan enthusiasm with eyewitness intensity:

> High over all on his bench in front, like the seventh avenging angel sitting on his cloud, sat the Honorable Albert B. Ander-

Warren T. McCray

son in his black robes, eyeing the defendant malevolently and smacking mental lips over the feast to come.... "Close the doors, and lock them, and have the United States Marines from the recruiting office patrol the corridors," decreed the Judge, and the trial began.[20]

McCray had been involved in a variety of businesses that centered on cattle farming. His credit was already overextended when a sharp economic downturn hit the state in the aftermath of World War I. To avoid bankruptcy, McCray conceived a scheme to borrow money from a number of banks, offering forged promissory notes that he claimed reflected cattle sales. If a bank was reluctant to accept his notes, the governor normally dangled the promise of the deposit of state funds as a further incentive. When notes came due, often after ninety days, the governor mailed new notes to many of the banks as a way of avoiding payment.

By the time he was indicted in late 1923, the governor owed well over one million dollars to 157 banks. McCray testified that some nights he stayed in the governor's office until 1:00 or 2:00 in the morning, so great was the volume of his personal financial correspondence. The most colorful moment of the trial was probably the testimony of W. J. Hendry, a farm manager whose signature McCray had forged on about $160,000 worth of notes. After denying any involvement in the scheme, Hendry was asked if he had assets equal to the value of the notes. "Well, I did own two heifers and coon dog," he replied. McCray's defense was that he had simply been striving to maintain a business in hard times. The jury convicted him in fifteen minutes. After a short lecture in which Anderson indicated he found no difference between McCray and the "lowest criminal," Anderson sentenced the governor to ten years in the federal penitentiary in Atlanta, Georgia.[21]

Industry and Organized Labor in Court

Despite the fact that he presided over several trials involving political questions, Anderson was probably better known in his own time for trials involving individual workers and labor organizations. The transformation of Indiana, as of much of the United States, from a rural/agricultural to an urban/industrial society was far advanced by his tenure. Anderson's docket often reflected the disputes and divisions of that industrial world. Early in his tenure, for example, the admiralty case of the *Conveyor*, which had sunk in the Ohio River, reached the district court. The ship was salvaged, and an insurance policy was paid to the owner who wished to use the money to repair the vessel. But the seamen on the vessel sued in Anderson's court, asking for their wages. Noting that such wages "are nailed to the last plank of the ship" as a pledge of payment, Anderson redirected the insurance settlement to them.[22] In 1912, clerk of court Noble Butler, sitting as special master in chancery, supported the Indiana Railroad Commission's attempt to replace oil headlamps on locomotives with acetylene or electric lights because of their greater documented brightness and resultant contribution of public safety.[23]

Another good example of industrial issues was the contentious question of liability for injuries occurring in the workplace. In general terms the issue was who was at fault when accidents, injuries, or even deaths occurred while workers were on the job. American law in the nineteenth century had traditionally approached this question through the fellow-servant rule. Essentially, the rule provided that if another worker (the fellow servant) could be shown to have contributed to causing an accident, an employer was not responsible. Employers frequently used the rule to avoid the payment of workers' compensation, and it was under intense attack by labor throughout the industrial states. Especially between 1910 and 1920, many states substituted a new form of guaranteed compensation that paid the actual expenses of the injury. During the transition, some employers chose to argue cases in federal courts where the older fellow-servant rule still applied.[24]

Anderson usually enforced the fellow-servant rule and reaped a harvest of criticism from organized labor and its advocates. Historian Martin Tuohy reviewed Anderson's handling of the claims resulting from the 1914 death of Albert Fellers. Fellers had died while doing electrical work on the interurban South Shore Line in Lake County, Indiana.[25] Tuohy opined that Anderson's rulings and jury instructions showed little sympathy for the claims of Fellers's family and offered this harsh assessment of the judge's conduct: "Anderson [had] developed a national reputation for arrogance, severity, and unflinching opposition to working-class protests against the personal hardships caused by the new industrial order."[26]

In such a climate of opinion, any labor-related case evoked strong opinion. This was especially true of those cases that involved violence because the turn of the twentieth century was a period of disturbing violence in America. The assassination of President William McKinley in 1901, the attempted murder of Theodore Roosevelt in 1912, and the assassinations of governors in Kentucky and Idaho in 1901 and 1904 were examples of national events that commanded popular concern. Other violent actions only added to the public perception that the rule of law was under challenge. Such was the case with a dramatic series of bombings and murders that culminated in 1912 in the most visible case to reach Anderson's courtroom.

On October 1, 1910, a bomb exploded in the alley next to the *Los Angeles Times* building in California, killing twenty-one night shift workers and injuring more than thirty others. The *Times* was a strongly antiunionist newspaper, and both its owner and the Los Angeles police assumed the explosion was an act of labor violence. Arrests soon followed, and one of the accused, Ortie McManigal, agreed to turn states' evidence. McManigal named two brothers, James and John McNamara, and claimed they had acted with the knowledge of the leadership of the International Association of Bridge and Structural Iron Workers. Quickly arrested, the brothers proclaimed their innocence. Samuel Gompers, president of the American Federation of Labor, believed their plea, feared the indictments were really an attack upon unions, and retained Clarence Darrow to lead their defense. Darrow, a nationally known attorney from Chicago, had represented other labor leaders in media-intensive trials. He initially planned a high visibility defense. But McManigal's evidence against the brothers was eventually corroborated, especially after a raid on the union's headquarters in Indianapolis found documents that supported his allegations. It was a mark of the tensions surrounding the case that the raid was not undertaken until President William Howard Taft had reviewed the request and indicated his support of the action. Darrow eventually entered into an agreement with California authorities that spared the brothers' lives in exchange for their guilty pleas, a bargain that earned the defense attorney the wrath of organized labor leaders who continued to proclaim the McNamaras' innocence.[27]

The bombing was one of a number of explosions, ultimately totaling nearly one hundred, carried out as part of a nationwide campaign by officers of the International Association of Bridge and Structural Iron Workers in an attempt to replace so-called open shops with union shops on steel girder construction projects. The deadly campaign arose from a 1905 union strike against the American Bridge Company in Ohio. The strike was an ugly affair, with violence on and off the construction sites. It eventually spread to numerous other sites where the American Bridge Company or its affiliates held contracts. The company showed no inclination to settle on terms acceptable to the union, and in December 1906 several of the union leaders decided to initiate a bombing campaign. The specific attacks later tried in federal court continued intermittently over nearly four years between January 20, 1908, and August 27, 1911.²⁸

The Los Angeles trial set the stage for a separate trial in Indianapolis, where about forty union leaders were tried for actions described in the documents seized from the union's headquarters. The case reached the U.S. District Court for the District of Indiana, where it was prosecuted as a "conspiracy to commit a crime against the United States, and of transporting, aiding, and abetting the transportation of dynamite and nitroglycerine in interstate commerce in passenger trains and cars between the several states." The case was prosecuted in Indiana because the union's national headquarters, where the conspirators often stored their explosives in a basement safe, made their plans, paid for their "batteries, clocks, fuse and attachments," and shipped their timed detonators (which the prosecution termed "infernal machines"), was in the American Central Life Building in Indianapolis.²⁹ Darrow, facing two successive jury tampering trials in California, did not appear in Indianapolis.³⁰ Instead, Chester Krum of Saint Louis took the lead in arguing the case for the defense.³¹

The prosecution claimed that the defendants monitored nonunion structural steel construction sites across the country and carefully targeted firms that could be harmed financially by the damage and delays wrought by the massive bombing campaign. Although the union activists had communicated by letters and telegrams as well as in person, they had carefully avoided speaking to outsiders or putting incriminating details of the bombings in writing. Thus the case against the defendants rested primarily on reports of conversations involving government informants. The government's case carefully focused on two elements: the web of circumstantial evidence that indicated the various defendants had "come to a mutual understanding" that constituted conspiracy, and the actual transportation of the explosives on a common carrier across state lines, which was illegal under federal law.³²

The trial, often called the Los Angles dynamite trial, was conducted under intensive media scrutiny. Reporters eager for exclusive copy sought human interest items. A razor smuggled to one defendant to permit an extra shave before a court appearance and verbal byplay surrounding the prohibition of gum chewing in the courtroom both made front-page news. More serious security concerns produced extensive precautions that included local police, special marshals, and Secret Service officers.³³ Government representatives were keenly aware of the potential for public disturbance. Most were careful, as was Anderson in his charge to the jury, to try to avoid the charges leveled by Gompers and others that the trial was an attack on unions themselves. Anderson noted in his charge to the jury,

> Men have the right to use their combined power through such organizations to advance their interests in any lawful way; but they have no right to use this power in the violation of the law. Organized labor is not on trial here, nor is the right of labor to organize an issue; but members of labor organizations owe the same obedience to the law and are liable to the same punishment for its violation as persons who are not members of such organizations.³⁴

Accordingly, the trial focused on the illegal interstate transportation of the explosives and resulted in the conviction of thirty-eight defendants. Most received stiff sentences, all but six of which were sustained upon appeal.³⁵ One of the most striking visual images to emerge from the district court's history was the procession of convicted men, each chained to a guard, returning in a long column from the Ohio Street courthouse to the Marion County Jail on Alabama Street.[36]

Dramatic as it was, the 1912 bombing case was not the only significant labor case to involve the district court. At the end of World War I, for example, the United Mine Workers (UMW) appeared several times in Anderson's court. The states from western Pennsylvania across Ohio and Indiana to Illinois were considered part of a major coal formation commonly called the Central Competitive Field. Coal was the essential industrial and residential fuel of that era, and mining was one of the largest nonfarm occupations in the country, involving hundreds of thousands of workers. In 1898 the United Mine Workers had successfully unionized the bituminous mines in the Central Field, and the UMW quickly became one of America's largest labor unions. Its national headquarters was located in Indianapolis. During and just after World War I the union experienced an internal struggle for leadership that brought to power as its president a charismatic organizer, John L. Lewis.[37]

Lewis and the UMW in 1919 and 1920 were in the process of facing two major challenges. One was the negotiation of a labor contract with the mine operators under the wage restrictions imposed by the federal government during the late war. The other was a lengthy struggle to extend UMW membership into nonunion coalfields, especially in several West Virginia counties. The two issues sometimes became entangled, especially when mine owners sought injunctive relief from UMW activities. When such disputes involved federal issues, they often reached the Indiana district court due to the location of the union's headquarters in Indianapolis or because the central field contract involved many mines in southwestern Indiana. Some angry union members believed the disputes came before Anderson because the mine operators considered him a friendly judge.[38]

Convicted dynamiters entering federal building to receive sentence

The first series of issues to reach Indiana's district court came in the context of a threatened coal strike in the autumn of 1919. The UMW had entered into a wartime agreement to accept its wartime wage level until April 1, 1920. But soaring consumer prices had eroded purchasing power, and union locals were demanding relief. The administration of President Woodrow Wilson did not want a strike, and various spokesmen of his administration had suggested upward salary adjustments ranging from 14 percent to 31 percent. Predictably the mine operators seized on the first figure, the union on the second. Probably fearful of political repercussions from making too large an initial award, but also fearful of a coal strike with winter approaching, the Wilson administration eventually offered to support a compromise of an immediate 14 percent increase and an additional later award through arbitration. Under pressure from its more militant districts, the union instead called a strike to improve its bargaining position. At that point, the government went into Anderson's court to ask for injunctions against the union leaders. Citing the 1917 Lever Act, which banned wartime interruption of the production of food or fuel, Anderson agreed on October 31.[39]

The injunctions were probably part of a strategy that allowed the parties to achieve a desired compromise while assigning any criticism to the district court. Whatever the strategy employed, the Wilson administration's proposal was negotiated in early November. But that did not prove to be the end of the injunction issue. Some of the individual union districts refused to accept the compromise and went out on strike, citing the economic hardship felt by their members. UMW officers appeared off and on in Anderson's court for nearly a year thereafter. The issue was further complicated when mine operators in West Virginia sought relief from armed union organizers.[40] It became more complicated still when Anderson acted favorably on an operators' request to ban dues checkoffs for union membership dues. The checkoff ruling was quickly overturned on appeal to the Seventh Circuit. But the underlying injunction issue caused the UMW in 1920 to retain the services of Charles Evans Hughes, former Republican presidential candidate and future Chief Justice of the U.S. Supreme Court, to appear on behalf of the mine workers.[41]

Hughes based his arguments on two issues. He questioned the postwar constitutionality of the Lever Act's wartime restrictions, and he noted an error in instructing the grand jury. Anderson accepted much of Hughes's first argument, ruled the Lever Act was no longer in effect, and dismissed most of the injunctions based upon it. But the second issue commanded more attention from observers:

Hughes confronted the judge with an error the judge had made in addressing the grand jury. The judge had identified John L. Lewis as having made an incriminating statement which had in fact been made by a non-union official. Although the judge refused to admit his error in open court, the charges against the defendants were subsequently dropped.[42]

The confrontation is often pictured as a tense moment, but Hughes's biographer notes that Anderson and Hughes visited pleasantly in the judge's chambers afterwards. Hughes told his clients after that private meeting he had not discussed the issue, but said they should not worry about being tried. They were not.[43] Hughes himself, in preparing notes for his autobiography, merely observed, "I argued the case on demu[r]er, in the District Court. This case was never brought to trial."[44]

Prohibition in the Context of New Responsibilities
A central change of the early twentieth century came as Congress expanded the jurisdiction of the federal courts. Between 1906 and 1919 several statutes brought additional cases to the court's docket. Most of the new laws reflected the reforming spirit that contemporaries identified with the progressive movement. Thus the Meat Inspection Act (1906) and the Pure Food and Drug Act (1906) sought to provide new protection to the consumer. The Migratory Bird Treaty Act (1918) reflected a conservationist concern for the natural environment. The Clayton Antitrust Act (1914) sought to clarify enforcement of the Sherman Antitrust Act (1890). The White Slave Traffic Act (1910), commonly called the Mann Act, made an obvious moral statement. The Opium Exclu-

sion Act (1909) proclaimed its purpose in its title. The Harrison Narcotics Drug Act (1914), in the guise of a tax law, extended the federal government's power beyond opium and its derivatives (heroin and morphine) to cocaine and its derivatives. The Sixteenth Amendment added the income tax to the list of federal taxes. Most significantly, the Volstead Act (1919) implemented the recently ratified Eighteenth Amendment's prohibition on the production and sale of alcohol.[45]

John Niblack suggested the consequences of such changes in a revealing anecdote.

> A little Italian from Gary pleaded guilty to bootlegging.
> "That will be a fine of $500.00 and costs! Take him away!" pronounced Judge Anderson.
> "Thatsa all right, Judge. I gotta that $500.00 right here in my hip pocket," said the defendant brightly.
> "Is that so?" snapped the Judge. "Just look in your other hip pocket and see if you can find six months!"[46]

Anderson gained a reputation for imposing stiff sentences on convicted bootleggers. He also publicly criticized both city and state authorities for their lax efforts at enforcement, placing himself in the tradition of moral reformation often found on the district court.[47] A moral man, Anderson often spoke in moral terms. Early in his tenure, for example, he was asked to discharge a bankrupt man from alimony payments to his former wife. Anderson indignantly refused, calling alimony a duty and not a debt: "Anything more disgraceful in a moral point of view than the complainant's attempt, by becoming a voluntary bankrupt and manifestly for the sole purpose of cutting off the alimony decreed to his wife, cannot be imagined."[48]

Cornerstone laying ceremony, 1903

But it would be a serious error to view changes in federal law as simply a matter of introducing a police court element into the district court. The historian of one Indianapolis law firm keenly recalled the effects of other changes in federal law on his firm:

> the 16th Amendment to the Constitution authorized the levy of an income tax without the requirement of apportionment between the states. . . . The amendment, effective February 25, 1913, not only gave the federal government access to an enormous source of revenue but, with judicial acceptance of the graduated tax, became a method of transferring wealth. The revenue laws by the thirties had become so complicated as to make the practice of tax law a specialty.[49]

U.S. Courthouse under construction, February 20, 1904

A New Courthouse

The new century saw the district court moving to new courthouses in several cities, starting with Indianapolis in 1905. The new building, erected at the northeast corner of Meridian and Ohio streets, was an excellent example of the thirty-five physically commanding structures that the federal government was erecting across America under the terms of the Tarsney Act of 1892. The building was designed in the Beaux Arts style by the Philadelphia architectural firm of John Hall Rankin and Thomas Kellogg. The style, sometimes called neoclassical, stresses horizontal visual lines, prominent facades (such as that along Ohio Street), pediments and Ionic columns evoking ancient Greco-Roman ideals, and corner entrances that provide bilateral symmetry. The Beaux Arts style had been popularized at the 1893 Columbian Exposition, although the design's adoption probably also reflected a desire to reference the tradi-

Postal workroom, circa 1905

tion of Roman civil law. The structure's linkage to Indiana was clearly affirmed by the use of limestone as its facing material. Four massive exterior sculptures, Industry, Agriculture, Literature, and Justice, were created by John Massey Rhind and installed in 1908.[50]

The original building represented roughly the southern half of the current structure and included a north-facing Palladian facade that has been replaced by later additions. In common with many federal structures of the era, the courts were expected to share space with the central branch of the U.S. Post Office. The east-west main floor corridor for many years housed postal service windows, the north facade long accommodated loading bays for postal trucks, and friendly rivalry caused both judges and postmasters to claim the structure as their own. Over the years a variety of other government agencies took up temporary or

Postal workers and vehicles along the north side of the building, circa 1905. This area was filled in with the 1938 addition.

permanent residence. The top floor once housed dormitories and club rooms for railroad postal workers staying overnight in the city. A variety of law enforcement offices, such as the local offices of the Federal Bureau of Investigation (FBI), were scattered throughout the facility, and narrow concealed corridors and observation slits were even added to permit postal inspectors to observe postal workers.[51]

The original interior designs and decorations are among the building's architectural achievements. Twenty-two different shades and types of marble were employed in creating two dramatic cantilevered staircases to the second floor, octagonal rotundas at the ends of the main floor cross corridor, two vaulted elevator lobbies, and a host of wall and floor features. Mosaics graced many ceilings and domes in the public areas; stained glass was found in many window spaces. The greatest efforts were lavished on the two original courtrooms at the southern corners of the second floor, originally designed for the use of the district and circuit courts. Marble, bronze, mosaic, stained glass, and original works of art were designed to give visual expression to the dignity and purpose of the law.[52] A charming legend, sadly lacking documentation, suggests that in 1902 a German engineer, imprisoned at Michigan City Prison, won a pardon by proposing the idea of the cantilevered curving stairs ascending to the second floor.[53]

Change and Continuity in Court Functions

The physical change of location for the district court came at a time when other changes were also affecting the legal profession. One was the growth of new styles of pleading. The legal profession entered the new century familiar with forms and practices that evolved over many years, incorporating many of the practices of the Indiana state courts. One

The original district court courtroom, circa 1907, recently renamed the Judge William E. Steckler Courtroom

Bass Photo Co. Collection, Indiana Historical Society

later practitioner, Harry T. Ice, of the Indianapolis law firm Ice Miller Donadio & Ryan, reported the recollections of his partner James Ross:

> Pleading in those early days was an art; a trial, a contest between counsel. Discovery was not unlimited as it is today. Surprise, therefore, was not uncommon in a trial. . . . Any slight error in pleading became ground for demurrer, or failure in proof for a motion for a directed verdict. Reputations were at stake in every trial. Trials were truly adversarial proceedings, with the lawyers as the principal actors.[54]

This began to change, partly as an outcome of the 1891 law establishing the modern court of appeals system in which Indiana became part of the Seventh Circuit. This new system emphasized the appellate court's role in reviewing and sometimes reversing district decisions. Because this review was conducted with the understanding that the trial judge and jury were expected to weigh argument and evidence, the appellate court's role became that of reviewing the district court's processes and procedures for reversible error. It was an obvious boon to court reporters and stenographers whose transcripts of testimony and judicial remarks were necessary to such review. But it also had the effect of causing attorneys to emphasize—their critics would say belabor—the proceedings with technical pleadings designed to provide them, if needed, with a basis for appeal.[55]

The change was made more gradual by the retention until 1911 of the older circuit court system, with its separate staffs and jurisdictions. It sometimes surprises observers to discover that both a circuit court and a separate court of appeals existed (in this circuit) for twenty years, until the former was abolished as part of a congressional reform act known as

Noble Chase Butler

the Judicial Code of 1911. Most original jurisdiction the circuit courts had enjoyed was now formally assigned to the district courts. The 1911 code not only completed the elimination of the old circuit courts, it also required simplification and uniformity in forms and pleadings and sought to allow grand juries to function for an entire district rather than just a division. The law also set new national court salary schedules, for example raising district judges' salaries to $6,000.[56]

Hand in hand with such changes went elements of continuity. One of the most important was the presence of Noble Chase Butler as clerk of the court for more than forty years, from 1879 to 1922. Butler is best known today to most Indianapolis residents for the home at 1204 Park Avenue where he resided for many years, later restored as the Morris-Butler House by Historic Landmarks Foundation of Indiana with funding from Eli Lilly. Students of his era are also grateful that he maintained an extensive collection of personal papers, the Noble Butler Collection, housed in the William Henry Smith Memorial Library of the Indiana Historical Society. Butler was a product of southern Indiana, born in Salem in 1844 and educated at Salem Academy, Hanover College, and the University of Louisville Law School. A veteran of the Civil War, he always lamented that his frail appearance caused him to be assigned to telegraphy duties rather than combat roles. After the war, he completed his legal studies in the law office of his father, John H. Butler, in New Albany, and became a law partner of his father and of Walter Q. Gresham.[57]

Butler gained a reputation as an expert in bankruptcy law, and as early as 1867 he was named the register in bankruptcy (equivalent to a modern referee) for New Albany by Chief Justice Salmon P. Chase. Twelve years later, when the position of Clerk of the Indiana District Court became vacant, Butler was appointed to the position by Gresham. In 1927 he recalled the differences he felt separated nineteenth- and twentieth-century court cases and practices.

> When I came to Indianapolis as clerk, the Circuit and District courts business was mainly civil cases—Of course, we had some criminal business, but not the wholesale amount we have now. It rarely exceeded a dozen cases involving violation of Federal statutes, light violation of the pension laws, the laws against counterfeiting, etc. The civil business was very important and involved the foreclosure of mortgages on the railway systems in the state, the reconstruction of railroads and a new adjustment of railway systems under foreclosure of mortgages and sales, etc.[58]

Butler's long tenure eventually made him a spokesman for the interests of clerks of the district courts, particularly on the issue of fees and salaries. At a time when Anderson's salary was set by law at $6,000, Butler's income was about $7,000—an indication of the importance he and others attached to the issue.[59] A skilled administrator adept in records management, Butler gave the court continuity well into the Prohibition era.

A North–South Division

Anderson was the last district judge who served the entire state of Indiana throughout his tenure. His elevation to the Seventh Circuit in 1925 set in process a division of the Indiana district into its modern southern and northern districts. That process proved to be fairly complicated and was not fully realized until 1928. Several political and organizational factors were involved.

The first step in the process was obviously the appointment of Anderson to his new position in Chicago. In some ways this was to be expected. He enjoyed a reputation as an incorruptible judge. One 1923 biographical directory observed, "At no time during his career has a defendant been able to play upon the sympathies of this man. Justice has been meted out in a fearless manner; punishment . . . the only existing corrector of evil, has been ordered for rich and for poor alike."[60] It had been common practice for a generation to name circuit appointees from the district bench. Two of Anderson's three predecessors had themselves been appointed to the Seventh Circuit; the son of the third had similarly served. The seats on the Seventh Circuit were informally apportioned by states, and the vacancy Anderson filled was considered assigned to Indiana. While he served on the district bench, Anderson had many friends on the federal bench. Several of them wrote on behalf of his appointment in 1925. Finally, Anderson was of the political party that controlled the presidency and Senate in 1925. The one unusual feature of his appointment was his age. Anderson was sixty-eight and would only serve about two years until he fell under the terms of a 1919 law that offered generous retirement terms to federal judges. This 1919 act offered any judge who was seventy years of age, and who had served ten years, the opportunity to retire at full pay, to have a replacement judge named, and to continue to hold court if he wished (with the approval of the presiding judge).[61] Anderson's Circuit Court of Appeals tenure thus proved to be brief, while ill health prevented him performing many duties while on senior status.

The post of district judge had previously attracted the attention of Indiana's congressional delegation, and the period surrounding Anderson's elevation was no exception. In 1924, as news of the upcoming vacancy spread, a number of recommendations reached Washington. By then it was a standard pattern for prospective candidates to prepare résumés and seek bar association endorsements, as well as to seek the traditional political endorsements. Faced with a flurry of names, Indiana's Republican delegation—and particularly Senator James E. Watson—began to discuss the possibility of naming two judges to succeed Anderson. At its inception the idea was thus seen as a matter of political patronage, with Watson considered by many observers to be encouraging nominations from the northern part of the state.[62]

The idea of two federal judges certainly gained ground when it became apparent that the two leading judicial candidates, Robert Baltzell and Thomas Slick, were from different ends of the state. This permitted Indiana's congressional delegation to consider dividing the state in a manner that reflected the long-established practice of holding court sessions in different localities. Soon a bill was introduced by Congressman Andrew Hickey of La Porte to divide Indiana's ninety-two counties into seven divisions of the Indiana district court, each with its seat in the city after which the division was named: Indianapolis, Terre Haute, Evansville, New Albany, Fort Wayne, Hammond, and South Bend. The central Indianapolis division would contain twenty-five counties; each of the other divisions between nine and fifteen. Each division would have a full-time clerk and hold at least two scheduled court terms per year on a timetable that permitted attendance by one of the judges. The second district judge, with the same powers as the existing district judge, was authorized in the same act. The bill was approved January 16, 1925.[63]

The contest for the new northern seat came down to a struggle between Thomas W. Slick of Saint Joseph County and Thomas Henegar of Tippecanoe County. Henegar was his county's superior court judge and enjoyed the support of the Lafayette bar. Slick was reported to have Watson's ear, and Slick's friends, according to one press report, questioned the geography of Henegar's county:

> They are saying that Lafayette is in the Indianapolis belt and does not belong to northern Indiana. They have recalled that the Tippecanoe County Bar Association opposed the Hickey bill and that it sent a representative, Clyde A. Jones, of Lafayette, to Washington to appear before the senate judiciary committee in opposition to the legislation.[64]

Slick was named to the new position by President Calvin Coolidge on February 6, 1925. Attorney General Harlan F. Stone, a future justice of the U.S. Supreme Court, summarized Slick's support base and its strong Saint Joseph County focus in a letter of recommendations to the president:

Mr. Slick is recommended by Hon. James W. [sic] Watson, Senator from Indiana. Mr. Slick has the endorsement of Hon. Arthur L Gilliam, Attorney General of Indiana, who declares that he has known Mr. Slick for 12 years; that he is a man of character and ranks at the top of the legal profession in Northern Indiana.

Mr. Slick's appointment is also endorsed by Rev. John Haxen White, Bishop of the Methodist-Episcopal Church; Mr. E. W. Taylor, President, Young Women's Christian Association of South Bend; Mr. T. A Hynes, President, South Bend Chamber of Commerce; Congressman Andrew J. Hickey of Indiana, Hon Cyrus E. Pattie; Hon. Fred Bingham, Hon. Lenn J. Oare, Judges, St. Joseph Superior Court No. 2; as well as numerous ministers of the church and prominent and distinguished lawyers of the Indiana bar.[65]

Slick was born in South Bend in 1869, taught school for a time, and earned a law degree from the University of Michigan. He returned to his hometown, developed a successful private practice, and served as the Saint Joseph County prosecuting attorney and later as South Bend city attorney.[66] Slick was initially appointed judge for the district of Indiana and from 1925 to 1928 had authority to hold court throughout the state. In fact, he sat for a time in Indianapolis and Evansville, and his southern Indiana counterpart held trials in South Bend and Hammond.[67]

The intent of Slick's appointment had clearly been to create a regional division in the state, and in 1928 a campaign was mounted to make the three northern divisions of the court into a district. There was apparently enough reluctance in Congress about this change, however, that at least one northern Indiana newspaper felt impelled to mount a campaign on behalf of the proposal. The *South Bend Tribune* assured its readers in 1927 that there had been a variety of administrative problems besetting the courts, including a seventeen-year-old boy held for three weeks in Hammond because a grand jury in Indianapolis forgot to transmit its decision not to indict him; an expert witness who failed to appear in Hammond because a subpoena issued in Indianapolis bore an inaccurate date; and a prisoner held in the Crown Point Jail whose paperwork was misdirected to South Bend instead of Hammond.[68] Two months later the paper summarized its position:

> Increased federal court business and the fact the South Bend, Hammond, Gary, Ft. Wayne and other northern cities are so far distant from Indianapolis, making it inconvenient for the federal officials with headquarters in the state capital to come to the northern part of the state, led to the appointment [of Judge Slick].[69]

The campaign succeeded, and Coolidge signed Senator Arthur Robinson's bill on April 24, 1928, making the division official. The northern district received the three northern divisions, covering the northern third of the state.[70] Occasional cases continued to be filed across district lines if a judge was absent,[71] but the separation was essentially complete.

Slick contributed to the separation by a variety of good-natured actions designed to emphasize the differences between the two emerging districts. He issued annual reports emphasizing the rapidly growing caseloads in his three divisions, particularly through aggressive prosecution of liquor violations. Slick proved almost as hostile to organized liquor interests as Anderson had been, although the errant individual drinker could usually expect probation and a warning; the only court officer Slick publicly dismissed was a U.S. marshal who was observed "imbibing" in a Fort Wayne saloon. The judge also was no friend of D. C. Stephenson, rejecting each attempt the former Ku Klux Klan leader made to obtain a writ of habeas corpus to be released from prison for his convictions in state court. Slick addressed the bar on the need for timely prosecution of caseloads and stressed new docket management procedures he had adopted. He praised the 1925 law that permitted federal judges to include probation in criminal sentencing. Judge Slick rarely jailed first offenders and sought to showcase the successes of his court's careful oversight of probationers. He implemented more formal sessions of the court, an attribute of the northern district that some legal practitioners suggest still prevails. And he created a separate court family in which he named the first woman in Indiana (and third in the nation) as clerk of the court in the South Bend division in 1925 and as clerk of the northern district in 1929.[72]

Margaret Lung Cowgill was born in Gas City, Indiana, in 1900 and graduated from Marion High School in 1917 and Marion Business College in 1918. She became deputy clerk of the Saint Joseph County court from 1919 to 1923 and then worked in the law office of Walter Arnold. Appointed on a temporary basis in 1925 to the South Bend division clerkship, she received permanent appointment to the division in 1928 and to the clerkship of the northern district in 1929. The *South Bend Tribune* observed, "Mrs. Cowgill earned a reputation for loyalty and efficiency unexcelled in the service, and has proved to be a popular official."[73] A subsequent personality profile observed, "getting the clerk's post was the biggest thrill of her life because it meant fulfilling an ambition she has had since the age of 16."[74] The northern district was clearly launched on its own course.

When asked in 1959 to recount the changes Slick introduced, Hammond attorney Timothy Galvin offered this summation:

I was a young lawyer in those days and I can tell you that for the most part the lawyers of northern Indiana didn't practice in the federal courts. I think many of us were somewhat afraid. The fact is, we had little opportunity to do so. Of course the jurisdiction of federal courts had not extended in those days to the broad field which it now covers. But apart from that the administration of justice in the federal courts in Northern Indiana was an altogether different thing the days before the advent of Judge Slick to the bench of the court. We had but one judge in the state. Practically all of the proceedings in federal court were carried on in Indianapolis. If we had matters that could properly be brought before the federal court, for the most part we had to go

Robert Baltzell

to Indianapolis. I suppose, without personal criticism of anyone and without personal knowledge of what I am going to tell you, but I have heard from hearsay that in the years before Judge Slick became Federal judge, that when we did have a term of court in Hammond—and I am sure the same thing was true in other cities in Northern Indiana, in Fort Wayne and South Bend—that the judge came and tried to finish all the business of the court in a day or two, and seemed to resent the fact if the business kept him longer. The result was that what cases we had from this section, the trials actually took place in Indianapolis. All that changed with the coming of Judge Slick to the federal bench.[75]

Judge Baltzell: The Prohibition Years
Less than three weeks before Slick was named to the second Indiana district judgeship, Robert Baltzell was appointed to Anderson's vacated seat by President Coolidge. The appointment was confirmed by the U.S. Senate on January 13, 1925. Six days later Anderson administered the oath of office to Baltzell in Indianapolis. The new jurist was born in rural Illinois in 1879, where he attended high school in Sumner and later taught for five years. From 1903 to 1904 Baltzell attended Marion Law School in Marion, Indiana, and then moved to Princeton to practice law. He was active in Republican politics, served on that party's state committee, and attracted the support of Republican state (and later national) chairman Will Hays. During World War I, Baltzell was commissioned a major in the Judge Advocate's Office and was assigned to administer the draft in Indiana. In 1920 he ran for circuit judge of Gibson County, winning election in a normally Democratic area. A year later he was the focus of attention when a violent coal strike occurred near Princeton.

Some 1,500 miners, many of them armed, marched to the home of an unpopular mine superintendent and forced his exit. Baltzell promptly convened a grand jury, insisted upon the indictment of any of the miners who could be identified, tried about 150 of them, and sentenced fourteen to prison. The series of events earned Baltzell a "hard-boiled" reputation that stuck with him throughout his later career.[76]

The actual process of Baltzell's appointment is not well documented. His appointment file with the Senate Judiciary Committee contains little more than the usual letter of support from Senator Watson and a transmittal letter from Attorney General Stone. Local newspapers added that Baltzell had been endorsed by the state Republican organization and by officers of the Women's Christian Temperance Union, and an earlier biographer of UMW president Lewis noted that President Coolidge had discussed the appointment with the labor leader, a putative Republican.[77]

The early years of Baltzell's service were heavily concerned with the enforcement of Prohibition, maintaining the long tradition of the Indiana court's enforcement of moral reform. In 1925 Baltzell attracted notice by imposing maximum sentences on Mayor William Callahan and ten other Bicknell, Indiana, men who had been convicted for liquor violations.[78] In his sentencing remarks he regretted "the law doesn't permit the court to give you sufficient punishment."[79] In 1926 he presided at the trial of twenty-eight men and one woman in the "Jack Daniels case," named for the bonded warehouse in Saint Louis where bootleggers siphoned thirty thousand gallons of whiskey from 891 barrels and sold part of the stolen alcohol across four states, including Indiana. The trial was held in Indianapolis because, more than two years before, a bulletproof truck containing part of the stolen whiskey had been seized by the sheriff of Marion County on U.S. 40.

The trial attracted regional attention to the Indianapolis court for numerous reasons. Several of the defendants were prominent in

Missouri politics and another was a collector for the Internal Revenue Service. The star government witness was a prominent Ohio bootlegger, George Remus, who felt he had been double-crossed by the conspirators and told his story in colorful detail. Baltzell conducted the proceedings in an expeditious, no-nonsense manner—and gained praise from the press for the stiff sentences he handed out to those convicted.[80]

That publicity, in turn, contributed to later assignments whereby Baltzell presided over federal trials in Chicago and New York, gaining favorable mention for the way he managed the administration of the trials and receiving praise from temperance advocates for the stiff sentences he imposed. A New York defense lawyer pointed out that his sentences exceeded those normally handed down in the Empire State. He replied, "a New York criminal is no better than an Indiana criminal and that's the way we treat them in Indiana."[81] In an appreciative summary of his prohibition activities, the *Indianapolis Times* observed,

> During the prohibition days he often sentenced as many as 20 persons at once, more than 100 persons appeared before him on arraignment days and he issued padlock orders closing 50 to 75 speakeasies at a time. He couldn't reconcile the viciousness of the criminals with his belief in Christian principals. Those principals still are evident during trials in his court. He strikes out at those who pray [sic] on the poor, the weak and the helpless.[82]

The *Indianapolis Star* provided another revealing anecdote.

> In a bootlegging case during the days of prohibition, the judge bucked top-level political pressure to give an influential defen-

dant a prison sentence instead of probation. He made the defendant's plea for probation look ridiculous in an examination of a defense witness, a physician, who at first claimed a prison term would injure the man's health. Before open-mouthed attorneys, the judge had the physician agreeing, finally, that a Federal penitentiary, with its fine hospital facilities, actually would be the best place for the ailing defendant.[83]

William Steckler summed up the perception of Baltzell as "very strict in criminal matters." In a later oral history, Steckler recalled one seventy-year-old defendant who received a sentence of twenty to twenty-five years. The defendant pleaded to Baltzell, "Judge, I'll never live that long." Baltzell leaned forward and replied, "Well, do the best you can."[84]

Although Prohibition ended with the ratification of the Twenty-first Amendment in 1933, other new federal statutes provided a source of cases that reached the southern district court. Some of the new laws were tied to a changing economy. The National Motor Vehicle Theft Act (or Dyer Act) of 1919 acknowledged the growing importance of the automobile by making interstate car theft a federal crime. The National Stolen Property Act of 1934 added all other interstate thefts over $5,000 in value. Other new laws reflected public and media perception of increased lawlessness. These included the Lindbergh Act of 1932, which made kidnapping a federal crime, and the National Firearms Act of 1934, which sought to reduce criminal access to machine guns. Some new laws reflected responses to the causes or consequences of the Great Depression that followed the stock market collapse of 1929. The Securities and Exchange Act of 1934 was one of many laws tied to New Deal policies of President Franklin D. Roosevelt, many of which addressed white-collar crime.[85]

The Barrett Murder Case

A particularly dramatic example of the federal interest that is sometimes involved in criminal cases involving firearms reached Baltzell's courtroom in 1936 when he tried what was probably the first murder case heard in an Indiana federal court since territorial times.[86] George Barrett, a suspect in a Kentucky car theft ring, was approached by two FBI agents on August 14, 1935, in College Corner, Indiana. Barrett drew a gun, fled into a nearby woods, and shot it out with the agents, killing Agent Nelson Klein before being wounded in the leg and captured. Barrett was brought to Indianapolis for trial and was prosecuted for murder. The government presented Barrett as a hardened criminal who had lost an eye in a shootout with revenue officers as early as 1913 and whose two trials for the murder of his mother and sister had ended in hung juries in 1931. The jury deliberated for two days before returning a guilty verdict, although a local court reporter was told by one juror they did so because they liked the meals the court provided them.[87]

Baltzell sentenced Barrett to death. Privately, the judge expressed concern that the event might assume a circus atmosphere, and publicly he set the time of the hanging for midnight. But local authorities proved unable to fully restrain the curious, and on the day before the execution more than five thousand individuals trooped through the tent in which the gallows was erected in the yard of the Marion County Jail. The hanging itself was conducted by the U.S. marshal acting under a warrant from the district court. The execution included grim touches. Unable to walk on his wounded leg, Barrett was carried to the gallows on a stretcher. A woman fainted as Barrett approached, and the stretcher bearers passed over her unconscious body as they reached the thirteen steps to the platform. The rope holding the gallows trap door was cut with one blow of an axe, and Barrett fell to his death at one minute after midnight. It remains the only federal execution ever held in Indianapolis, and one of only ten conducted in America in the 1930s.[88]

The case deeply affected Baltzell.[89] Steckler discussed the case with Baltzell in the late 1940s, and forty-five years after that still recalled the judge's words with vivid intensity:

> Young man, there's one thing I pray you'll never have to do.
> [Steckler] said, what's that, Judge Baltzell?
> I hope and I pray that you'll never have to sentence a man to die.[90]

In another conversation with Steckler, Baltzell went even further in expressing his personal convictions:

> This, I [Steckler] recall, when I conferred with him about taking over the court.... [W]e were talking about the unpleasant things that a district judge is required to do.... He [Baltzell] looked at me with tears in his eyes, and said, "I often wonder whether I will reach heaven as a result of having to pronounce a death sentence."[91]

The Ladoga Canning Case

Not all the cases that reached Baltzell were so dramatic, but some were of considerable local significance. In the history of his law firm, Harry Ice detailed the effects one civil case had on both a client and its law firm. The case that originated when one of the original partners of the firm, James Ross, accidentally discovered in an unrelated discovery hearing that the American Can Company had been paying a rebate to Indiana's largest canner of baked beans, Van Camp Packing, for its volume purchases of tin cans. Ross employed this discovery when he was approached by a smaller canner, Ladoga Canning, which received no rebates when it purchased cans from another tin can manufacturer. Ross's partner, Solon Carter, subsequently filed a series of cases that invoked the 1914 Clayton Anti-Trust Act and argued that small canners were victimized by the rebate arrangement. Baltzell initially ruled against the small canners because they purchased from a different seller. This line of reasoning was eventually overturned on appeal by the U.S. Supreme Court. A series of damage cases then were filed in the southern district court, with a key jury trial resulting in a decision supporting the small canners. American Can eventually negotiated a large settlement.[92] Ice's memoir vividly describes the Indianapolis courtroom as he remembered it in the Ladoga Canning jury trial:

> [Carter] swept his hand toward the defense table with its several attorneys and behind it the staff table with several clerks and a row of file cabinets brought into the courtroom to hold the volumes of documents which had inundated the jury. . . . He recounted in detail the losses of Ladoga of its "pork and bean" business to VanCamp. He converted the accounting figures to pennies per can on the grocery shelf, pointing out that the can cost more than the contents.[93]

Procedural Changes

Changes in the court's jurisdiction were accompanied by a variety of procedural changes. Most important among these to trial attorneys was the introduction of the modern federal rules of civil procedure in the 1930s. Before that time the Conformity Act required the courts to conform, as near as possible, to the procedural rules of the state in which the cases were heard. But the very lack of national uniformity this produced was increasingly vexing as more and more cases involved plaintiffs and defendants with interstate businesses and problems. In 1934 Congress passed an Enabling Act that allowed the U.S. Supreme Court to name a commission to review these procedures. Headed by Charles Clark, dean of the Yale Law School, the commission reported in 1938 and the rules were promptly adopted. The new rules reflected Clark's own advocacy for rules that were simple, flexible, and designed to advance, and not impede, legal proceedings. The rules drew heavily on equity practices and, in effect, merged civil and equity procedure. They introduced the modern concept of discovery, in which evidence must be revealed in advance of trial, and contributed to a shift from courtroom pleading to pre-trial negotiation. A judge's skills as negotiator and arbitrator were more likely to be called forward. Soon a smaller and smaller portion of civil cases actually came to trial.[94]

This change in trial procedure is sometimes identified with a resistance to reliance on formal procedure as a means to win a court judgment, a movement known as legal realism. This new approach asked judges and/or juries to look beyond the formal language of the law and study the social implications and consequences of institutional behavior. It encouraged expert testimony within certain parameters. It appealed to a sense of fairness that was often called "social justice" and was in many instances a reflection of the reformist spirit and quest for social order so politically influential from the Progressive Era onward.[95] It certainly owed much to a spate of litigation created by the expansion of government power during the New Deal and can be seen when the court addresses public works construction programs.

Sherman Minton

Sherman Minton—Supreme Court Justice

Another way that the discussion of realism and formalism touched Indiana, and indirectly the district court, was in the career of Sherman

Minton,[96] the first Hoosier to be appointed to the Supreme Court. (The second was Chief Justice John G. Roberts Jr. in 2005). Minton was from southern Indiana, where he had opened a successful law practice in New Albany after returning from service in World War I. The populist philosophy of William Jennings Bryan attracted Minton to the Democratic Party as early as 1896. By the 1920s the young lawyer had a reputation as an effective political organizer and a wise political counselor, and in 1934 he rode the popularity of the New Deal to election to the U.S. Senate. There his organizational talents and his support for President Roosevelt's interventionist economic programs won Minton leadership positions. In 1937 Roosevelt, in the thinly veiled guise of a retirement program, sought to gain a majority on the Supreme Court by expanding its size by six members—and thereby reverse the court's opposition to most New Deal measures. Opponents dubbed it a "court packing plan"; defenders argued it was necessary to allow democracy to function in the economic crisis of the Great Depression. Minton became one of the leading advocates of the plan, winning many friends in Roosevelt's circles but going on to lose reelection in 1940.

Minton was soon rewarded with a seat on the Seventh Circuit, the practice of elevating district judges having not been universally followed since Anderson. There he continued to serve as an informal adviser to Democratic leaders on both patronage and policy questions, while maintaining an office at the New Albany division courthouse. In 1949 Minton was named to the Supreme Court by President Harry Truman. Ill health rendered his later service less effective and may account for a growing sense of judicial restraint, but there is little question that his involvement in the debate over the role of politics in judicial decision making in the 1930s captured the reform spirit of his time.[97]

Administrative Developments

A number of administrative developments affected the new southern district court. As part of a burst of construction projects tied to the New Deal government's attempts to create jobs in the middle of the Great Depression, a new federal building was constructed in Terre Haute. The old building was demolished in 1933 and its replacement opened in 1935. Designed in a vertical, streamlined style by Warren Drake Miller and Ralph O. Yeager Sr., under the authority of the supervising architect of the United States Treasury, it continued to combine court and post office functions in a restrained, efficient presence.[98] The Terre Haute structure owed much to Baltzell. As the *Indianapolis Times* later reported in a retrospective on the judge's seventieth birthday,

U.S. Courthouse, circa 1918

Forty-six defendants were involved in a national prohibition law violation case which was tried in Terre Haute in 1930. The defendants and the witnesses were so numerous that many persons had to stand on the sidewalk outside the building, the small courtroom being packed to capacity. It was as a result of this case that Judge Baltzell requested the federal building department to build a new federal building at Terre Haute, which was done a few years later.[99]

A new federal penitentiary was constructed outside Terre Haute in 1940, hastening the end of the practice of boarding federal convicts in state prisons. The stark walls and cells suggested that a sense of punishment was more important than penitence in the minds of the designers.[100]

In Indianapolis, new construction added a major addition to the northern side of the federal building. Designed by architects McGuire and Shook, the new addition was built between 1936 and 1938. It added offices and space that later became jury rooms and courtrooms, as well as such safety features as enclosing open elevator shafts. The government's attempts to provide employment in the 1930s also extended into the arts, where the Treasury Relief Art Project (TRAP) funded new murals on the third floor by twenty-four-year-old Grant Christian. His south wall featured post office themes, while the north wall presented six panels depicting early and present-day Indianapolis.[101]

The court had many responsibilities. The naturalization of citizens continued to be a significant activity of the federal courts in the 1920s and 1930s. In Baltzell's obituary, the *Indianapolis Star* noted, "More than 5,000 aliens received citizenship through Judge Baltzell."[102] Naturalization ceremonies in the courtroom became a regular feature of the court's docket and an opportunity for Baltzell to speak about the responsibilities of citizenship. When two young men appeared before him early in his tenure, Baltzell noticed they had been arrested for speeding. The United Press reported the judge's admonition prior to admitting them as citizens:

> Auto drivers who disregard the speed laws are not good prospective timber to become citizens of the United States. When you disregard the speed laws you place yourself in the class of law breakers and law breakers are not good citizens.[103]

Probation also came to assume considerable administrative attention. Permitted since 1925 in criminal cases, it required officers of the court to monitor many offenders and eventually led to the creation of a separate probation office. The *Indianapolis Star* commented on the time Baltzell, "genuinely pleased ... congratulated a Negro laborer, reporting his probation, on a bank book entry showing savings from a slim pay check."[104]

The death of Butler, longtime clerk of the Indiana district, came at a time of other changes. He was succeeded by another attorney, William Kappes, who served until 1928. Kappes, in turn, was succeeded by the first non-attorney to serve as clerk. Albert C. "Soggy" Sogemeier served until 1951. He was highly regarded for his records management skill and thus personified the growing administrative demands of the clerk's office. Under the aegis of the Conference of Senior Circuit Judges (later the Judicial Conference of the United States), circuit judges began in 1922 to monitor the caseloads of district courts with an eye to assuring speedy resolution of cases on court dockets.[105] After more than seventy-five years of laboriously entering every fee charged to an attorney, district clerks were allowed to simply total the charges at the end of a case and charge against a deposit filed with the court.[106] Skills of office procedure and records management became important criteria for selection. As Slick bluntly put it in explaining his appointment of Margaret Cowgill, "selection . . . is made purely on the grounds of efficiency."[107]

Depression, New Deal, and World War
America in the 1930s plunged into the Great Depression, which was quickly felt through an increase in bankruptcy filings. When Baltzell's staff totaled his caseload for his twenty-four-year tenure, it included 7,293 criminal cases (disproportionately Prohibition violations), 7,507 civil cases, and a striking 6,721 bankruptcy cases.[108] One local law firm, Locke Reynolds, credited "major cases involving business failures" as a source of the firm's growing stature in the 1930s.[109] One such case was *Hack v. American Surety*, which twice made its way to the Seventh Circuit as the parties argued the applicability of a blanket bond in a bank failure caused by the corrupt dealings of the bank's officers. Another was an Indiana farmers' publishing company, whose antitrust claims against rival publishers eventually required an opinion by the Supreme Court.[110] Simultaneously, the growth in the economy added to the scale of monetary issues. In the late 1940s the district court heard the case of Turner Glass Company of Indianapolis, an antitrust suit in which large glass companies were accused of fixing prices to drive Turner Glass from the industry. Where the 1816 district court had been limited to $100 claims, the sum of damages sought by Turner in its successful action was $5 million and treble damages.[111]

Other important changes in the operation of the southern district court came through the continued expansion of federal jurisdiction. A host of statutes ostensibly designed to regulate and reinvigorate economic activity added greatly to jurisdiction of the federal courts. Baltzell's court oversaw, with no apparent controversy, the condemnation proceedings that removed 363 slum houses to make possible the Lockefield Gardens housing project. This apartment project was the first significant African American public housing project in Indianapolis and one of the first such peacetime projects anywhere in America. The complex was built between 1935 and 1938 on a tract south of Indiana Avenue on the west side of Indianapolis by the Housing Division of the Federal Emergency Administration of Public Works.[112] Predictably, Baltzell expected high standards from government workers. In 1939 he tried eleven defendants, including Kokomo city officials, who were convicted of defrauding projects of the Works Progress Administration (WPA).[113] In 1940 he oversaw the conviction of a WPA officer in Marion County who had used WPA funds and workers to open streets in a planned subdivision owned by a relative of the administrator.[114]

Liquor continued to be an issue on Baltzell's docket, although now as a civil issue related to the constitutionality of the wholesale marketing rules adopted by the state of Indiana after enactment of the Twenty-first Amendment. In 1933, for example, Baltzell rejected a challenge to the state's regulation of wholesale distribution because the petitioners were simultaneously in state court on what Baltzell deemed a concurrent issue. In 1935 he again supported the state's wholesale regulations as consistent with national practice and the commerce clause. Then in 1950 he upheld a suit by wholesale purchasers against prices established by manufacturers that set a minimum below which prices could not fall.[115] Prohibition was dead, but regulation had not gone away.

Other forms of moral regulation appeared before the district court. In 1939 Irving and Rose Lewis were convicted of Mann Act violations for transporting three young women, aged fourteen and fifteen, across the Indiana-Illinois state line to perform nude in a carnival show ostensibly proclaiming the theme of the evils of white slavery. The defendants' defense, which argued that hootch shows did not meet a legal definition of debauchery, as required in the law, impressed neither the jury nor the court of appeals.[116]

The outbreak of World War II also made itself felt. The restoration of Selective Service in 1940 brought a flow of conscientious objectors before the court, among them Jehovah's Witnesses, Mennonites, and Quakers. The condemnation of land for defense projects came as well, including Camp Atterbury, the Wabash Valley Ordnance Plant, and the Crane Naval Depot.[117] In 1942 the most serious security case since the Civil War reached Baltzell when William Dudley Pelley appeared in court. A former leader of the Silver Shirts, a pro-Fascist group active since the 1930s, Pelley was charged with insurrection and sedition. He and a codefendant had written and published several thousand copies of the *Galilean Magazine* and a pamphlet titled *We Fight for This Republic Only*. Both were violently antigovernment tracts that the prosecution asserted violated federal laws that prohibited "false reports or false statements with intent to interfere with the operation or success of the military or naval forces of the United States or to promote the success of its enemies." Expert witnesses compared Pelley's arguments to the main themes of German propaganda, while others refuted each of his specific claims. Pelley's defense, essentially arguing that he was just offering opinion and "loose talk," did not convince the jury, and he was sentenced to fifteen years in prison. The Seventh Circuit, adding a strong affirmation of the concept of "clear and present danger," affirmed the conviction.[118]

Judge Baltzell's Final Years

Baltzell continued to serve the southern district until 1949, when he reached the age of seventy and qualified for retirement benefits. His last years had been a time of ill health, so much so that it was sometimes necessary for deputy marshals to assist him up the steps to his seat on the bench. Friends who had known Baltzell in earlier days still looked upon him as "hard, but firm," a judgment he had earned in the 1920s. But those who practiced before him in his last years, as his docket fell behind and his health problems manifested themselves in personal acerbity, sometimes took a less favorable view. One anecdote, widely repeated and possibly true, concerned Baltzell's unwillingness to excuse prospective jurors whatever their reason. One day a man appeared, timidly raised his hand, and asked to be excused because his wife was about to give birth. Baltzell reportedly responded, "There are two times when a man needs to be with his child—when it's conceived, and when it's delivered," and excused the man.

In a more serious vein, William Steckler offered this analysis:

> He was in failing health. . . . He was a person that most lawyers, I don't believe, fully understood. He had a certain number of lawyers who were very, very capable. I call them the elite of the local profession here in Indiana. Judge Baltzell would like to have those lawyers in the courtroom. They did a great deal of the work for the Judge, and made it possible for him to achieve and retain respect during his failing years. They would do a lot of his motions—orders—prepare the orders, draft those orders. Today we have law [clerks] who prepare those orders for us.[119]

Baltzell's retirement was to usher in a period of significant change on the Southern District Court.

CHAPTER FOUR

A Multi-Judge Court Develops

1950–1979

A PROFOUND GENERATIONAL CHANGE OCCURRED in Indiana, as in much of America, after World War II. When the veterans returned home, they quickly seized control of many elements of society. As family members, they helped create the postwar baby boom. As consumers, they revolutionized the economy with demands for new homes, new cars, new appliances, and modern medicine. New lifestyles, publicized by the new medium of television and practiced in a vastly expanded suburbia, became a feature of an expanded and optimistic middle class. But not all groups in society enjoyed the benefits of these transformations or respected the leadership that championed them. The civil rights movements eventually resulted in discrimination claims by various protected groups including minorities, women, the elderly, and the disabled. Liberalized societal views challenged standards on narcotics and controlled substances. In growing numbers voices of challenge and protest found their way to a southern district court that was itself experiencing growth and administrative transformations that mirrored the society it served.

Congress Creates a Multi-Judge Court

Since the formal separation of Indiana's two judicial districts in 1928, a single judge had served the southern district. Beginning in 1954, Indiana was included in a nationwide expansion of the federal district courts. This was accomplished in Congress primarily by the enactment of five statutes between 1954 and 1978. Each statute reflected both the political success of the party in power in Washington in appointing additional members of the federal judiciary and the growing docket of the districts. In 1954, 1961, 1966, and 1978, the southern district was authorized an additional judge, becoming the five-judge court that it is at the present time. Only in 1970, when Indiana's congressional Democrats resisted President Richard M. Nixon's opportunity to make a judicial appointment, was a new southern district judge not authorized.[1]

Many believed that the congressional decision to create a second judgeship for the district had been forestalled by a political impasse for several years prior to 1954. As Judge William Steckler recalled,

> There was always that great need for more than one judge for the Southern District of Indiana. I often stated after I was

appointed that it was apparent that Judge [Robert] Baltzell had declined assistance. Indeed, I found a certain amount of communication here that indicated he did not want an additional judge appointed, at least not so long as the White House was under Democratic leadership.[2]

The relatively rapid expansion in the number of judgeships reflected some consistent features. First, the expansion was publicly justified by reference to caseload statistics. These tabulations of caseloads had been kept by the Judicial Conference and its predecessors since the 1920s and typically revealed that the southern district was above the national averages. Judge Baltzell's reported resistance to the enlargement of his court during a time other districts were gaining new judges almost assured that his workload burdens would increase. Second, the expansion was more enthusiastically supported by state and congressional leaders who were of the same political party as the president of the United States.

The Politics of Appointment
Under the U.S. Constitution federal judges are appointed by the president of the United States, and partisan politics have of course been a part of the selection process. Whether as a reward for past services, as a statement of a societal philosophy, or in furtherance of a particular political viewpoint, each appointment mirrors to some degree the tone of the era when it was made. For nearly a century prior to 1950 there had been one constant in the district court for the southern district of Indiana: each of its judges had been named by a Republican president. No Democrat had been appointed to the bench since 1842. Between 1950 and 1979 four

Democratic presidents made four of the five new appointments, and different political philosophies and approaches began to appear in the second half of the twentieth century.

William E. Steckler. President Harry Truman nominated William Steckler to replace Baltzell on February 14, 1950. Born in Mount Vernon, Indiana, on October 18, 1913, Steckler was thirty-six years old at

William E. Steckler

the time of his appointment, making him one of the youngest federal judges to be named during his tenure. He was also the first judge of the southern district court born in the twentieth century. Educated at Benjamin Harrison Law School (now Indiana University School of Law in Indianapolis), from which he graduated in 1937, Steckler mixed law with politics in his early career. In the 1936 election he volunteered his services to the Democratic Party, and more specifically to the faction of that party led by Indianapolis banker Frank McKinney and prominent attorney Frank McHale. Steckler soon developed expertise in Indiana election law, eventually serving as a member of the Marion County and then the Indiana state election boards and rewriting portions of the state's election code. He also gained a reputation as a skillful administrator in a series of public utility rate adjustment cases in 1949 and 1950 when he was public counselor of Indiana in the administration of Democratic governor Henry F. Schricker.[3] More than sixty prominent leaders endorsed Steckler's candidacy, including John G. Tinder, who was at the time Indiana Commander of the Veterans of Foreign Wars,[4] newspaper publisher Eugene C. Pulliam, and numerous attorneys and Democratic Party leaders. In later recalling the process, Steckler said,

> Three days before my name was finally submitted to the president, I was still uncertain about having my name submitted. But, I couldn't let down my friends, the political leaders, who had gone so far in my behalf. At that time, Frank McHale was the Democrat National Committeeman. He was in a power struggle with another faction. The two senators, Senator [William] Jenner and Senator [Homer E.] Capehart, were Republican, and President Truman was in the White House. This meant Mr. McHale carried great power with the White House. However,

my friend Frank McKinney appeared to be personally closer to the President.⁵

Steckler's nomination file, maintained by the U.S. Senate Committee on the Judiciary, of which Senator William Jenner was a member, highlighted the recommendations from Howard Burns, chairman of the American Bar Association's Standing Committee on the Federal Judiciary, and Telford Orbison, president of the Indiana State Bar Association, noting as well that "no witness personally appeared in opposition to nominee" at his April 1, 1950, hearing.⁶ Steckler later recalled that Truman had informed him that a favorable bar association recommendation was a requirement of confirmation.⁷

Cale J. Holder. President Dwight D. Eisenhower nominated Cale Holder on August 2, 1954, to the newly created second seat on the southern district bench. Holder was born in Lawrenceville, Indiana, in 1912. He attended Benjamin Harrison Law School, served in the U.S. Navy in World War II, and built a varied legal practice. He and his brother opened a law firm in Beech Grove, and he served terms as Marion County Deputy Prosecutor, Special Attorney to the State Personnel Board, and Deputy Indiana Attorney General. Holder also served for five years as secretary of the Indianapolis Bar Association and was well known in legal circles. He was one of many World War II veterans who participated in a generational shift in Indiana politics, bringing youthfulness and energy to the state's leadership.⁸

Holder's appointment, the one Republican selection of the postwar period, was perhaps the most bitterly contested nomination in the district court's history. The controversy was in large measure a result of Republican factionalism, exacerbated by the vehement opposition of a

Cale J. Holder

prominent newspaper publisher. In 1949 Holder, with the support of Senator Jenner, had been chosen as Indiana Republican State Chairman. Holder was a skilled organizer and adept at balancing competing individual and regional interests within the state. He was credited for organizing a major off-year general election victory in 1950. But in 1952 even Holder's considerable skills were insufficient to avert a bitter intraparty fight that divided the Republican primary electorate and the state's delegation to the Republican National Convention over two presidential candidates. Many party regulars favored conservative U.S. Senator Robert Taft of Ohio; many insurgents supported Eisenhower. Many observers were thus surprised in 1954 when Eisenhower acceded to the recommendation of the state's two Republican senators, Jenner and Capehart, and nominated Holder for the newly created Indiana judgeship. As Steckler later recalled,

> It was always rather surprising to hear that while Judge Holder was a great Taft man ... Judge Holder would be named by President Eisenhower. But that goes back to the power of the Senators, and the Senators had their own favored individuals. The Senators were able to dominate in the outcome of those appointments.[9]

That was normally the case, but in 1954 the confirmation process was not easily resolved. Several Republican insurgents vented their deep disagreement with the Holder nomination. The key critic was Pulliam, powerful publisher of the *Indianapolis Star* and *News*, who filled his newspapers and personal communications with relentless attacks on Holder's legal background, his integrity, and his personal efforts soliciting endorsements from members of the local bar. Pulliam took prominent Indianapolis attorney Kurt Pantzer with him to Washington, D.C., to state his case directly to Attorney General Herbert Brownell Jr. and to attempt to persuade the two Indiana senators to withdraw Holder's name. But Jenner, a key member of the Senate Judiciary Committee, was unmoved, and Pulliam's opposition proved unavailing.[10]

A very different picture of Holder appears in the endorsement letters that Pulliam had so vigorously attacked. Numerous Indiana judges and lawyers as well as individuals involved in public affairs and politics enthusiastically endorsed Holder, among them Lieutenant Governor Harold W. Handley, U.S. Attorney Jack C. Brown, Indiana Attorney General Edwin K. Steers, former governor Ralph F. Gates, all five members of Indiana's supreme court, and all but one of the judges of what was then known as the appellate court of Indiana. A sizable number of Indiana's superior court judges, bar association presidents and members, and local businessmen also supported the nomination.[11]

Hugh E. Reynolds Sr., who was then a member of the Judiciary Selection and Tenure Committee of the Indiana State Bar Association and a partner in the Indianapolis law firm Slaymaker, Locke & Reynolds, stated that Holder was "a man of high morals and good character with an excellent family background and fine legal training. He has acquired the habit of industry and his disposition and temperament fit him ideally for this judicial office." Reynolds's partner Theodore L. Locke wrote that Holder was "a fine lawyer, possessed in the fullest measure of the cardinal qualities of loyalty, sincerity and absolute integrity."[12]

At least two of Holder's references directly responded to Pulliam's criticism. Wray H. Fleming, general counsel to the Indiana State Press Association Inc., spoke to media issues:

> It was the Hoosier State Press Association which first questioned the cloak of secrecy set up by the past national regime

in the administration of public welfare. When this controversy rocked the session of the Indiana legislature in 1951, it was Mr. Holder who aided our organization and led the fight to abolish secrecy of public records. Without his leadership, we would not have won and for that he has the unending gratitude of Indiana newspapers.[13]

Walter Leckrone, editor of the *Indianapolis Times,* responded to those who were opposed to Holder "on grounds amounting to party disloyalty." Leckrone explained that "no accusation could be farther from the truth, and I can only assume any such had been made as a last resort by persons who could obviously find nothing to criticize Mr. Holder's personal or professional qualifications." Leckrone cited the number of endorsements of Holder and directly addressed Pulliam's accusation of party disloyalty:

> Mr. Holder personally conducted and directed with great vigor the campaign for Mr. Eisenhower in Indiana. His leadership brought together divergent wings of the party within a State into a united effort many of us had believed was impossible to attain in 1952. The results, the most sweeping Republican victory in Indiana in many years, for President Eisenhower, the entire State ticket and even most of the local and municipal tickets in the State, clearly speak for themselves.

Leckrone concluded with the observation that he believed that the administration would not be "misled by a personal vendetta into overlooking [Holder's] other outstanding qualifications for the post or the tremendous contribution he has made to party harmony and success."[14]

Holder's Washington supporters stood firm, and despite the controversy he was confirmed to take the seat on the southern district.[15] But the ill will generated by the Pulliam campaign lingered for some time, as evidenced by the *Star*'s account of the reception at the Columbia Club following Holder's swearing-in ceremony:

> Nothing like this ever before has happened in the history of the Indiana judiciary. And so, as was expected, the ugly head of political favoritism raised its somber warning in the coronation services which made Cale Holder the king of the Federal judges in Indiana.[16]

S. Hugh Dillin. President John F. Kennedy nominated Samuel Hugh Dillin to the newly created third seat on the court on September 14, 1961. Dillin was born in 1914 in Petersburg, Indiana, where his father practiced law. He earned an AB in 1936 and an LLB in 1938 at Indiana University. While in law school he was elected to the Indiana House of Representatives as part of the Democratic sweep with Franklin D. Roosevelt in 1936. Dillin eventually served four terms in the statehouse and two in the state senate—his political activity interrupted by a stint as captain in Army Ordnance in World War II.[17] As a practicing attorney, in partnership with his father, Dillin built a general practice that included much courtroom work, involving land titles, mineral (oil and coal) claims, and personal injury settlements. In the Indiana legislature he gained a reputation for effective party leadership that earned him serious consideration for nomination for governor in 1956. As a friend and ally of U.S. Senator Vance Hartke, Dillin's appointment sailed through Congress in 1961, but only after some final politically charged maneuvering between Congress and with the Kennedy White

S. Hugh Dillin

House over the allocation of judicial seats had been completed.[18]

Judge Dillin later recalled the situation:

> When I was appointed things were a little unusual. Senator Hartke nominated me for the Southern District and David Kiley for the Northern District. District judges were supposed to be senatorial patronage. The president usually didn't butt into those things. So we were sailing along, David and I, and all of a sudden, the White House told Vance that, in order to get the bill

creating 143 new judges through in a hurry, they had promised the ABA [American Bar Association] that they would appoint a reasonable number of Republicans. Bobby Kennedy, who was Attorney General, said: "We don't feel that we owe Indiana anything as it went for Nixon in the election. So we will take one of your nominees but the other one you're going to have to abandon. We will appoint a Republican in that slot." ... Bobby Kennedy and Hartke were deadlocked for a long, long time. Finally, Hartke said, "Okay I believe you, so I will go along with a Republican as long as it's my Republican." Bobby said, "We'll go along with your Republican as long as he is a real Republican." So that's how Jesse Eschbach, a law school friend of Hartke came into being as a Republican [Northern] district judge.[19]

James E. Noland. President Lyndon B. Johnson named James Noland as district judge to the newly created fourth seat on October 6, 1966. Noland was born in 1920 in LaGrange, Missouri, where his early memories were of hard farm labor in a depressed rural landscape. The Noland family moved to Spencer, Indiana, during the Great Depression, where Noland's father sought to build a dental practice and involved himself eagerly, but usually unsuccessfully, in Democratic politics. The younger Noland's career soon combined education and military experience. Noland earned an AB from Indiana University in 1942, an MBA from the Harvard Graduate School of Business Administration in 1943, and an officer's commission in the Army Transportation Corps where he served between 1943 and 1946. The future judge returned to Indiana to earn his JD from Indiana University School of Law in 1948. The Noland name was familiar to voters in southern Indiana from his father's campaigns, and Noland ran three times for the U.S. House of

James E. Noland

Representatives, winning once in 1948. He took pride in passing the bar examination and entering Congress in the same winter.[20]

Defeated for reelection in 1950, Noland returned to Indianapolis and built a successful private practice. He also held a variety of government positions ranging from assistant state attorney general and first assistant Indianapolis city attorney to a membership on the state election board, where he coedited at least one edition of the state election code.[21] When later asked which of these many experiences most influenced him, Noland identified his Harvard training, "which did have, I think, a very strong impact upon my thinking and upon my conviction that the free enterprise system should be given as much leeway as possible to permit business and industry to continue without being trammeled with excessive regulation."[22]

Noland's appointment process followed the now-familiar path of selection and confirmation. Members of the bar and of the community attested to his legal judgment and his community service, chief among them the party and public officials who enjoyed access to the administration of President Johnson. As congressman Andrew Jacobs Jr. succinctly captured the process in memorial remarks at the time of Noland's death in 1992,

> I think it is appropriate to point out that two people, more than any others on earth, are responsible for the correct decision to appoint James E. Noland to the Federal bench. One, Jim Beatty, who was then the county chairman here; and two, the real mover and shaker, who was animated by Jim Beatty, the honorable Birch E. Bayh.[23]

Gene Edward Brooks. The southern district court completed its complement of five authorized judges with the appointment of Gene Edward Brooks by President Jimmy Carter on July 27, 1979. Brooks was confirmed by the U.S. Senate on October 4 of that year. Brooks was an Indiana native whose family had resided in southwestern Indiana since territorial times. He was born on the family farm near Griffin in Posey

County on June 21, 1931. Brooks graduated from Indiana State Teacher's College (now Indiana State University) in Terre Haute in 1953, served as a lieutenant in the Marine Corps from 1953 to 1955, and returned to attend Indiana University School of Law, from which he graduated in 1958. He financed much of his education by pitching professional softball and later noted he built many of his political friendships on intramural teams. Brooks entered private practice in Mount Vernon, Indiana, and ran successfully for the first of three terms as county prosecutor in 1959 on the Democratic ticket. For ten years he balanced the duties of a part-time prosecutor with a general private practice and extensive political activity, much of it in support of his law school intramural softball team's catcher, Birch E. Bayh.[24]

Brooks first joined the court in 1968 when he was named U.S. Bankruptcy Referee for the southern district of Indiana by Judge Steckler. In an oral history, Brooks recounts a bankruptcy appointment process that merged the politics of Congress with the personalities of the district court. The process began when Brooks was called by Senator Hartke and asked to accept the position. Brooks promptly contacted Bayh and asked his opinion. Bayh noted that with the retirement of the current part-time referee, the position was being made full time. While Bayh had been unaware Brooks was interested, the senator told Brooks he would certainly consult with Hartke to advance the appointment. Brooks quickly learned, however, that the formal appointment rested with Steckler, who had no love for Hartke and who had never met Brooks.[25]

Interested in the job, but unsure what to do, Brooks consulted a friend of Steckler, local editor Arvin Hall. Hall advised Brooks to "just drop by" the Indianapolis courthouse to say hello to Steckler and to assert the offer originated with Bayh. Brooks reluctantly followed the advice, was ushered into Steckler's chamber for "just a minute," and stayed more than

(Front row, left to right): John D. Tinder, Gene E. Brooks, Sarah Evans Barker, Larry J. McKinney, David F. Hamilton. (Back row, left to right): William E. Steckler, S. Hugh Dillin

two hours talking with the judge. When asked who was behind the idea of the appointment and of this discussion, Brooks named Bayh. Steckler reportedly said that was good. No offer was tendered at the time, but when Brooks returned to Mount Vernon that evening, he called Hall: "Arvin said, 'You got the job.' I said, 'I have'? He said, 'Steckler called me right away.' He said, 'I liked that boy.' He wouldn't call me, but he called Arvin and told Arvin he liked that boy."[26]

Brooks's appointment coincided with a period when the bankruptcy functions of the federal courts were in flux. Partly this was because caseloads were driven upward by consumer debts that reflected the rapid expansion of charge cards and other forms of consumer credit; partly it was a response to the economic instabilities of the 1970s, which witnessed one sharp recession followed by a period of double-digit inflation; partly, too, it was a response to the effective lobbying efforts of the United States bankruptcy judges, who sought greater status and independence within the judiciary.

A word about titles may be in order here. Since 1978 the title of "judge" has applied to those sitting on the bankruptcy bench. It was informally used by many before that time, not least among whom were the bankruptcy judges themselves. But on some courts, including the southern district of Indiana, the title's use was resisted by some district judges (and other court personnel), who sought a clear distinction.[27] Brooks, with a mixture of humor and annoyance, recalled the subject of his position's title during the 1970s:

> District Judge Noland was tough on that. He felt strong [sic] about being called bankruptcy judges. He used to tease me all the time in a joking sort of way. He would say to Judge Steckler, "Here's a referee, Referee Brooks is here." He made a point out of it.[28]

Brooks sensed a more serious issue at work in this conflict. He believed the heart of the matter was the disappearance of the few important surviving elements of patronage in the judicial system, the ability to appoint receivers to administer commercial bankruptcy. Brooks later claimed that all of the then-serving judges expressed varying degrees of interest in cases of large value.[29] But, in particular,

> Judge Holder did know. There wasn't any question about it. Holder found out before anybody else did. And he wanted—he controlled it. . . . He appointed one single firm and one single

accountant every single time.... Holder drew about four of the biggest cases there were in a row.... Once it was Holder's case, I get a phone call from Holder and he would say the trustee will be in to see you.[30]

Brooks attributed his acquiescence in these arrangements to his need to seek reappointment each six years, as law then required. Brooks's criticism of his colleagues' behavior should certainly be viewed with the knowledge that he eventually served as the president of the National Conference of Bankruptcy Judges, and that during his service the conference successfully lobbied for a new bankruptcy law that incorporated provisions relating to the newly prescribed title, terms of office, and the trustee system—and called for bankruptcy judges to serve not during good behavior but for fourteen-year terms and to be appointed by the president and confirmed by the Senate. (The final version of the legislation actually provided for appointment by the court of appeals).

New procedures made it easier for individuals, as well as businesses, to seek bankruptcy reorganization. In addition, a U.S. Bankruptcy Court was created as an adjunct of every district court. A trustee system designed to replace receiverships was to be implemented, first on a pilot basis.[31] The 1978 law, as Lawrence Friedman has argued, responded to the easy access to credit available in modern society and to the lack of social stigma attached to most bankruptcies in a culture that respects and often encourages risk taking. Its practical consequence was a dramatic increase in personal bankruptcies nationally to more than a million a year by 1990.[32]

In 1979 Brooks moved from the bankruptcy court to the recently created fifth seat on the district court. His appointment looked to some outside observers as a simple promotion, reflecting his continued friendship with Bayh. The reality was slightly more complicated, since it came as a result of a new selection procedure involving informal review by a committee composed of members of the bar but appointed by the senator. Brooks recalled the process this way in his oral history:

> We went through a process. You had a committee. Then you had thirty-five people. Then they narrowed it down to twenty-five people and then they finally got it down to five. Then the five they recommended to Birch and he was going to make the final decision on it. We had to all go down to D. C. and talk to Birch and he gave no indication to anybody who he was going to give the job to. . . . There was a lot of speculation. Reading the papers some days it was going to be me and then some days the other one. He called me on the phone one day. . . . He said, Gene, I am going to have to get you out of that job as bankruptcy judge. You screwed up as much as you can do it. I'm going to have to get you out and get you another job. That is how he told me.[33]

Political Questions Before the Court

Party affiliation clearly influenced the selection of judges. But when asked if it also shaped the decisions made by those judges, Steckler later gave this assessment:

> They still talk about the importance of the district court to a political party. I think that is true to the extent that receiverships, when they are actually used today, and there are very, very few of them today, could favor the party from which the district judge came when appointed. . . . The importance of political affil-

iation in decision-making is true only if a judge wishes to favor a party in writing his opinion, but that is subject to reversal on appeal.[34]

If there was such a case, Steckler added, it would be the Unigov decision, which "was favorable to the Republican Party."[35]

Unigov, short for Unified Government, was adopted in Indianapolis and Marion County in 1969 with the strong support of the Republican Party. The act allowed the mayor to be elected on a countywide vote, created a single City-County Council, and assigned a wide variety of civic functions and powers to the new entity. At the same time, the act provided less than total unification. Police and fire services and school corporations were among the government activities little changed by the act. Desegregation questions later made the schools a central topic. But in the initial lawsuits, including one brought by Patrick Chavis and supported by the Central Christian Leadership Conference, the issue was the potential dilution of minority voting. The plaintiffs argued that by combining the predominantly white voters of suburban Indianapolis with those of the pre-Unigov city, the voting power of central city blacks was reduced. The plaintiffs were unable to convince a three-judge panel that the issue was more than local, confined to a single county[36]—as they were unsuccessful in persuading the court in most later reapportionment cases involving the dilution of minority voting.[37]

Another moment when the court was asked to rule on a political question came with its decision in the 1970 U.S. Senate race between Hartke and his Republican challenger Richard Roudebush. The November 3 race was close, 4,383 votes, causing the challenger to seek a recount of ballots in eleven counties, including Marion County. Roudebush based his request on Indiana election law, which specifically allowed such recounts. Hartke based his objection to a recount on article one, section five, of the U.S. Constitution, which states, "Each House shall be the Judge of the Election, Returns and Qualifications of its own members." Judges Steckler and Dillin, speaking as the majority of a three-judge panel, issued an injunction preventing the recount. They determined that any state recount would necessarily require breaking wax seals and otherwise compromising the integrity of the evidence created by precinct election boards, denying Hartke his constitutional right to have the election judged by the Senate. Stevens, the third panelist, dissented in a way that emphasized the importance of the decision, observing "No federal court has ever done so [enjoin a Senatorial recount] before."[38] The U.S. Supreme Court, in a five to two decision, later reversed the district court's decision, ruling that recounts are part of the legitimate exercise of a state's power to conduct elections and that a recount does not usurp the Senate's ultimate decision-making power.[39] The Senate ultimately seated Hartke.

Not all cases involving political affiliation were of such magnitude. Dillin recalled with amusement a case early in his tenure when a corporate airplane, flown by a pilot without the permission of his employer, somehow crashed into a private home in Evansville. The home owner, Dillin recalled, had an exaggerated opinion of the recoverable amount of damages and persistently refused fair offers of settlement:

> One of the lawyers told me, "This lady is a precinct committee lady for the Democratic Party and she says that the only white person in the world that she'd trust would be Senator Hartke." Hartke, of course, had been mayor of Evansville for a number of years. So the day of the trial came and I had the lawyers in and I said now bring your client in. I want to talk to her. So I visited

with them for a while. I said, "Well, you know Senator Hartke appointed me to do this job." "Oh, he did," she said. I said, "I happen to have his telephone number in Washington. Why don't we call the Senator and see what he says about this case." She agreed to this so I called him. I gave him the facts and of course I emphasized the *ultra vires* aspect of the case. He said, "You want me to tell her to settle, don't you?" I said yes. He said put her on and so forth and so forth. That's how we settled that case.[40]

The Press of Court Business

Despite the rapid expansion in the number of its judges, the court's operations were dominated in this era by the pressures of an ever-expanding docket. Starting in 1950, the court began to change its practices and procedures in an ongoing effort to keep current with its caseload. Reflecting upon these changes, Steckler recalled that his thought, when first appointed judge, had been to strike a balance between tradition and innovation. "A following judge," he noted, "does not want to stray too far away from the policies and practices of his predecessor."[41] Yet Steckler also felt that the weight of cases required innovation. His solution was to turn to the group of attorneys that he identified as "the elite of the legal profession," who had previously worked with Baltzell. Most of these individuals—Hubert Hickum, Jerry Belknap, Kurt Pantzer, and Tom Scanlon—were members of the law firm Barnes, Hickum, Pantzer and Boyd (today Barnes & Thornburg). This informal advisory group began by recommending that the judge place himself visibly at the center of the process of change. Symbolically, they helped him do so by purchasing a judicial robe that they presented to Steckler to wear at his swearing-in ceremony. It was, Steckler later recalled, one of the first instances where any judge outside the Atlantic seaboard wore a robe in court.[42]

Administratively, this informal advisory group suggested that Steckler concentrate on two aspects of trial procedure: the pretrial conference and the court's instructions to juries. Baltzell, they noted, seldom welcomed attorneys to his chambers and never provided advance copies of his jury instructions to lawyers trying cases in his court. Steckler agreed that under his predecessor, "These chambers had been something like the inner sanctum sanctorum." Moving much of the give-and-take discussion of the courtroom into the judge's chambers hopefully would shorten trials. In addition, having the jury instructions available to them in advance gave opposing counsel the opportunity to discuss concerns and possible changes and thus reduce the challenges occasioned by such instructions. New procedures placed greater reliance on discovery of evidence, moving many issues from the courtroom to the "law offices and telephones" of the participants. The changes also caused Steckler to expand his chambers at the expense of the court library, installing a long conference table to accommodate the many new conferences with counsel.[43]

Other changes followed. Soon the district court and its advisers were preparing kits of forms designed to standardize court motions and pleadings and proposing guidelines designed to shorten multiweek civil trials. As Steckler put it, "You should avoid any trial that's longer than the longest vacation a juror has taken." Steckler described many of these changes at seminars conducted by the U.S. Judicial Conference and thereafter served on a number of that group's committees promoting the national adoption of practices pioneered or developed in the Indiana court. Steckler also was responsible in 1968 for the original proposal for a bulletin of the Federal Judicial Center, which has continued to be published as *The Third Branch*. Many of the innovations of the southern district of Indiana found their way into the federal rules and gave the court one of its most important sets of achievements.[44]

Not all the changes were so momentous. Dillin later recalled that

> the judge [Steckler] has several firsts. . . . One is that he is the first judge to ban cuspidors from the federal courtroom. They were beautiful objets d'art, but after a bailiff stepped in one and fell down, it was determined that they had to go. Then there was the case of the distracted jurors. The judge's witness box used to have an open front, and when mini skirts were in vogue many a female witness found the attention of the jurors riveted on something other than her words. Accordingly, he became the first judge to use a witness box entered from the side.[45]

The practice of law before the court reflected other changes as well. Law schools now dominated the training of young attorneys, ending the traditional path of "reading law" as an apprentice in a lawyer's office. The adoption of a uniform state bar examination in 1931 put obvious pressure on law schools to provide instruction consistent with the evolving standards of the bar and made the examination a benchmark in every attorney's early career. Interestingly, one of the chief proponents of the examination was Dillin, a young state representative at the time. As law firms grew in size and in specialization in response to the growth of their business, they increasingly adopted such practices as the "billable hour" in measuring attorney fees. But as late as 1950 Steckler could recall,

> the federal law practice in that day was largely concentrated in the hands of a few large law firms here in Indianapolis, and in the hands of a few lawyers, some of whom had been Assistant United

States Attorneys, or United States Attorneys. The few big law firms that had the federal practice, I dare say you could count on two hands.... The other lawyers who got in and out of the federal court would be in only occasionally, and I was among them.[46]

Service in the U.S. Attorney's Office remained an important step on the career ladder of a number of lawyers. As more and more women and minorities were admitted to the legal profession, this also was reflected in the office. Future judge Sarah Evans Barker was the first woman to serve as an Assistant U.S. Attorney in the southern district, from 1972 to 1976, and as First Assistant U.S. Attorney from 1976 to 1979.[47] In 1977 President Jimmy Carter named to a four-year term as U.S. Attorney Virginia Dill McCarty, making her one of the first women to serve in that position. McCarty, who was from Plainfield, was an honors graduate in 1950 of Indiana University Law School in Indianapolis. In addition to private practice, her credentials included service as a deputy attorney general (1965–69) and a member of the Indiana Board of Law Examiners (1971–76).[48] As U.S. Attorney, she joined her predecessors in participating in the widening range of legal business that came before her office. In 1977 and 1978, as one example, her office participated in a series of hearings that obtained information on the costs of drug production at Eli Lilly and Company.[49]

Commissioners Become Magistrates

The district court continued the practice of maintaining a part-time commissioner in each of its divisions. Several commissioners, such as John Cody Jr. in New Albany and Robert Duffy in Terre Haute, served for many years. On the other hand, Gilbert Shake served in Vincennes from 1952 to 1956, but resigned for lack of business—and the court simply eliminated the position.[50] By the 1960s, however, the office of commissioner was caught up in national debate over how to best handle the growing press of business before the courts and became transformed into the new position of magistrate.

The Federal Magistrates Act of 1968[51] was the product of nationwide discussion involving the Judicial Conference and the judiciary committees of Congress. The act responded to perceived problems in the existing office of commissioner, which had been part of the federal judiciary since the 1790s. These problems included payment by a fee system and the lack of uniform criteria for selection or appointment. Under the 1968 act, commissioners were renamed magistrates, assigned eight-year terms (four years if part-time), and required to be members of the Bar of the highest court of their state. Powers of the magistrates were significantly expanded in pretrial proceedings, discovery, and posttrial relief. With consent of the defendants, magistrates could conduct misdemeanor criminal trials and serve as special masters in civil actions. After a three-year pilot program administered by the Federal Judicial Center, district judges were empowered to implement the new system in every district.[52]

The new law offered the Judicial Conference the opportunity to review its staffing of the office. It was a significant compliment to both the southern district court and to Noland that he was named to serve on the Judicial Conference Committee on the Administration of the Federal Magistrate's System from 1973 to 1982.[53] In most cases, the part-time nature of the magistrate's position was maintained. Two serving commissioners were appointed magistrate for their division: John Cody Jr. in New Albany and Robert Geddes in Indianapolis. Two new magistrates, Joseph Woody Annakin and D. Joe Gabbert, were named in the Evansville and Terre Haute divisions, respectively. Other existing commissioner positions were eliminated. One new full-time position of chief magistrate was created in the Indianapolis division.[54]

The first chief magistrate in the southern district of Indiana was Thomas J. Faulconer. He was an Indianapolis native born in 1923, a

Thomas J. Faulconer

1945 graduate of Butler University, an army veteran, and a 1948 graduate of Valparaiso University Law School. Faulconer had followed the path of Democratic political involvement, where he initially allied with Indianapolis mayor Philip Bayt. In 1958 Faulconer was elected a Marion County criminal court judge. There he presided over the trial of Connie Nicholas for the murder of Eli Lilly and Company executive Forrest Teel. Nicholas's "abandoned mistress" defense attracted national media attention, which in turn resulted in Faulconer becoming one of the first criminal judges in America to allow television cameras in the courtroom.

The fact that the judge had remained an active participant in party politics, his service in the 1960s as chief judge of the Indiana court of appeals, and his innovative judicial reputation, won him the magistrate's appointment.[55] The *Indianapolis Star* was blunt, "The Democratic judges selected him."[56]

As chief magistrate, Faulconer participated in significant national changes in the powers of the federal magistrate's office. In 1976 Congress allowed magistrates to conduct evidentiary proceedings in habeas corpus actions. A 1979 law gave magistrates consent jurisdiction, allowing them to conduct civil trials with the consent of the parties. The 1979 act also provided for merit selection panels to advise district judges.[57] Faulconer later recalled that the pressure of pretrial work and of the review of prisoner petitions was greater than he expected and prevented him from exploring other potential areas of activity of his office. Faulconer's most unusual responsibility was serving as magistrate for all crimes on a federal military property, Fort Benjamin Harrison.[58]

Old and New Courthouses
The district court was witness to significant change in its facilities during this period. Each new judicial seat created the need for additional

offices, chambers, and an additional courtroom in Indianapolis. The judges' library yielded to space needs in 1969. Shortly thereafter, two new federal buildings, the Minton-Capehart Federal Building and the South Street Post Office, allowed other government offices to be relocated and permitted the court occupancy to expand in the Ohio Street facility.[59] Steckler recognized the struggles over space when he recalled a proposal by the post office to reconfigure the Ohio Street facade of the building by cutting down the trees and installing an automobile ramp and a central postal patron entrance. Steckler recalled,

> I cited to the Postmaster and General Services Administration the inscription on the south side of the building which reads "United States Courthouse and Post Office," proving that this building was a courthouse first and post office second.[60]

Change also occurred in the divisions. Dillin remembered a revealing episode when he reflected upon the judge's chambers in the old New Albany federal courthouse:

> At the time I first came on the bench, Sherman Minton . . . was a Justice of the Supreme Court of the United States. Minton's home was in New Albany when the court was in recess. There was a double desk in the judge's chambers there in the courthouse that we used when we were down there. One side of the desk was for the use of the district judge and the other side was for Justice Minton and nobody as far as I know ever dared to open Justice Minton's drawers . . . . He finally died and it was my turn to go down to New Albany and hold a term of court. I thought, "Well, there might be something in here that his widow

would like to have ... so I had better open it." So I did, and there wasn't much in there except a bunch of telegrams congratulating him on his reelection as United States Senator—because it was like Dewey and Truman.... So here was a whole drawer full of those things and carbon copies of his responses to the letter and telegrams, which were invariably humorous.[61]

That older building was replaced by the New Albany Federal Building on West Spring Street. The new facility was designed in 1965 by the firm of Walker, Applegate, Oakes and Ritz and dedicated in July 1966. Similarly, in 1969 the older Evansville facility was vacated for a new federal building on Martin Luther King Boulevard.[62]

Administrative Practices

The changes in court practices and procedures undertaken by the judges of the southern district were paralleled by changes in the administrative responsibilities that fell on the staff of the court. Not only were the number of cases filed increasing, but also the complexity of many civil cases was adding substantially to the motions, pleadings, and notices that made up much of the paperwork of the court. Management of the docket and scheduling of trials and conferences became a serious consideration for each judge. Holder, in particular, took personal pride in the tight schedules he was able to plan and maintain.

The individuals who served as clerks of the court, in particular, found their activities changing in significant ways. First, they were increasingly called on to manage the accounts and budgets of the court, under the oversight of the Administrative Office of the United States Courts (which had been created in 1941). Second, the clerks were required to supervise a growing variety of personnel matters. Between 1950 and 1982, the number of court employees grew from 25 to 146. Because court employees were employed under judicial rather than executive authority, they were supervised in a manner different from the civil service. Judges, for example, long considered the appointment of the clerk of the court and other court staff an appropriate exercise of the independence of the judiciary. Third, the clerk of the court was expected to develop, or to employ subordinates who had developed, specialized skills to support the court's work in areas of law such as bankruptcy. Finally, the clerks were expected to adapt and improve records management. Bound docket books yielded in this period to loose-leaf binders. Card files became a common form of indexing for large cases. Records storage and retrieval became a particular challenge as the case files filled, and threatened to overwhelm, available storage areas. Microfilming became more and more attractive as the 1950s progressed, as did federal documents repositories in the 1960s.[63] Many of these changes were embodied in newly published rules of court.[64] Substantial portions of the records of the southern district were deposited in Record Group 21 of the Great Lakes Regional branch of the National Archives and Records Administration in Chicago.[65]

Steckler, as senior judge on the court after 1954, carried the designation of chief judge. At the time the title did not rotate among the serving judges, as it later would do. As chief judge, Steckler generally appointed the court's personnel. He could, of course, have been challenged in this power if a majority of the judges sought a different individual. But until Dillin's appointment, Steckler always prevailed over the more junior Holder. Dillin then routinely supported Steckler, later observing:

> I never disagreed with Steckler. Holder was in the Bill Jenner wing of the Republican party . . . extremely partisan. We didn't

have any real bitter arguments while it was the three of us. Steckler had always made all the appointments around the court and he still did. I wasn't going to team up with Holder to do something else. I was never very interested in patronage anyway. I learned early on in politics that the people who were involved in patronage—every time they made a friend, they made about a dozen enemies.[66]

The appointment of Noland made some difference in this arrangement. Dillin recalled, "We all got along, although we had our differences. We had an argument or two over who was going to be clerk after Bob Newbold retired." Dillin added, "Actually, being a district judge, at least around here, was a pretty lonely business in the sense that you would run your calendar and every body else would run his calendar the way he wanted to and you really didn't get together all that often."[67]

On the Bench
Clad in the robes of office and seated on an elevated bench in dignified well-appointed courtrooms, judges usually evoke respect—or more—from many of those who appear before them. The judges of the new multi-judge court were no exception. Judge Barker's good-natured assessment was that "They were really first rate judges. They had remarkably fine judicial skills and each brought a different 'skill set' to the bench,"[68] which captures the memories of many. Reviewing that era in a 2003 symposium held as part of the court's historical celebration, several panelists reflected on their experiences before the judges of this period.[69]

Although within the experience of the panelists, it was hardly a modern era. On the practice of court reporting, James Voyles recalled,

"Bertha Harrison was the court reporter, and she had a voice mask. She spoke every word that every lawyer was speaking in the court at the time. That is how it was recorded."[70] On the larger issue of civility on the part of attorneys, Barker noted that the judges

> had another weapon that I think is maybe not available, or not as easily available today. And that is the judges knew the lawyers in the practice group from which the lawyers came who were appearing before them who were misbehaving. And it was not unusual, I'm told, for calls to be made to a senior partner in the firm to re-educate this young lawyer into some sort of civility.[71]

Steckler's patience commanded special notice. As Barker noted, "He set a high standard. But he was a very patient, kind man who let the process unfold basically at a pace that the lawyers either chose or the proceedings themselves yielded."[72] Attorney James Strain added that Steckler was "patient well beyond what the lawyers might think would be required for the particular problem that was before him. But he would hear argument right on up until there wasn't any further argument on sometimes the most minute issue."[73] Voyles recalled of the judge, "I learned decorum.... I watched one day, we were standing there, and somebody had walked into the well of the courtroom, and he asked them to be removed because they weren't a lawyer."[74]

Holder, in Strain's words, "worked as hard as any person I have seen at trying to get an order out that could not be reversed by the 7th Circuit.... Everything conceivable that could be put into the order was put into the order, so that on some ground—all it takes is one—the order might be affirmed."[75] Barker recalled, "Judge Holder was a very tough, demanding judge, but sort of courtly in his own way."[76] Holder's attention to precise legal language, such as the difference between an offer and a motion to submit evidence, was remarkable. Voyles remembered, "But he would also say to us, if you were in front of him and you would make . . . a mistake of making a motion instead of an offer, he would say, 'Now, Mr. Voyles,' he said, 'you are making tracks on my record. You don't want to make—or double dribbling on my record.'"[77] The judge's tough sentences for criminals were well known. In Barker's recollection: "One sleepy morning his sleepy law clerk, who was serving as bailiff, came in and gaveled the Judge in and said, 'The Honorable Cale Jail Holder presiding.' A lot of requests for continuances came next."[78]

In a 1983 memorial address, attorney Karl Stipher recalled a personal-injury lawsuit brought by a Union Station baggage handler. Testimony eventually revealed that the plaintiff, although claiming never to have had a prior injury, actually had filed a number of nearly identical lawsuits in different jurisdictions. The baggage handler's embarrassed attorneys, claiming no knowledge of the fraud, agreed to have the suit dismissed with prejudice so that it could not be refiled. Holder then took a lengthy recess before returning to his courtroom, and according to Stipher,

> So he called the jury back in and called the plaintiff in, and he says, "Young man, come up here." And he said, "What have you got to say about your conduct in the federal courtroom today: These lies that you've been talking about? What have you got to say for yourself?"
>
> He [the plaintiff] said, "Well, I don't have much of anything to say."

And he [Judge Holder] said, "Well let me tell you: You are not going to make a fool out of this jury in this federal court; you are not going to make a fool out of the federal court; and you're not going to make a fool out of me. I am sentencing you to ten days in jail for your perjury in this court. Marshal, take him away."[79]

Reflecting upon Judge Holder in a 2003 summary, attorney William Welch added,

> as the dockets ... grew ... Judge Holder devoted considerable effort to managing his docket; and as a part of that effort, he developed a reputation for strong encouragement of, if not outright insistence upon, settlement. One heard from time to time the comment that lawyers who practiced before Judge Holder yearned for the opportunity to try their cases rather than settle them.[80]

Dillin gained special marks in his quest for efficiency. "One of his most famous expressions was, 'Can't you summarize it?'" Barker recalled.[81] Strain added that when Dillin "had heard enough basically he would tell you he had heard enough, and then he could give you a ruling."[82] Attorney John Kautzman noted, "And if he didn't like something about the ways things were going in the courtroom, it didn't matter if it was the plaintiff's lawyers or the defense lawyer, he would immediately take over the questioning from the bench."[83] In a 2003 assessment Welch simply noted, "In other words, in the vernacular, he did not suffer fools gladly."[84]

Noland's kindness and good humor gained special marks, as did his sense of decorum. "He had a great sense of the propriety that ought to attach itself to court proceedings," Barker noted. Newly fashionable pastel shirts and long hair had no place in his courtroom.[85] Assistant U.S. Attorney Charles Goodloe added, "He was very patient and generally, I think the lawyers were basically very comfortable and at ease before him."[86] According to Voyles, Noland's turns of phrase were memorable: "He would say, 'Now Mr. Voyles, you know the train is getting ready to take off from the station. Is your guy going to get on the train?' Took me awhile to have him explain that to me. But [what] he wanted to know was if there was going to be a guilty plea."[87]

Voyles also recalled Noland's enduring sense of humor:

> I tried a case in [his] courtroom. . . . I don't know if I should explain the case. It was a case where a sexual object had been sent through the mail that had exploded, and we tried that case with the postal inspectors, and it was a big case because it was a very dangerous situation. But through the trial Judge Noland—we would have these periodic little breaks because of the humor that were [sic] in the case, and we would see Judge Noland would be covering his mouth, or he would call us to the bench.[88]

Noland shared in the practice of encouraging settlement through negotiation. Former governor Evan Bayh, who had served as one of Noland's law clerks, recalled one negotiation that had drawn on for hours when the defense made what the judge considered a reasonable settlement offer. The judge looked at the reluctant plaintiff's attorney and said, "Mr. Smith, you are aware of the provisions in the southern district of Indiana for remitter, are you not?" The case was settled within an hour.[89] Dillin summed it up, "Judge Noland disliked long briefs, long trials, and long arguments by counsel."[90]

Interchanges among the judges often highlighted their special interests. Barker recalled,

> the judges worked together and knew each other for a long time, so they would teach each other and, obviously, behind each other's back make little remarks. . . . One time there was going to be a judges' meeting up in Noland's chambers, and he had this elegant chambers . . . [that] had had this long table with chandeliers and it had on the desk a quill pen and there were candelabra. . . . But I remember I was talking to Judge Dillin about something and he says, "Well, I must go now to the Williamsburg suite."[91]

Criminal Cases

The federal courts, the southern district among them, saw significant changes in criminal law. Steckler noted,

> We have witnessed the extension of the exclusionary rule prohibiting the use of evidence seized in violation of constitutional rights. We have seen established the right of indigent defendants to appointed counsel, the right to consult an attorney before responding to interrogation, and the extension of procedural safeguards to juveniles.[92]

The district court continued to deal with a variety of federal crimes, of which interstate automobile theft and narcotics usually produced the largest caseload. The passage of the 1970 Comprehensive Drug Abuse Prevention and Control Act assured that the latter received special attention. The act reclassified a number of controlled substances into five schedules, provided penalties tied to the anticipated extent of the abuse, and distinguished between quantities intended for use and for sale to others. Seen by many as a reaction to the highly publicized drug culture of the 1960s, the act was intended to toughen federal enforcement. Its effect on plea bargaining, by adjusting proposed sentences using these many legal distinctions, was considerable. The act also placed considerable responsibility on the U.S. Attorneys to define categories of offenses and to negotiate plea agreements in which defendants who were guilty accepted appropriate definitions of their offenses.[93]

The new sentencing guidelines reduced the discretion previously exercised by many judges. Predictably, such guidelines were viewed with some skepticism by many judges, who felt an outside judgment had been substituted for their own closer acquaintance with cases that came before them. Dillin left no doubt regarding his thoughts on the subject:

> I find the sentencing guidelines much more difficult because I don't think they are accurate at all. There are many cases where I would give a much harsher sentence than that provided by the Guidelines and in others I would put the defendant on probation and they won't let me. . . . I don't know why somebody doesn't come with something like a candy machine where you punch in the ingredients and a card comes out at the bottom and tells you what the sentence is because that is about what it amounts to.[94]

But for all the changes, some issues remained familiar. Steckler remembered his "moonshine" cases, brought to him because excise tax had, of course, not been paid:

We had a number of moonshine cases, especially down in the Evansville Division and the New Albany Division. . . . Some of those people made very fine moonshine whiskey, according to the reputation that we heard. . . . There is a lot of wooded area down there. It is rather wild in places. We had one defendant from Bedford, and he took great pride in the still he had built—the brick firebox and all the other things he had built to manufacture alcohol.[95]

The Civil Rights Era

Civil rights was a central issue of American discourse during this era, but it was hardly a new issue in Hoosier society and politics. Many of the important civil rights organizations in Indiana predated 1950; for example, the Indianapolis branch of the National Association for the Advancement of Colored People (NAACP) had been organized in 1913. Many civil rights leaders harkened to issues that had surfaced at least as early as the Great Migration that had begun from the rural South during World War I, or during the growth of segregation—especially in the southern half of the state—during the 1920s. Many of the topics debated in civil rights discourse after 1950, such as access to public accommodation in restaurants and theaters, were argued in the context of black participation as soldiers and workers in World War II. If there was a difference after 1950, it was in the leadership skills and political sophistication of those who insisted on the end of Jim Crow.[96]

The 1950 census documented that Indiana's African American population lived primarily in cities such as Indianapolis, Evansville, and Muncie. The civil rights campaigns in the state similarly focused on those communities. Urban issues, such as minority access to education and employment, were important elements of such campaigns. Equal state laws, and their equal enforcement, were central to most civil rights programs until the mid-1960s. Yet even in the 1950s, Steckler made one important civil rights decision in the southern district court, deciding a public housing case in Evansville.

The 1953 Evansville case was initiated by the NAACP in an attempt to establish a federal precedent allowing equal access to public housing projects. Thurgood Marshall, a future U.S. Supreme Court justice, was lead counsel for the plaintiffs, aided by the local efforts of Constance Baker Motley and Henry Richardson. They argued that the administrators in charge of the project, in Steckler's words, either "reluctantly recognized that persons of the black race had the right to be housed in a public housing project, or the authorities absolutely refused to recognize the needs of the black community who needed housing facilities." The Evansville Housing Authority assigned black families to separate projects inferior to those provided to white families. In 1953 a new low-rent project open only to white residents was built, resulting in the filing of a lawsuit on behalf of several black women who sought entry. Steckler noted that he "had no great amount of precedent to apply," but concluded on the basis of the Equal Protection Clause of the Fourteenth Amendment "the black citizen had equal rights to be housed in a public housing project—the same rights as those of the white citizen."[97]

School desegregation cases came within a new federal view in the 1960s with the passage of the 1964 Civil Rights Act, although the U.S. Supreme Court's 1954 *Brown v. Board of Education* decision had already sparked a number of cases in district courts in the southern states.[98] The 1964 law established a series of steps that could result in a Justice Department lawsuit to correct abuses. First, the law allowed a parent, or a group of parents, to complain in writing to the U.S. Attorney General that their children, as a class, were being deprived of the equal protection of the laws. Second, the law instructed the Justice Department to determine if the complaint had merit. If it did, the offending school corporation was required to correct the conditions within a reasonable length of time. Third, should a school corporation fail to make a satisfactory response, the law required the Justice Department to bring a civil suit in district court to correct the abuse. Modern court practice assigned cases on a random basis and brought such issues of segregation in the Indianapolis Public Schools (IPS) before Dillin in May of 1968. At that time IPS and its superintendent were named as defendants in a lawsuit alleging the school system was guilty of such abuses. The case, in its various manifestations, continued to appear on the court's docket until the late 1990s.[99]

The IPS desegregation case did not actually reach Dillin until August 1971, as both sides attempted with little success to negotiate a settlement. When it was argued, the IPS case required Dillin to answer a series of legal questions. In 1971 the initial question before the court was to determine if the underlying complaint of *de jure* segregation had merit. The plaintiffs, with aid from the NAACP, argued that it did, pointing to a dual system, part white and part black, maintained with internal boundaries often redrawn along racial lines and operated in part by busing of black students to exclusively black schools. The defendants responded that the situation of single-race schools instead reflected patterns of neighborhood housing and was *de facto* but not *de jure*. Dillin found that housing patterns indeed contributed to the problem. But he also found for the plaintiffs on other issues. He called attention to the fact IPS boundaries had been redrawn 360 times since 1954 and that 90 percent of the changes had the effect of increasing racial segregation. Dillin seemed particularly concerned that a single black high school,

Crispus Attucks, had been expanded while new suburban white high schools were built.[100]

Dillin was blunt in his later oral history: "Well, of course, there wasn't any question but that the school board for years and years and years had intentionally segregated the Indianapolis schools." He continued, "of course, at that time under *Brown v. Board of Education*, the schools just had to be desegregated. That was it, so I desegregated them."[101] Twenty-three years after the event, Dillin vividly recalled the public reaction, "We did get a lot of threats and we did have marshals who stayed with us at home for about a week, but that was it. Fortunately, I spell Dillin in a different way 'i-n' instead of 'o-n' so a lot of people couldn't find me in the phone book." The judge chose instead to emphasize the support he received. "I got a lot of encouragement out there really and I got encouragement from [William] Hudnut," who was Dillin's minister and later mayor of Indianapolis.[102]

Once the issue of segregation was decided, Dillin needed to seek a remedy that was consistent with recent case law. Central to the remedy was the extent to which busing, formerly used to maintain a segregated system, should be used to desegregate IPS. In his 1971 ruling, Dillin ordered faculty and staff reassignments, a review of transfer policies, desegregation of Crispus Attucks, and negotiations with the suburban schools.

Dillin, himself a former state legislator, sought to involve local citizens and state legislators in working toward a resolution of the situation. Two general courses of action were needed. One required that local citizens be motivated, in the nonpartisan elections held for school commissioners, to elect candidates supportive of policies and administrators committed to desegregation. According to Dillin, this was necessary because most school commissioners for the majority of the last half century had supported racial separation as a policy. The other course of action required that the Indiana General Assembly be induced to review the relationship of IPS, in central Indianapolis, to the suburban city and township systems surrounding it. This was necessary because Indiana school districts are products of state legislation, and because the absence of suburban participation through some type of cross-district enrollment would almost certainly lead to the demographic shift commonly called "white flight." Dillin was particularly concerned to avoid a "tipping point" where the withdrawal of white students from IPS would leave a largely black system and undo the effects of any desegregation plan.[103]

Dillin saw some success in the first area. Newly formed citizen committees began to run, and elect, slates of commissioners by the mid-1970s who sought to work with the district court. But in the second area, Dillin experienced less success as legislative session after legislative session made only token changes in state law. As a consequence, the judge added the suburban school systems and the state of Indiana as defendants in the ongoing case. In 1973 the Seventh Circuit generally approved Dillin's decision (and the Supreme Court denied an appeal by IPS). The appellate decision also approved Dillin's decision to add additional defendants and made possible a second trial that summer. In the second trial Dillin concluded that the state of Indiana had contributed to the problem of segregation, even if the suburban systems generally had not. However, to achieve the goals of desegregation, Dillin saw few alternatives to some form of busing. He ordered one-way busing of black students to township schools; the state legislature responded by providing funding formulas that would pay for the busing but not merge the systems.[104]

A series of appeals and hearings followed on related questions. In 1974 and 1975, for example, much attention was focused on the role of the Unigov Act in promoting segregation. The 1969 law had, of course, merged many civil jurisdictions of city and county without including the school systems. Most press accounts focused on the testimony of former Indianapolis mayor Richard G. Lugar that the merger of schools would have doomed the legislation. Ruling that such evidence made the townships a party to the issue, Dillin proceeded with his orders for busing. Generally, the judge was upheld by the Seventh Circuit, including his use of the fairly unusual device of an interdistrict remedy, although the appeals process and the ongoing political negotiations delayed the implementation until the early 1980s in the era of the modern court (chapter five).[105]

Other civil rights era cases that reached the court attracted less public attention but confirmed the court's involvement. In 1966 Steckler ruled on a case involving standards prohibiting the employment of women in physically strenuous occupations.[106] In 1967 Holder approved a settlement of another NAACP lawsuit brought against school authorities in Kokomo. Part of Holder's order closed two predominantly black elementary schools.[107] In 1970 Dillin approved an Evansville-Vanderburgh County plan for continued desegregation, which included two-way busing and closed two black elementary schools, transferring the students to previously white schools.[108] Holder similarly conducted hearings dealing with school desegregation issues in Kokomo.[109] The knowledge that the district court did not hesitate to act in such cases was surely a consideration in the minds of other local authorities as they considered negotiated settlements of civil rights cases in their communities.

At least once the court was called upon to deal with media portrayals and assessments of the issues of the times. In 1973 Lincoln Theodore Perry argued that he had been defamed in a Columbia Broadcasting System (CBS) 1968 telecast, "Black History: Lost, Stolen, or Strayed." Perry was a prominent black actor in the 1930s, appearing under the stage name of Stepin Fetchit. In the telecast commentary, narrated by actor Bill Cosby, Perry's movie persona was described as "the lazy, stupid, crap-shooting, chicken-stealing idiot." Perry sued for defamation, but the court held that he failed to meet the stringent tests of a slander action. The court granted summary judgment to CBS, ruling that Perry was a public figure whose movie career was of public interest and that CBS had not recklessly disregarded the truth in its telecast.[110]

Civil liberties cases also came before the court on occasion. In 1960 the district court ruled that Wyatt Jennings, a prisoner at Terre Haute Penitentiary following his court-martial conviction, was incorrect in arguing that the alleged fact that the Korean War was fought under the United Nations flag did not deprive the U.S. Army of jurisdiction over criminal offenses by one of its soldiers.[111] And in 1978 the court ruled that under the First Amendment Hare Krishna advocates could enter the Indiana State Fairgrounds to "talk to members of the public about their religion, to gratuitously distribute their religious literature, flowers or other items of nominal symbolic value, and to solicit contributions" provided they paid admission, stayed on pedestrian thoroughfares, and acted only during normal hours of operation.[112]

Indiana Issues in Court

The distinctive character of the Indiana economy is often seen in the nature of civil cases that reach the district court. Cases involving agriculture, transportation, mining, and manufacturing regularly have been on the court's dockets. After 1950 additional economic enterprises important to the Indiana economy presented still more cases of interest. Many fell into the categories of light industry, service, and entertainment, reflecting a growing, ever-changing economic variety that was energizing many areas within the southern district of Indiana.

Limestone. A good example of a traditional industry involved in a district court case came in 1958, when Mary Lucille Sandidge sued for damages under the Clayton Anti-Trust Act. The plaintiff owned a limestone quarry near Mitchell, which she had leased to produce crushed stone. Her suit involved alleged damages that resulted from the defendants' actions on and around her property in the early 1950s, when a competing quarry was opened, allegedly causing her own to be flooded and closed. Part of the case asked Holder to decide if the statute of limitations precluded action. The other part asked the court to decide if the closing of her single quarry constituted a move toward a monopoly in crushed limestone. The defendants won on both issues. Much of the decision became a review of the Indiana limestone industry, whose potential production from seven broad belts of stone in the state caused the court to conclude no one quarry could have a meaningful impact on the consumer.[113]

Movie Theaters. In 1948 the Supreme Court extended the operation of antitrust laws to motion picture distribution in *United States v. Paramount*.[114] The District Court for the Southern District of Indiana soon joined in the implementation of this decision when Syndicate Theaters, a local group, sued Greater Indianapolis Amusements Inc., a four-theater chain that claimed to enjoy, in Steckler's words, "great advantage in the motion picture exhibition business, by reason of being able to obtain so-called 'big box office' or 'blockbuster' first run motion pictures." Because the defendant was at the end of a chain that included several major studios such as MGM, as well as other producers and distributors, the case involved a voluminous amount of evidence and became a proving ground for many of the innovative procedures being implemented by the court.[115] The twelve-member jury (six members only later became standard practice) eventually found for the defendants, who successfully argued that they were following standard business practices that did not provide "preferred treatment or advantage."[116]

Time Zones. Drive-in theater operators also appeared before the court, arguing about the enduring question of Indiana's proper time zone. Semiofficial "railroad time" had operated in the state since 1883, and national time zones had first been mandated under an act of Congress in March 1918. That act had been replaced in 1966 by the Uniform Time Act, which required the Secretary of Transportation to determine time zone boundaries. The secretary had eventually drawn a line that placed twelve counties near Gary and Evansville in the central zone and the remainder of the state in the eastern zone. The act also required daylight saving time in the summer months, unless a state law decided otherwise. Drive-in theater operators, concerned that the ensuing 9:30 p.m. sunset would cut into their business, first tried for state legislative remedy, but the governor vetoed the bill. The operators then sued in district court, arguing the time zone boundaries were arbitrary and capricious. Dillin denied a plaintiff's motion for a preliminary injunction, and his decision was sustained on appeal.[117]

Auto Racing. Few activities are more identified with Indiana than auto racing. No single sporting event attracts more spectators than the Indianapolis 500 on Memorial Day weekend. Not surprisingly, a variety of cases related to racing have reached the court. The most publicized in the mid-twentieth century was the 1968 case filed by Andy Granatelli, the STP Corporation, and the Studebaker Corporation against the United States Auto Club (USAC). The plaintiffs had designed a new type of racing engine, a turbine similar to the engines used to power airplanes. In the 1967 race, the Granatelli engine had proved to be superior to the piston engines commonly driven in the Indianapolis 500, although a mechanical failure in the race car had denied it a victory. USAC, attempting to maintain a competitive balance between turbine and piston cars, changed its rules for 1968 to require Granatelli to modify his engine. Granatelli sued to obtain an injunction to prevent the enforcement of the new rules.[118]

Steckler heard the case and later recalled Granatelli as a "colorful figure" in the best Horatio Alger rags-to-riches tradition. But the judge ruled in favor of USAC. Steckler based his decision on the fact that many events that require "competitive equivalency" are conducted under the rules of sanctioning bodies, and that "Granatelli was a member along with the other race car owners." Steckler agreed that it was a legitimate exercise of a sanctioning body's power to assure a "competitive relationship ... so that there would be a race."[119]

Pharmaceuticals. Over the past century a variety of industries and businesses have, for a time, made Indiana a center of their activities. Insurance, railroading, meatpacking, and automotive assembly all left their mark on the Indiana economy. One industry that has continued to play a major role is pharmaceuticals, which made several contributions to patent law before the district court. An important example after 1950 was the lawsuit that determined the proper patent holder of procaine penicillin.

Penicillin had gone through a long, rather slow period of development between the world wars. Among its problems was the burning sensation that early injections produced, a sensation that many manufacturers sought to overcome by mixing penicillin with procaine, a painkiller, in an aqueous solution. One penicillin manufacturer, Eli Lilly and Company, encountered the further problem that their product, when refrigerated in solution, produced crystals not found in other manufacturers' output. Company researchers eventually discovered that the crystallization was the result of the purity of the product. Impurities in other manufacturers' output had prevented that reaction. More important, Lilly research further discovered that if the precipitated crystals were ground (or micronized) and placed in solution, the resulting solution would maintain a consistent level in a patient's blood over a longer period of time. Lilly promptly filed for a patent, and several of its competitors protested. The case was tried in 1953 and permitted the principal Lilly scientist, Harley W. Rhodehamel Jr., to review the process of research that led him to a concept that the court concluded was "novel and original with him and constituted invention of a high order," making Lilly the first company to conceive and reduce to practice the invention—that is, be able to produce a product based upon the new concept.[120]

Herbal Remedies. Steckler also remembered with some amusement a very different type of drug case. In the early 1950s, an "herbal doctor" named Cox was twice prosecuted by the Food and Drug Administration (FDA) in the Terre Haute division for selling brown paper bags filled with herbs that the dealer contended had medicinal value when brewed as a tea. Steckler said, "We pronounced it both 'herbs' and 'erbs' throughout the trial." In the second trial, Steckler recalled that the FDA-appointed prosecutor made the mistake of announcing to the jury that the herbs were "nothing more than weeds." A quick-witted defense attorney promptly accepted the prosecution argument and argued in closing that a few weeds never hurt anyone. "What the defense wanted was to have the jury overlook the offense of misbranding. While the jury found the defendant guilty, it took a long time in reaching its verdict."[121]

A Summary Judgment

Less than thirty years might seem like a short time in the history of a court. Yet the decades from the 1950s through the 1970s clearly constituted a dramatic period of change in the southern district's history. The addition of four new judges' positions, the transformation of commissioners into magistrates, the substantial revision of the bankruptcy court, the trend-setting revision of court practices and procedures, and the rapid expansion of both staff numbers and responsibilities made the district court of 1979 very different from its 1950 predecessor. Strong, effective, and individualistic judges and other members of the court family had wrestled with an ever more crowded docket that extended into such "hot button" areas as civil rights. The court that entered the contemporary era was one of the busiest in the United States.

Reviewing the work of the new multi-judge era in 2005, Barker offered this assessment:

> Each served for a long time and presented a formidable legal presence. It should not be forgotten that during their tenures the law was rapidly developing in many areas including voter rights and increased work place rights. These judges had to adapt to significant changes, as did the rest of society, but the onus was on each of them to make the law work in individual cases.[122]

CHAPTER FIVE

◘

The Modern Court Develops

1979–2005

THE PACE OF JUDICIAL CHANGE THAT HAD BEEN SO great after 1950 slowed in some ways after 1979. No new judgeships were added, fewer reorganizations of court functions occurred, and no new courthouses were built in the divisions. In other ways, however, the pace of change remained great and sometimes even accelerated. Each of the judges in place in 1979 was succeeded in the next quarter century, court procedures experienced a dramatic overhaul in the era of electronic filing and the computer, and the sheer volume of business reaching the docket continued to expand rapidly. New faces and new practices were accompanied by some of the most visible and significant decisions in the district court's history. International art theft, pornography, public corruption, desegregation, environmental protection, economic development, highly visible crimes, and the rights of prisoners all appeared among the remarkable variety of cases the court was asked to hear.

Judicial Succession

Between 1983 and 1998 all the sitting district judges were replaced by successor appointees.[1] Judge Cale J. Holder died on August 23, 1983. Judges William E. Steckler and James E. Noland each assumed senior status on December 31, 1986; Noland died on August 12, 1992, and Steckler passed away on March 8, 1995. Judge S. Hugh Dillin assumed senior status on March 31, 1993, and died on March 13, 2006. Judge Gene Edward Brooks retired to private practice on December 31, 1996, and died on April 28, 2004.[2]

In response, five individuals were appointed to the court, each filling one of the vacancies created by the death, retirement, or assumption of senior status of the predecessor judge. Sarah Evans Barker[3] was nominated by President Ronald Reagan and sworn in on March 30, 1984, to fill the Holder seat. Larry J. McKinney[4] was nominated by Reagan and sworn in on July 27, 1987, to fill the Steckler seat. John D. Tinder[5] was nominated by Reagan and sworn in on September 10, 1987, to fill the Noland seat. David F. Hamilton[6] was nominated by President Bill Clinton and sworn in on October 28, 1994, to fill the Dillin seat. Richard L. Young[7] was nominated by President Clinton and sworn in on March 25, 1998, to fill the Brooks seat. In 2005 all five of these appointees were serving.

All of the current judges were born in the Midwest during or shortly after World War II: Barker in Mishawaka, Indiana, in 1943; McKinney

Sarah Evans Barker

in South Bend, Indiana, in 1944; Tinder in Indianapolis in 1950; Young in Davenport, Iowa, in 1953; and Hamilton in Bloomington, Indiana, in 1957. Of their combined university and law degrees, four were earned at Indiana University and six at institutions outside Indiana. Barker earned her bachelor of science degree at Indiana in 1965 and her juris doctor

Larry J. McKinney

(JD) at the Washington College of Law at the American University in Washington, D.C., in 1969. McKinney earned his bachelor of arts degree at MacMurray College in 1966 and his JD at Indiana University School of Law three years later. Tinder received a bachelor of science degree from Indiana University in 1972; he received his JD from Indiana

University School of Law in 1975. Hamilton graduated with a bachelor of arts from Haverford College in 1979 and a JD from Yale Law School in 1983. Young earned his bachelor of arts at Drake University in 1975 and received his JD from George Mason University School of Law in 1980.[8]

All five judges spent some portion of their careers in private practice and also had extensive experience in the public sector, much of it directly involving the state and federal courts, prior to their appointments. Two were serving as county circuit court judges at the time of appointment, McKinney in Johnson County and Young in Vanderburgh County. Barker and Tinder were each serving as U.S. Attorney for the southern district of Indiana at the time of their respective judicial appointments, and both also had prior stints as Assistant U.S. Attorney. Hamilton clerked for Judge Richard Cudahy of the U.S. Court of Appeals for the Seventh Circuit and held the position of counsel to the governor of Indiana.[9] The five appointees, in the aggregate, brought more than forty years of prior public service to the bench, indicative of their familiarity with the judicial process.[10]

An unwritten rule developed in the modern appointive process for federal district judges. It provided that the final recommendation be made by the two highest officials of the president's political party within a particular state. If the U.S. senators were of the president's party, it thus rested with them; if not, the governor or ranking members of the U.S. House of Representatives of the president's party were generally consulted. This practice was followed with regard to all recent appointees. U.S. Senators Richard Lugar and Dan Quayle were thus consulted by Reagan, and Governors Evan Bayh and Frank O'Bannon, along with members of Indiana's democratic congressional delegation, enjoyed a similar opportunity under President Clinton regarding the selection of Judge Young.

Richard L. Young, President Bill Clinton, and Roseann Young in the Oval Office in September 1998

This was an era when the highly visible seats on the U.S. Supreme Court were often the object of controversial hearings before the Senate Judiciary Committee, frequently characterized in starkly contrasting views of judicial philosophy and specific social issues such as abortion. No such partisan or philosophical conflicts occurred with any of the modern southern district nominees. Each experienced a brief and favorable appearance before the Judiciary Committee, where several nominees remembered being asked "softball" questions by the senator chairing the committee. Unanimous Senate confirmation routinely followed. Barker was spared the process of a vetting by the Justice Department preceding her Senate confirmation hearing, but later appointees underwent that process. All recalled their telephone conversations or photo opportunities with the president who made their appointment.[11]

This is not to say that the nominees were not subjected to considerable other scrutiny prior to appointment. In 1981 Lugar established a nonpartisan Merit Selection Committee to assist in the task of reviewing his potential nominees. The committee process, which culminated in Barker's appointment, received applications from individuals seeking consideration and asked applicants to respond to a variety of questions related to their legal background. Similar panels performed this function for later appointees. McKinney, for example, recalled being reviewed concerning decisions he had made while on the bench that had later been overturned on appeal. The Federal Bureau of Investigation (FBI) always conducted detailed background investigations prior to nomination by the president. Each of the five current judges was also subjected to unofficial review by the media, the bar, and sometimes by other private organizations such as the National Association for the Advancement of Colored Persons (NAACP).[12]

Political Issues Reach the Court

A lack of divisive political confrontations in the appointment process was later mirrored in the relatively small number of highly charged political cases—such as federal election or reapportionment disputes—that reached the district court. Those cases that did involve partisan argument most commonly involved hiring or promotion practices that had been based in some way on an individual's political party affiliation. In 1986, for example, the Indiana State Employees Association filed suit against the Indiana Republican State Central Committee over the issue of political clearance cards. At least since the 1930s, it had been the practice of both major parties to perform some form of review of many individuals' political affiliations or beliefs before approving their hiring by state

David F. Hamilton

government. Such a practice became an issue in the case of non-merit, non-policy jobs during the governorship of Robert D. Orr, and the court ruled that plaintiffs had standing to pursue their case.[13] The case did not come to trial because the state government discontinued the practice. Later cases, revolving around reassignment and promotion of individual employees, were not usually a major feature of the court docket.[14]

The most visible patronage case was filed by Peter Americanos, an Indiana Deputy Attorney General (DAG) and a Republican, who lost his position shortly after Pamela Carter, a Democrat, was elected Indiana Attorney General in 1992. Americanos argued that because he did not personally perform political functions as a DAG, his removal was improper. The court, citing case law, found that the inherent powers of the DAG position included meaningful participation in decision making and determination of priorities for the office, and it ruled for the attorney general.[15]

Much more important in defining the stance of the court toward public officials was its handling of cases of public corruption. One of the most notable cases of public corruption came before Noland in 1982, when the former president pro tem of the Indiana State Senate, Phillip E. Gutman, was tried for using his official position to extort bribes. Testimony showed

John D. Tinder

that Gutman had approached the executive director of the Indiana Railroad Association in 1973 and set in motion a payment of one thousand dollars a month for the next three years from the association to Gutman. He, in turn, shared the money with two other state senators. Gutman's defense was that he had been paid a legal fee, but his decision to manage the money from a private account probably contributed to his conviction—as did the detailed testimony of the lobbyist. Gutman's appeal to the Seventh Circuit, based on the psychiatric problems of a witness and the publicized guilty plea of a codefendant, was unsuccessful.[16]

Another highly visible public corruption case, this time involving the state judiciary, reached Barker's court in 1989 when Marion County superior court judge Michael T. Dugan II was tried for a pattern of racketeering that extended to mail fraud, wire fraud, extortion, and bribery. The government brought three basic claims against Dugan: that he demanded kickbacks from individuals that he, as a judge, had appointed as receivers and appraisers; that he illegally paid for vacations in California from public funds; and that he manipulated the governance of an insurance company in receivership in his court for a personal gain of nearly $200,000. He was convicted by a jury on twenty-five counts and sentenced to eighteen years in prison.[17] The Court of Appeals for the Seventh Circuit upheld Dugan's conviction and sentence.

The court was also confronted with corruption in its own ranks. Charges were filed on May 8, 1989, against former Chief Bankruptcy Judge Nicholas W. Sufana. The government alleged that Sufana did "directly and indirectly ask, exact, solicit, seek, accept, receive and agree to receive an item of value" and also "knowingly and willfully did make, and did cause to be made, a false, fictitious, and fraudulent statement and representation of a material fact in a matter within the jurisdiction of the FBI" while a judge with the Bankruptcy Court.[18]

The first charge related to Sufana's March 1985 solicitation and acceptance of a $10,000 cash non-interest bearing loan from Mike Strange, the former owner and operator of Midwest Liquidators.[19] The loan was supposed to be repaid within ninety days but was not paid until more than one year later, when Sufana became aware of a federal investigation involving Strange. The second charge related to an in-chambers interview of Sufana by FBI agents in February 1987, during which Sufana denied ever being offered or receiving anything of value from Strange or Midwest Liquidators. A subsequent interview in January 1989 yielded a different response. In fact, Sufana admitted he had not told the truth in the earlier interview and that he had received gifts and favors from Strange, including the $10,000 loan and a $9,300 car. Later, in interviews with the government, Sufana "acknowledged that he knew that Strange provided him the $10,000 loan, car, and other favors and gifts to him because of his position as Chief Bankruptcy Judge (and) he knew Strange was attempting to 'curry favor' from him due to Midwest Liquidators heavy reliance upon Bankruptcy Court Business." The charges against Sufana stemmed from these and subsequent FBI investigations.[20]

On June 22, 1989, Sufana, in an appearance before Judge Larry McKinney, pleaded guilty to and was convicted of receiving an item of value and making a false statement. He was sentenced to six months imprisonment on the first charge, and, on the second charge, was sentenced to eighteen months probation and fined $50,000, as well as given a special condition of probation requiring that he perform one hundred hours of community service. Because of his age (seventy-six years old) at the time of his sentencing and due to a number of health issues, Sufana served his sentence at the Medical Center for federal prisoners in Rochester, Minnesota.[21]

Magistrates Become Magistrate Judges

The position of federal magistrate judge changed as it developed. In 1990 the Judicial Improvements Act changed the title of the position from magistrate to magistrate judge.[22] As in other district courts, the southern district magistrate judges assisted with the court's varied and growing workload. Within the range of criminal responsibilities that could be assigned, the court emphasized motions on criminal misdemeanors and a variety of preliminary felony proceedings. In its 2002 reporting year, Administrative Office statistics showed that an exact 1,000 pretrial misdemeanor criminal matters were handled, 905 of them ruling upon motions. During the same period, 1,850 preliminary felony proceedings took place, with judicial activities as varied as issuing warrants for searches and arrests, conducting hearings for detention or appointments of counsel, and holding preliminary examinations and bail review.

Civil matters also occupied much of the magistrates' time. Here case management predominated, with emphasis on the many aspects of pretrial procedure. At the same time each case was assigned (on a random basis) to a district judge, it was also assigned to a magistrate judge. It then normally became the responsibility of the magistrate judge to expedite the judicial process. Pretrial conferences were conducted, possibilities of settlement were explored, and the process of discovery and written depositions was refereed. Case management plans were developed, deadlines were agreed upon by the parties, and diversions were explored. All of these tasks demanded time and management skills and made the magistrate judgeships an essential feature of modern civil procedure.[23]

The Indianapolis division was authorized three magistrate judge positions during this period.[24] In 1979 the serving magistrate judges, in order of their appointment, were Thomas Faulconer, John Paul Godich, and J. Patrick Endsley. They would be succeeded during this period, again in order of appointment, by Kennard P. Foster, V. Sue Shields, Tim A. Baker, and William T. Lawrence. Faulconer served until his 1986 retirement. Foster, who had previously served as an assistant U.S. attorney on such high profile cases as the Brett Kimberlin case, succeeded him. Foster served until his retirement in 2002 and stayed on as a recalled magistrate judge for several more years. Lawrence, formerly judge of the Marion County Circuit Court, then succeeded him. Endsley served until his retirement in 1993 and was replaced by Shields, then serving on the Indiana Court of Appeals. Godich set the modern record of length of magistrate judge service in the district by continuing in his position from 1973 until 2001, when he assumed recall status. He was succeeded by Baker, who had formerly devoted his time to civil matters in the office of the U.S. Attorney. David Miller served the Evansville division on a part-time basis until 1986. His successor, Brian Williams, served until 1988. The position was then converted to a full-time appointment, held since then by William G. Hussman Jr. The New Albany division position continued to be part time throughout this period, first held until 1995 by John Cody Jr. and since then by Michael G. Naville. Jordan D. Lewis has held the part-time Terre Haute division position continuously since 1979. The part-time post at Muncie, held by Sam Reed, was discontinued in 1984.[25]

The Evolving Bankruptcy Court

Bankruptcy judgeships went through a period of uncertainty in the early 1980s as Congress and the U.S. Supreme Court wrestled with the constitutional question of the extent that an independent bankruptcy court

(Bankruptcy judges, 2004, clockwise from top): Anthony J. Metz III, Frank J. Otte, Basil H. Lorch III, and James K. Coachys

enjoyed the protections, such as life tenure and immunity from salary reduction, of article 3 of the Constitution. In 1984 a compromise was reached. It assigned bankruptcy to judges specifically appointed to deal with that responsibility and defined a series of bankruptcy categories (whose chapter numbers became a key feature of late-night television after a change in the bar's canon of legal ethics permitted lawyers to advertise). The law also addressed the status of bankruptcy judges by providing that future appointments be made by the courts of appeals, declared bankruptcy judges to be judicial officers of the district court, and reserved some review powers to the district judges.[26] Growing numbers of bankruptcy cases were a significant area of the southern district activity. For the 2003 reporting year, the bankruptcy court accounted for 7,475 business filings and for 33,935 nonbusiness filings. The southern district of Indiana's bankruptcy filings were, on a per capita basis, among the highest in the nation.[27]

The transition to the new bankruptcy court in 1978 and 1979 was made with little public fanfare. Nicholas W. Sufana, who served as a referee in the Indianapolis division since 1963, and Richard W. Vandivier, referee in the Evansville division since 1973, were the first appointments.[28] They were joined in 1978 by Robert L. Bayt in the Indianapolis division and in 1980 by Michael H. Kearns in the Evansville division. In addition to their legal experience, all had strong ties to the Democratic Party and, in particular, to Senator Birch Bayh.[29]

The most troubling aspect of the new system was the lengthy eight-year pilot testing period for the new trustee system. During the transition, many of the practices of the former bankruptcy system remained in effect. The court became the subject of a lengthy and uncomplimentary series of investigative articles in the *Indianapolis Star* in April 1987. The series culminated in a recommendation that the new bankruptcy trustee system, supervised by the U.S. Justice Department, was necessary to serve as a check on favoritism in appointments and fees awarded to certain attorneys and accountants. To document its case, the *Star* devoted much of its fourteen-part series to allegations of abuses in the southern district's bankruptcy court. Several articles focused on alleged favoritism in the appointment of lawyers and receivers, inconsistently high awards of fees, inadequate record keeping, and the poor business practices of some receivers. Several of the bankruptcy judges provided interviews as the series was prepared. They denied any impropriety and attributed any problems to the difficulty of transition to the new law and system.[30] Bayt, for example, said, "In hindsight, maybe different trustees should have been selected. But in 1978, 1979, the administrative office in Washington wanted experienced people, and that's what they got."[31] With the introduction of the new trustee system, supervised by the Justice Department, the issue disappeared. Judge Brooks, by then serving on the district court, was himself a target of the series for practices he carried over from his service on the bankruptcy court. In his oral history he noted:

> Now every bankruptcy judge that I talk to thinks it [the trustee system] is the greatest thing that ever happened. We didn't realize it because all the troubles are handled by the trustee. The bankruptcy judge doesn't have to get involved in all that stuff.[32]

The current bankruptcy judges, Frank J. Otte, Basil H. Lorch III, Anthony J. Metz III, and James K. Coachys, have dealt with a continuing increase in the numbers of liquidations and bankruptcy reorganizations.[33]

Altered Divisional Roles

Brooks's appointment as district judge in 1979 brought changes in the Evansville division. As bankruptcy judge, Brooks had based himself in Evansville and traveled to the Terre Haute and New Albany divisions. When Brooks was appointed a district judge, Senator Birch Bayh oversaw legislation authorizing this seat as a permanent judgeship in Evansville, the first in the southern district located outside Indianapolis. Changes in court staffing and in the assignment of magistrate judges, bankruptcy judges, assistant U.S. attorneys, and deputy U.S. marshals soon followed.

In 2005 the court had to confront the possibility of closing all or part of the Terre Haute division due to budget constraints. The Terre Haute Federal Building had been constructed in the 1930s in the typical manner that located the courtroom above a post office. In 2000 the Terre Haute Post Office moved to a new location, leaving the court as the main occupant of a sizable building, which required costly improvements and initiated discussions with other potential tenants. The precise resolution of the problem remains in question.[34]

The Indianapolis Courthouse

The 200th anniversary of the convening of the first territorial court in Vincennes was observed by a special ceremony in Indianapolis, followed in subsequent years by a series of dinners, special programs, and symposia that recognized the history of the court and its courthouses over those two centuries. The Historical Society of the United States District Court for the Southern District of Indiana was created. It sponsored both the historical observances and the development of public outreach on behalf of the court.

In 1995, following the death of Steckler, whose forty-four years of service on the bench was one of the longest terms in American history for any district judge, the district courtroom in Indianapolis (sometimes referred to as the West Courtroom) was renamed the William E. Steck-

The Indianapolis Courthouse

ler Ceremonial Courtroom. In 1986 a combination of age and water damage had required extensive restoration of its frieze murals. This was followed in subsequent years by many other renovations undertaken by the General Services Administration (GSA), which managed the facility. Beginning in 1992, the GSA invested approximately $9 million to renovate and restore the Indianapolis courthouse, within the design goals of "probity, permanence, clarity and restraint."[35] Regular guided tours permitted the public to view many of these features.[36]

Overseeing the needs of such a majestic building was often a daunting task. Dillin, in his 1992 eulogy for Noland, recounted Noland's stewardship over the Indianapolis courthouse during his years as chief judge:

Well, as has been said, Jim developed civility to a high degree. He could disagree without being disagreeable. And since ours is a disputatious profession this is a little bit on the unusual side; however, he could be blunt if the situation called for it. And the best example of this, perhaps, in [sic] this enduring monument and his dealing with General Services Administration on this building in which we sit. And he finally worked out a truce with them and got them to the point they would agree to the remodeling that is now going on. It is a ten year project. So now we are getting three new magistrate judge courtrooms, four new bankruptcy courtrooms, and another district judge courtroom, and so on and so on. Judge Noland was the chief architect for this project, but I should add also that the money for it came from Washington through the good efforts of Congressman Jacobs, who purports to be pretty stingy with a dollar.[37]

Many improvements were undertaken during, and as a part of, the 2003 bicentennial observances. Judge Barker was influential in the planning and organization of those events and worked in cooperation with the Administrative Office of the United States Courts and General Services Administration on substantial efforts to renovate, modernize, and expand courthouse facilities.[38] The beautiful design work and the architectural details that reemerged during this process did not obscure the work of the busy court. Much of the modernization of the courthouse came in response to the need for contemporary improvements.[39] Safety considerations produced new fire doors and other features. Building security was increased, particularly after the September 11, 2001, terrorist attacks. Computer connections and other electronic services were installed. A twentieth-century building became home to a twenty-first century court.

The Court Family

The publication of court procedures and activities, including access to its dockets and cases, remained an ongoing part of the southern district's activities. Updates of the court's *Local Rules* appeared once or twice each year, and an *Attorney's Handbook* was added in 1995.[40] Working in conjunction with the Seventh Circuit, pretrial guidelines continued to be refined. In 1990 the U.S. Attorney's office for the southern district produced *Inside Federal Court*, a nine-minute video designed to assist children in understanding their role when testifying before the court.[41] McKinney participated as a coauthor of the Seventh Circuit's updated handbook of pretrial procedures.[42]

Judges of the southern district court were recognized several times through appointment or election to national judicial groups. Noland was a member of the special Committee on the Bicentennial of the Constitution of the United States from 1985 to 1992. He also served as a judge on the Foreign Intelligence Surveillance Court from 1983 to 1990 and as presiding judge of that court from 1988 to 1990.[43] Barker served as a member of the U.S. Judicial Conference from 1988 to 1991, as a member of the Sentencing Commission of the Judicial Advisory Committee from 1995 until 1997, as a member of the board of directors of the American Judicature Society from 1992 to 1998, and as president-elect on the executive committee of the Federal Judges Association beginning in 2001.[44]

An emphasis on collegiality developed throughout the court family. Attorneys who practiced before the court were provided a set of guidelines encouraging civility, and most who practiced before the court found its atmosphere hospitable in comparison to other districts. The court family was shocked and saddened in 1986 by the murder of probation officer Thomas E. Gahl, the first probation officer ever killed in the line of duty. The U.S. Probation Office was later dedicated in his honor and memory.⁴⁵

Not every initiative was a long-term success. Between 1991 and 1994, the southern district of Indiana was one of six districts (of the ninety-four districts in the nation) that participated in an experimental program to televise civil trials. The proposal, championed by Robert Kastenmeier, chair of the U.S. House subcommittee that oversaw the administration of the courts, was implemented on a pilot basis by the U.S. Judicial Conference's Committee on Court Administration and Case Management. Individual cases were televised at the discretion of the presiding judges, and relatively few problems of conduct in the courtroom were identified. The most serious concern expressed locally was that the experiment did not lead to continued coverage that illustrated the actual process of federal law, but instead tended to result in brief newscast snippets of courtroom activity or in the use of the courtroom scene as a backdrop for media commentators. Whatever the local experience, the pilot had opposition from many members of the conference, including the late Chief Justice William Rehnquist, and was not continued.⁴⁶

One obvious success was the growing diversity of the court family. While the idea of "firsts" may seem commonplace to some after the fact, many firsts occurred in the court's modern history. Barker and Virginia Dill McCarty were the first women to serve, respectively, as assistant U.S. Attorney and as U.S. Attorney for the southern district. Barker thereafter became the first woman to serve as district judge for the southern district. Shields was the first woman to be named magistrate judge in the southern district. Charles Goodloe and Harold Bickham were among the first African Americans to serve as assistant U.S. attorneys; Frank Anderson (later Marion County Sheriff) was the first African American to serve as U.S. Marshal for the district. Such diversity was partially a reflection of the growing number of women and minorities entering the legal profession, but it was even more a compliment to the talent and energy of the individuals who earned those appointments.

The volume of cases sometimes served to highlight the court's pro bono program. As Tinder has noted, "It is a long-standing custom among lawyers in this community to be generous in providing representation to the indigent." Organized under Local Rule 4.6, the court created a Civil Legal Assistance Panel, comprised of volunteers who would represent litigants lacking the resources to retain counsel. Initially designed to assist individuals in need of representation, the program proved popular with younger attorneys seeking litigation experience. It was also welcomed by judges who saw litigants helped through otherwise confusing procedures such as responding to motions or taking depositions, as well as actual trials.[47] The southern district, and those who litigate before its judges, have also benefited substantially from the significant efforts of Mike Frische, the court's long-serving Pro Se Clerk, who for a number of years has provided significant assistance to the court in cases involving prisoners and other pro se litigants.

The shift from trying cases to seeking resolution through mediation or settlement conferences, already prominent before 1978, continued with the modern court, where less than 2 percent of civil cases were resolved before a judge and jury. This process of negotiation, combined with a desire to make the court's work readily accessible, encouraged the search for innovative management techniques. Beginning in the 1990s, there was a growing reliance on the computer and the World Wide Web. In less than a decade the court's activities became almost paperless. The docket and filing was primarily electronic, scanners and PDF (portable document format) files presented most written evidence, and library law books were replaced by the electronic sources of Lexis and Westlaw.

The court's Web site was an increasingly important source of information and records through which both the legal profession and the public could monitor the work of the court. Teleconferencing was routine. The range of information management opportunities was exemplified by the more than 800-case Bridgestone/Firestone multidistrict litigation that was being heard by the court as this study was prepared. Such cases, touching on plaintiffs in many district jurisdictions, are now assigned by the Judicial Panel on Multidistrict Litigation to a single district court, the sheer volume of the ensuing documentation demanding modern case management plans.[48]

Appearing Before the Bench

Over time, fewer and fewer cases culminated in an actual trial. In the year 2000, for example, out of 2,996 filings, only 170 civil and criminal trials were required to resolve them.[49] Dismissals, summary judgments, and negotiated settlements continued to represent the overwhelming majority of dispositions. Recollections of courtroom proceedings were as entertaining and colorful as ever, but statistically they actually represented a small part of the court's total workload. The more senior judges, their style developed prior to 1980, were those most frequently recalled. Charles Goodloe recalled Holder's precision in his senior years in the 1980s:

> So he was constantly concerned with the record that was being made, and mechanically, to him, it was vastly different to have someone say they were making a motion regarding something than to just simply offer, for example, an exhibit in evidence, and he treated them differently.[50]

(Magistrate judges, 2004, front row left to right): Jordan D. Lewis, Tim A. Baker, William G. Hussmann Jr., V. Sue Shields, and William T. Lawrence; (back row, left to right): Kennard P. Foster, Michael Naville, and John Paul Godich

Goodloe also recalled Judge Brooks's manner:

> In the District Court he was philosophical, witty, and liked to tell humorous stories. But sometimes when he was doing that he could mislead you. You might be sitting there and lose track of what is going on, and that could be a mistake because he was usually keeping track of the process.[51]

Brooks saw himself as a risk taker, reflecting a spirit that pleased some but greatly annoyed others. Early in his tenure he experimented with new ways to make evidence available to jurors, especially in complicated trials. "I would let the jury from time to time take in the exhibits before the trial was over.... Let them look without discussion, just look at the exhibits." The key exhibit in one of his trials proved to be a two-page letter. Part of it dealt with the subject matter of the case, a death in the Terre Haute Penitentiary; another part dealt with the unrelated matter of the defendant's membership in "the Mexican mafia." Somehow the entire text of the letter was placed in view of the jurors, and then the letter disappeared. After the defendant was convicted, a defense attorney asked jurors why they had acted as they did—and the jurors named the Mexican mafia connection. "Brooks said, I called the jury back. It was the only time I ever did." Brooks learned that several jurors had seen the full text. He acknowledged that "When it went up to the Seventh Circuit, they reversed it, and they were very critical of me for letting the jury see any of the exhibits before the trial was over.... So I just stopped the practice."[52]

Few states have a better claim to humor than Indiana, especially when cast in the skeptical wit Hoosiers so admire. That style often appeared in the court's celebratory proceedings and still occasionally makes its way into its decisions as well. Barker brought a whimsical humor to some of her decisions. In one case involving a scuba diver's lawsuit for an injury sustained while diving in the Cayman Islands, Barker used the theme song from the television series *Gilligan's Island* as a metaphor for her reasoning in a case.[53]

The Press of Cases

Caseloads both increased and changed after 1978. As it has done for many years, the Administrative Office of the United States Courts kept track of caseloads, even assigning different weights to types of cases based on the likely time commitment involved. Their statistics for 1992 through 2004 were revealing. In 1992, 2,880 total filings were made in the southern district, 2,887 terminations took place, and 2,264 cases were pending. In 2004, by comparison, filings totaled 3,364, terminations 3,434, and pending cases 2,995. Weighted filings per judge went from 496 in 1992 to 729 in 2004; pending cases per judge increased during the same time period from 453 to 591.[54]

In 1992 the *Indianapolis Star*, citing a backlog of civil cases tied to pending motions, interviewed several judges and other local attorneys on ways to speed up the process. The newspaper noted that in 1990 Congress passed the Civil Justice Reform Act, requiring district courts to form advisory groups to address the matter. That advisory panel had met and filed a series of recommendations adopted by the court, most of which related to encouraging speedier trials or alternative methods of resolution. But, as judges and attorneys noted in the article, speedy trial rules gave first precedence to criminal trials, the number of "federalized" crimes was growing, and the complexity of many civil motions remained great—the press of business remained a modern challenge.[55] In explaining the press of cases, Barker observed,

> The Court is truly the point of access to government action for most individual citizens and is the point of access for individuals to vindicate their rights. It is available to accept the business that real people bring to it. The judicial branch has been and continues to be the branch of government that is the most responsive to the individual's request for services so long as the individual is able to frame a claim under the Constitution or an applicable statute. It is worth noting that the Court's responsiveness is in sharp contrast

to the legislative and executive branches of government, which can choose the contexts to which their efforts are directed.[56]

And in explaining the changing character of the caseload, Dillin noted:

> When I first came on the bench, practically everything we were trying was a diversity case. I mean on the civil side. We were trying one personal injury case after another. These days I don't suppose I try, well I don't try any automobile cases anymore. . . . All the automobile cases are settled because they do a complete discovery and are able to evaluate them very closely and they settle. . . . The big number of cases that we are trying now are cases that are civil rights cases of one kind or another, old age cases, sex discrimination, race discrimination and all that sort of thing. Those are harder to settle and they are more cumbersome in many ways because they are hardly ever clear cut.[57]

Changes in the Practice of Law

In this changing environment, the practice of law itself continued to change. Not only did the number of practicing attorneys and the size of many law firms continue to grow, but also new categories of employees such as paralegals and computer specialists appeared as case management assumed an ever-increasing place in legal practice. These new teams of legal professionals became commonplace in many large cases and on occasion are themselves documented in the findings of the court. Such an example of the practice of law appeared in one court decision as an outgrowth of a highly publicized disturbance in downtown Indianapolis.

On August 27, 1996, a group of off-duty Indianapolis police officers in civilian attire became involved in a fight on Meridian Street that resulted in the beating and arrest of two men, including Richard Craig. Many of the witnesses criticized the officers' behavior immediately before the brawl, alleging some had made "loud and vulgar remarks, many with offensive sexual and/or racial content." The confrontation between the officers and the two arrestees ensued. Investigation showed that most of the officers had been drinking previously in the mayor's suite at Victory Field and at two local bars. The "Downtown Police Brawl" spawned much media coverage and a series of criminal and civil lawsuits. Eventually criminal charges against Craig were dropped, and the criminal trial of four of the police officers in state court resulted in a hung jury. The civil cases were consolidated into a case filed in district court. A negotiated settlement included a $30,000 payment to Craig after the city of Indianapolis agreed that the officers "acted under color of state law and within the scope of their employment." It was further agreed that if the parties could not agree on fees and costs, the matter would be submitted to the court.[58] The parties indeed could not agree on fees and costs, and the court was required to decide the matter.

As an unintended consequence of the lawsuit, the resulting decision offers a useful insight into the practice of law in the 1990s. The court scrutinized a request for $251,899.70 in fees and $12,453.15 in costs, eventually allowing $168,990.20 in fees and $13,845.95 in costs. In doing so, the court reviewed the types of activity a law firm undertook in a high visibility case: answering media and press inquiries, defending counterclaims, seeking depositions, researching claims of policy and custom, defending against criminal charges, and striving to be identified as the "prevailing party, and, thus, eligible for fees and costs." The court examined the work of participants including the lead counsel and other attorneys, law clerks, secretaries, paralegals, and a private investigator. Computer records, not always well kept, were reviewed. The "market rate" for legal services in Indianapolis for this type of case was identified as the "lodestar" in setting hourly dollar rates ranging from $275 for lead counsel to $50 for a paralegal.[59]

Interesting as these numbers might be, the most important changes in the practice of law extended well beyond questions of staffing and fees to the remarkable scope of the cases that modern federal law assigned to a district court. Much of the interest and significance of the court's modern history can best be seen through the wide variety of cases and decisions that touched the lives of individual Hoosiers and simultaneously addressed the broader legal issues of the era.

Citizens' Rights

Civil rights continued to be an issue of public concern. The Indianapolis school desegregation plan under Judge Dillin's oversight was the most visible case before the district court for much of this period. Local desegregation entered a new phase in 1981 when the long-awaited implementation of cross-district busing went into effect. The plan provided one-way busing of black students from transfer areas within the Indianapolis Public Schools (IPS) boundaries to six suburban townships that did not have significant numbers of minority children enrolled. Although civic leaders generally urged public support and racial incidents were rare, a variety of matters remained before the court. Initially the court was asked to fix the responsibility for funding busing and to reassign IPS teachers and other personnel as the students they served were reassigned. The role of the Indianapolis Housing Authority also proved an issue when Judge Dillin ruled that public housing construction in the county, which had been exclusively within IPS boundaries, was contributing to the racial divide between central city and outlying townships. Eventually the costs of busing were paid through an agreement with the state government, staffing adjustments were made by allowing IPS employees preference in filling a number of new positions in the townships, and the Indianapolis Housing Authority undertook "housing initiatives to expand affordable housing choices throughout Marion County." In 1998 Dillin brought closure to the case, approving a plan to end busing over a thirteen-year period beginning no later than 2004–5, with students already in the IPS transfer areas allowed to attend their current township school until graduation.[60]

Civil rights issues since the 1960s had most often been discussed in the context of race. Yet the language of several key laws of the era also excluded gender, age, and personal disability as valid reasons for drawing distinctions in society. Especially after a series of decisions by the U.S. Supreme Court in the 1970s began to define the parameters of the issue more clearly, the federal district courts encountered a growing number of such cases.[61] Many such cases involved the daily activities of individual Hoosiers and seldom involved the stuff of which headlines are made. But as is so often true in the courtroom, the cases were of intense personal importance to the affected individual and sometimes provided insights about the questions a court must resolve. A revealing example, which involved a worker with a disability in conflict with his union's seniority system, was the case of Terry Eckles. Eckles was a Conrail employee who was working in a third-floor tower accessed by an external staircase when he was diagnosed as an epileptic. Citing the provision of the Americans with Disabilities Act (ADA) that calls for "reasonable accommodation" of a disabled worker, Eckles asked for reassignment. But the nature of his workplace was such that he would either have to bump a more senior worker or be exempted himself from being bumped through seniority. Hamilton ruled "the ADA did not require as a reasonable accommodation actions that would have violated a bona fide seniority system at the expense of other employees."[62]

The rights and responsibilities of youths also reached the court's docket, most visibly in a lawsuit by the Indiana Civil Liberties Union (ICLU) in 2000 that caused the court to review Indiana's curfew law. The challenge came after four Indianapolis teenagers who had attended a school soccer game stopped for a hamburger at a Broad Ripple restaurant and stayed past 11 p.m. on an evening when the Indianapolis Police Department was conducting a summertime sweep for curfew violators. Testimony revealed that the police administered urine and Breathalyzer tests without probable cause and without advising the students of their rights. Tinder ruled that this constituted a violation of Fourth Amendment protection against unreasonable searches. The judge further ruled that the law failed to accommodate activities protected under the Constitution, such as political activities. "It is the constrictive narrowness of the permitted exceptions to the Indiana curfew law that is its downfall, not the fundamental effort to set reasonable hours for minors."[63] While an appeal of Tinder's decision was pending, the State of Indiana responded with a new curfew law in 2001, which the district court allowed to stand. However, the Court of Appeals for the Seventh Circuit ultimately declared the law unconstitutional.[64]

Church and State Issues

The line between church and state sometimes proved unclear, especially when religious observances were held at public events or on public property. In 1996, a group of faculty and students at Indiana University

(Bloomington) sued the school's administration over the inclusion of an invocation and benediction at the university-wide commencement ceremony, alleging that it violated the Establishment Clause of the First Amendment. The court reviewed the complaint, applying the two tests: the *Lee* test and the *Lemon* test.[65] Regarding the *Lee* test, Barker found that, while Indiana University was involved in organizing the invocation and benediction, the plaintiffs were not coerced into participating in these events. The plaintiffs, Barker wrote, had "the ability to think independently, to analyze arguments skeptically and to disregard social pressures, peer or otherwise."[66]

Barker also applied the *Lemon* test in her decision. The test's three prongs require that "a state action (1) must have a secular purpose, (2) must neither advance nor inhibit religion, and (3) must not produce excessive government entanglement with religion in order to pass constitutional muster." Referring to the first prong, Barker found that graduation (and the accompanying benediction and invocation) was primarily a secular act. She also found that, given the brief and nonsectarian nature of the prayer, the event did not endorse any religion or influence anyone's religious beliefs. Finally, Barker decided that no enduring and therefore entangling relationship existed between the government and any religious institution in this case. The plaintiffs' motion for summary judgment was denied, and the decision was affirmed by the Court of Appeals for the Seventh Circuit. The Supreme Court denied the plaintiffs' petition for a *writ of certiorari* and the case came to an end.[67]

The court invoked the *Lemon* test again in 2000 and 2001 when it was twice called upon to deal with the placement of a large limestone monument depicting the Ten Commandments on the lawns of the State Capitol Building and later the Lawrence County Courthouse. The designers of the monument to be placed on the State Capitol lawn had sought to meet the first prong of the *Lemon* test—having a secular purpose—by including texts of the Bill of Rights and of the Preamble of the 1851 Indiana Constitution on other faces of the structure. But their failure to show a clear connection between historical and sacred text caused the court to rule that the monument's purpose was to advance religion. The monument's designers also had hoped to meet the second prong of the *Lemon* test—neither advancing nor inhibiting religion—by the design of the monument. But again the court ruled against them, considering that a reasonable observer would deem a six-ton stone monument prominently located at the seat of government to be a governmental endorsement of the Ten Commandments.[68]

The responsibility of churches to pay federal income and social security taxes was brought before the district court by the Internal Revenue Service (IRS) in the case of the Indianapolis Baptist Temple (IBT). This large congregation and its buildings, located on the south side of the city, operated as an incorporated entity until 1983. IBT had then undertaken a series of administrative reorganizations that culminated in declaring itself an unincorporated New Testament church. IBT's leadership further asserted that, in its new capacity, the church was exempted from federal taxation and ceased withholding in 1987. The IRS disputed the exemption claim and eventually sued for back taxes and penalties that totaled more than $5 million by the late 1990s. The court's analysis focused on the IBT claim that it could "evade federal tax law by metamorphosing into various different forms of entity." The court answered, "On this, it is sadly mistaken." Nothing in the Free Exercise or Establishment Clauses, the court concluded on the basis of case law, prevented a neutral, secular, and minimally intrusive federal tax.[69] The Court of Appeals for the Seventh Circuit upheld the decision, and the Supreme Court declined to hear the case. The decision attracted much of its media coverage during the ensuing foreclosure process, and U.S. Marshal Frank Anderson earned high marks for his patient and peaceful handling of the situation.[70]

Environmental Impact

Federal regulatory legislation tended to come in bursts in the twentieth century. One such burst is identified with the Progressive Era early in the century, another with the New Deal in the 1930s. Another such burst of new laws and ensuing regulations occurred in the 1960s and 1970s as Washington addressed a variety of public concerns tied to health, safety, and style of life. Spearheaded by such legislation as the Motor Vehicle Air Pollution Control Act of 1965 and the Air Quality Act of 1967, the environmental emphasis of many of the new laws was given central direction by the National Environmental Policy Act of 1970. The contamination or pollution of air, soil, and water became a significant issue on many public agendas, and environmental questions soon began to appear on federal dockets.[71] The most important of these in Indiana's southern district was the handling of trash.

Indiana landfills were receiving substantial shipments of out-of-state trash by the 1980s, prompting political debate and changes in state law. A new Indiana statute banned a shipment unless it met a series of requirements such as documenting the state of origin, paying fees equal to the fees charged in that state of origin, and certifying that the trash contained no hazardous medical waste. These truck cargos were often popularly identified as "New Jersey" trash, both because the Indiana initiatives were the subject of strong criticism by Senator Bill Bradley of that state and because the issue became the subject of a series of television advertisements spoofing New Jersey during the 1990 U.S. Senate race in Indiana. The Indiana law was actually challenged in the southern district of Indiana by two Pennsylvania haulers, Government Suppliers Consolidating Services Inc. and Jack Castenova Inc.

When tried in the spring of 1990, the case centered on the state government's responses to a 1978 U.S. Supreme Court ruling that held trash shipment to be a form of interstate commerce governed by the U.S. Constitution's Interstate Commerce Clause. Tinder ultimately ruled that Indiana could impose health restrictions on material dumped in its landfills, but only if such restrictions applied equally to Indiana residents and nonresidents. Because the requirements of documenting origin, charging fees, and certifying against hazards did not also apply to Indiana shippers, the judge found that the law was unconstitutional.[72]

The state government tried again the following year, passing a new municipal trash hauling law in response to the district court's concerns. Central to the new law were restrictions on cross hauling, the practice of carrying trash in trucks that were then used to haul other products such as food. Because most Indiana trash moved in dedicated vehicles, such as garbage trucks, in-state haulers were little affected. McKinney found the state's position generally consistent with case law and approved most of the new regulations. But the Seventh Circuit, concerned by a lack of evidence that public health was threatened and by the presence of "unreasoned" public fears, overturned the entire act.[73]

Many of the environmental cases that reached the southern district court reflected attempts by corporations, communities, and public officials to strike a balance between two considerations. One of these was to preserve economic activities and jobs in traditional industries dating from the smokestack era; the other was the desire to comply with new environmental regulations. The industries that most often attracted attention were those that mined or burned coal.

Southwestern Indiana had been a major coal producer for over a century, and mining still provided the chief livelihood in many Hoosier counties. But Indiana coal was high in sulfur content and when burned in factories or power plants often was blamed for acid rain and other environmental damage. It was technologically possible to "scrub" or remove the sulfur, but the ensuing cost was often higher than the alternative cost of transporting low-sulfur coal from mines at a greater distance. Some state officials attempted to respond by granting preferential treatment to Indiana coal. A 1990 Indiana law, for example, required in-state electric utilities, when complying with the federal Clean Air Act, to use high-sulfur Indiana coal in preference to low-sulfur out-of-state coal, even if the final cost was higher. In 1995 the southern district court overturned portions of that law. Following similar decisions in three other district courts, the court found that the preferential treatment of Indiana coal was a violation of the Interstate Commerce Clause.[74]

Indiana's industrial heritage left a number of environmental problems. Some again came before the district court. In December 1982, to cite one example, the court approved a consent decree for the surface cleanup of roughly sixty thousand barrels of toxic chemicals and their accompanying bulk storage and contaminated soil in Seymour. Finding that the decree was legal, fair, and reasonable, that the need for abatement was immediate, and that no other prompt solution appeared to be available, the court found that the public interest was adequately protected by the consent decree.[75] Fifteen months later the court, upon receipt of evidence of government agency approvals of the cleanup plans, ordered the disbursement of funds that it had held for the cleanup and for a public drinking water system in a neighboring residential subdivision.[76]

Economic Initiatives in the Rust Belt

The problems of traditional industries such as coal and chemicals—and the migration of many individuals and jobs to the Sun Belt—caused a number of midwestern states, including Indiana, to be given the derisive title of the Rust Belt. This was a reference to the decline of many traditional industries and the ensuing economic problems and dislocations that communities that once had depended upon the smokestack industries experienced. Efforts to avert job losses by sustaining older industries or encouraging alternative new economic activities that would spur job creation assumed a significant place on the agendas of many local and state political and economic leaders. On occasion aspects of these efforts reached the district court.

By the late twentieth century, the income of many families yielded a substantial surplus after paying for housing, food, clothing, transportation, and other essential forms of subsistence. The ensuing discretionary funds were a major factor in fueling the expansion and variety of service industries, which often proved the fastest growing part of the economy. Entertainment proved to be one of the most attractive of these industries.[77] As it attracted customers and investors, it predictably attracted litigation.

A number of Indiana cities took advantage of a change in the Indiana Constitution in the 1980s (and subsequent state law changes in 1993) that permitted riverboat casino gambling along Lake Michigan and the Ohio River. The profits at stake in such developments were large and sometimes became the subjects of litigation. In 2000 nationally known gambling promoter Donald Trump found himself in district court in Indianapolis for breach of contract. Two politically influential Indianapolis investors contended they had a valid contract with Trump that would pay them a substantial reward if they assisted him in obtaining a state gambling license for a Gary casino. A jury awarded the two $1.4 million in damages, but Trump prevailed on appeal. The Seventh Circuit found that the correspondence that had been the basis of the trial constituted merely an "agreement to agree" that lacked the force of a contract.[78]

The desire for economic development extended to the quest for amateur and professional athletic competitions that anchored new stadiums and related sports and convention facilities. Indianapolis in particular showed strong interest in this initiative. In 1984, for example, the Capital Improvement Board of Marion County succeeded in negotiating a lease with Robert Irsay that brought the Colts, his National Football League franchise, from Baltimore to Indianapolis. Irsay and eight moving vans of team equipment left Maryland late on the night of March 29, hours before the governor of that state signed into law a bill that acquired the team by condemnation. The newly renamed Indianapolis Colts quickly appeared in the southern district seeking to avoid the ensuing Maryland lawsuits. Steckler accepted the Colts's claim they were within the Indiana court's jurisdiction, only to be overturned by the Seventh Circuit. When heard in Baltimore, however, that district court ruled the City of Baltimore could not exercise eminent domain.[79]

Hoosier interest in automobile racing, which remained strong in the face of competition from new sports and venues, continued to generate cases before the court. In the early 1980s Dale Fazekas, a leading "Showroom Stock" driver, sued the publishers of *Auto Week* magazine for libel. Fazekas alleged that he had been falsely accused in the magazine of making significant modifications, forbidden by the rules of the Sports Car Club of America, to his 1979 Porsche 924. The court, applying existing case law, found for the defendants. The court ruled that such reporting was a matter of general interest within the racing community, that Fazekas was a public figure, and that he had not proven actual malice by clear and convincing evidence.[80]

Health care proved to be another source of litigation in a service economy. The "graying," or aging, of both the state and the national population created a growing market for health-care products and services ranging from pharmaceuticals to insurance. Complex and time-intensive cases of patent law introduced potentially high dollar verdicts, while issues of personal health care brought ill and injured individuals forward with pressing personal concerns. Because medical expenses for many families were the most rapidly increasing portions of their budget, and control of those costs was just as important to the consumer as it was to many providers, insurance issues seemed to recur most often. Steckler particularly remembered his participation in a significant antitrust suit brought by eighty Indiana hospitals against Blue Cross and Blue Shield. At issue was the defendant's creation of a preferred provider system, by which the insurer wrote policies that paid 100 percent of hospital and doctor bills for those who agreed to abide by the system's maximum rate and fee schedules—but only 75 percent of the bills of hospitals and doctors who had not agreed to participate:

> At first blush it appeared to be a very valid lawsuit, but after we had tried the matter and gotten into it deeply, I came to the conclusion that the plaintiffs did not have a case.... I ruled that the preferred provider program was a valid concept and a valid means of bringing under control the ever-increasing hospital charges and medical bills for physician services.[81]

Tinder encountered a different aspect of medical insurance when asked to rule on the case of Judith Harris, who was the victim of an aggressive form of breast cancer. Harris was convinced that her best option lay in an expensive experimental treatment that would cost $150,000 or more. Her insurance carrier, however, declined to approve the treatment because its experimental nature placed it outside the terms of her policy. Harris sued, asking the court to rule that a procedure that might save her life was covered by insurance. Tinder denied her request, ruling that the insurance plan was unambiguous and thus the denial by the carrier was not arbitrary or capricious. His decision also expressed the great pressures that are often occasioned by the tension between applying legal principles and exercising compassion:

> Despite rumors to the contrary, those who wear judicial robes are human beings, and as persons, are inspired and motivated by compassion as anyone would be. Consequently, we often must remind ourselves that in our official capacities, we have authority only to issue rulings within the narrow of the law and the facts before us.[82]

Patent Law: Zyprexa

One category of cases, which required the court to commit significant resources, and which typically presented complex issues, were patent cases. Trials in patent cases generally took longer and involved complex legal and scientific issues. Although not a typical case, Young's decision in *Eli Lilly and Company v. Zenith Goldline Pharmaceuticals* illustrates the level of complexity of patent law cases. As the owner of the patent for a chemical compound that was used to treat schizophrenia, the Lilly company sued several companies that were seeking to manufacture generic versions of the drug, claiming that the companies were guilty of infringement. At issue was the patent right for Zyprexa, which had been used by more than sixteen million individuals since it was first marketed in 1996, reportedly Lilly's best seller, with 2004 worldwide sales of approximately $4.4 billion.[83] Lilly was especially concerned because a few years earlier it had lost a patent battle relating to Prozac, the well-known antidepressant that was then Lilly's top drug.

The Zyprexa trial was lengthy, lasting from January 26, 2004, through February 12, 2004. At the trial's conclusion, the parties submitted post-trial briefs that Young eventually described in his written opinion as "helpful given the breadth and complexity of the disputed issues."[84] During the trial, Lilly lawyer Charles Lipsey described Zyprexa as Lilly's "life's blood," which was probably accurate given press reports that U.S. sales of Zyprexa accounted for approximately 17 percent of Lilly's total revenue.[85]

The companies that challenged Lilly's patent made six principal arguments against its validity, among them that the patent was anticipated, that it was obvious, that it was invalid under the double-patenting doctrine (which prohibits one from obtaining a second patent for an earlier invention or an obvious modification of an earlier invention), that it was invalid due to a prior public use, and that the patent was unenforceable due to Lilly's alleged inequitable conduct. Fourteen months after the hard-fought trial, Young handed down the court's decision, finding that the defendants failed to prove any of their six claims.[86] The press memorialized the moment:

> Young's 222-page decision was released at 4:50 p.m. electronically on the court's Web site and earlier in document form to attorneys from both sides. A handful of Lilly's lawyers, some of them smiling, left the Downtown Indianapolis federal courthouse without comment about 4:30 p.m. One clutched the inch-thick bound judicial opinion.[87]

The judge's lengthy opinion contains a detailed table of contents of the court's numerous findings of facts and conclusions of law. The opinion reviewed the history of drugs that have been used to treat schizophrenia, the importance of drug testing in animals, the history of the Lilly patent, and "the process by which generic drug companies gain approval from the FDA to bring generic pharmaceuticals to market."[88] After Young's decision was handed down, the drug companies that had sought to invalidate Lilly's patent immediately announced their intent to appeal to the court of appeals for the federal circuit, in Washington, D.C., which hears patent appeals.[89]

Prisoner Issues

Criminal issues were also important and occupied large amounts of court attention. Dillin introduced the court's modern concern with the death penalty this way in his 1994 oral history:

> We have a great many prisoner cases in this jurisdiction because we have several prisons in the Southern District of Indiana. We're going to have a flood of stuff out of the federal prison at Terre Haute because the Bureau of Prisons in its infinite wisdom has decided that all death sentence federal prisoners are going to be housed and executed in Terre Haute. So we're going to have a lot of habeas corpus cases out of Terre Haute, I'm sure.[90]

Federal executions are very uncommon. The lethal injection at the Terre Haute prison of the Oklahoma City bomber, Timothy McVeigh, on June 11, 2001, was the first federal execution since 1963. There have only been two additional federal executions since McVeigh's.[91] Nevertheless, each individual imprisoned on "death row" is entitled to a review of his case, a review that could involve a number of substantive and procedural issues. McKinney captured the importance of the issue when he noted that no cases, save possibly the most complicated intellectual property lawsuits, demand such time and attention.[92]

Other convicts besides those under sentence of death could of course seek legal relief. Hamilton's decision in the case of Jerry E. Watkins illustrates some of the issues and eloquently captures the powerful conflicting emotions surrounding such a decision. In *Watkins v. Miller*,[93] Hamilton granted federal habeas relief to Watkins, who had been found guilty in 1986 in an Indiana state court of murdering eleven-year-old Peggy Sue Altes, the younger sister of Watkins's wife. Altes was abducted, raped, murdered, and dumped at the edge of a rural field. After her body was discovered, Watkins pled guilty to having molested her two months before her disappearance. He was later convicted of Altes's murder and sentenced to sixty years in prison. Watkins thereafter unsuccessfully sought postconviction relief based on DNA evidence that was not available at the time of his trial. However, Watkins did not prevail in a variety of state court settings. Watkins subsequently filed a pro se petition for habeas corpus in federal court, although the district court later appointed counsel to represent him.

Hamilton began his opinion in *Watkins* with the observation that "[t]he United States Constitution requires a fair trial but not a perfect one."[94] Applying the rule announced in the U.S. Supreme Court's opinion in *Brady v. Maryland*, which holds that the government may not convict and imprison an individual while concealing from him material evidence which "tends to show that he is not guilty," Hamilton detailed the evidence and argument presented during Watkins's trial. Most importantly, the judge described the evidence, which the State had not disclosed to Watkins's lawyers. As observed by Hamilton, the State suppressed evidence:

> (a) that an undisclosed witness saw Peggy Sue being abducted at a time for which Watkins has a solid alibi, and by a person who could not have been Watkins; (b) that another suspect in the case failed a polygraph test; and (c) that investigators received reports of other men who had known Peggy Sue and who either told others they had killed her or turned up with blood on their clothes the night she disappeared.[95]

Additionally, while the Indiana Court of Appeals had found that the previously unavailable DNA test results only "suggest[ed] the possibility" that another individual had raped Altes, Hamilton pointed out that "[i]n fact those results prove beyond a reasonable doubt that someone other than Jerry Watkins raped the victim when she was murdered."[96] Hamilton observed that while the State had argued at trial that "There is no evidence whatsoever that anybody else ever molested Peggy Altes," that statement "is now conclusively proven wrong" by the DNA evidence.[97]

Hamilton observed that "in the American criminal system, no one should be sentenced to 60 days in prison, let alone 60 years, on the theory and evidence the state relies upon in this case to keep Jerry Watkins in prison."[98] The judge concluded his opinion, which ordered Watkins's custodian to release Watkins from custody within thirty days, with the following paragraph:

> Watkins did commit the despicable crime of molesting Peggy Sue Altes. He pled guilty to that crime, and the State of Indi-

ana punished him for it. Her murder was a separate crime. Watkins is not guilty of one simply because he is guilty of the other. The prosecutor told the jury in closing argument, "The spirit of Peggy Altes is here in Court with us today and her spirit cries for justice." . . . This court could not agree more sincerely. However, because the prosecutor failed to comply with his constitutional obligation to see that Jerry Watkins had a fair trial, Watkins' conviction and imprisonment have not answered that cry for justice. A writ of habeas corpus shall now issue.[99]

The State of Indiana initially tried to retain Watkins in custody while it sought to conduct new tests on DNA samples that it had long held in its files, but Hamilton denied the request, ruling such tests should have been done years before.[100] The state dismissed its appeal of Hamilton's decision after additional DNA tests confirmed the original tests, and Watkins was released from prison.[101]

Not all prisoner cases have involved habeas corpus. Prisoners themselves have sued their warden, as their custodian, over various prison conditions, and others have sued over other prison practices. The McVeigh execution, for example, called on Tinder to consider Entertainment Network Inc. and Liveontheweb.com's requests to broadcast the event live over the Internet. Tinder reviewed the history of media access to executions, found several Supreme Court rulings that the press had no greater access to information than the general public, and denied the request. "No court in this nation has ever ordered relief of this nature before. . . . The medium is not the message."[102]

The court recurrently encountered the issue of prison overcrowding at both the state and the local level. In 1982 Dillin ruled that the overcrowding at the Indiana Reformatory at Pendleton, coupled with other conditions, constituted cruel and unusual punishment. He noted the "Eighth Amendment embodies broad concepts of decency and humanity against which penal measures must be evaluated."[103] In 1992 Tinder heard the case of David M. Jones, who had been severely restrained in the Madison County Jail after a suicide attempt and then had been left chained on a cell floor for several days without being evaluated by a mental health professional. The judge found the practice at the jail infrequent, "but . . . nonetheless barbaric."[104] In 2002 and 2003 Barker held two successive Marion County sheriffs in contempt for overcrowding at the county jail. The judge also oversaw the preparation of detailed plans for the fiscal and operational reforms necessary to correct the problem.[105]

In another prisoner case, the court ruled against a convicted serial killer who filed a libel suit against an author who wrote about his crimes. In 1990 Avon Books published *Hunting Humans: The Encyclopedia of Serial Killers*, written by an Indiana resident, Michael Newton. Among the individuals discussed in the book was Gerald Schaefer, then serving concurrent life sentences in a Florida prison for two murders. After examining a variety of court and media sources, the author further stated that the plaintiff was "linked with the murders of at least 20 persons." In ruling against the plaintiff, the court found that Schaefer had not proven actual malice and that his two murder convictions met the legal definition of serial killing.[106]

Few issues before the court attracted more attention than those surrounding Fred C. Sanders. His case began in August 1988 when neighbors complained about Sanders's noisy dogs running loose. Indianapolis patrolman Matt John Faber arrived at Sanders's home and attempted to resolve the problem. But that meeting turned violent, and Faber was slain by a bullet fired by Sanders after entering Sanders's home. Other officers fired and wounded Sanders and then severely beat him after he was arrested and handcuffed. Charges and countercharges ensued. Sanders alleged that he was the victim of police misconduct—illegal entry and excessive force. The government charged Sanders with murder. Sanders accepted a plea agreement, pleading guilty to involuntary manslaughter and eventually served three years of a seven-year sentence. After his release, Sanders brought a civil suit in district court for damages against the city and the officers for violation of his civil rights and the use of excessive force. The jury that heard Sanders's case found in his favor and awarded him $1.5 million damages.[107]

The size of the award, and the evidence available to the jury on which to base it, became the subject of posttrial motions that Barker ruled upon. The judge ruled that the verdict was "excessive beyond reason." She continued,

> This verdict so far surpassed its evidentiary basis, one cannot help but wonder whether the larger national social and political climate entered into the thinking of individual jurors, whereby they sought, through this case, to counter-balance other perceived wrongs to other citizens by other police officers in other places. Whatever the jury's rationale, one thing is clear: they most assuredly abandoned their sworn duty to determine damages in accordance with the evidence and the court's instructions on the applicable law.

The judge noted that Sanders had dropped his claim for punitive damages months before the trial and was essentially dealing with "pain and suffering" questions. The jury's "monstrous" award was substantially reduced to $78,000 (with the option to the plaintiff of a new trial). The case ultimately caused the judge to observe:

How is it, the layman may ask, that a judge can override the fruit of a jury's labor, its verdict, after the jury has listened to witnesses and the arguments of the attorneys, and deliberated long and hard and finally reached a decision? The answer lies, of course, in the allocation of responsibilities between judge and jury. The jury's duty is to determine what the facts are, apply the applicable rules of law to those facts, and render a verdict. The judge's duty is to ensure that the law is fairly administered.[108]

The Indianapolis Pornography Ordinance

Throughout its history, the district court has been called upon repeatedly to interpret, and often to enforce, laws and regulations that rest on deeply held moral beliefs. Abolitionism and Prohibition each commanded attention in their eras. In 1984 a subject new to the court's jurisdiction appeared when Barker heard arguments regarding the constitutionality of an Indianapolis city-county antipornography ordinance.[109]

The ordinance was presented by the city as addressing the issue of gender discrimination. The city argued that it should be allowed to severely regulate pornography because it graphically presented the explicit subordination of women, harmed their opportunity for equal rights as citizens, and made them targets of a variety of crimes. The plaintiffs, a coalition of publishers, booksellers, and civil libertarians, argued that the city had overstepped the boundaries of First Amendment protections of free speech.[110] The court was asked to weigh the merits of two important societal interests. Barker noted, "It is difficult to quarrel either with the Council's underlying concern . . . or with its

(Left to right): Clerk of Court Laura A. Briggs, Magistrate Judge V. Sue Shields, and District Judge Sarah Evans Barker

premise that some legislative controls are in order. This case," she added, "comes to the court amidst heated public and private debate over the problems of pornography and sex discrimination in American society."[111]

The judge focused her decision on the narrower issue of the constitutionality of the ordinance—and ruled against the city. Barker began by ruling that pornography, as defined by the ordinance, constituted speech rather than conduct. The ordinance, she observed, specifically included "words" in its definition of what was prohibited. She noted that there were limited categories, most obviously obscenity, where regulation of speech was permitted. But the judge found that the definition of pornography in the ordinance was significantly broader than that normally applied by the courts, and did not apply such tests as the lack of redeeming literary, artistic, political, or scientific value. The judge also found the ordinance definition sufficiently vague to leave the average citizen in doubt as to its meaning. Finally, Barker found that its enforcement involved unconstitutional prior restraint. By such tests, the ordinance was unconstitutional.[112]

Barker's decision recognized that the city was, in effect, attempting to add a new class of constitutionally unprotected speech. She accordingly reviewed various recent rulings of the Supreme Court and found none that supported the city's case. Then the judge speculated on the implications of using limits upon speech to protect categories of persons.

> It would signal so great a potential encroachment upon First Amendment freedoms that the precious liberties reposed within those guarantees would not survive. The compelling state interest, which defendants claim gives constitutional life to their Ordinance, though important and valid as that interest may be

in other contexts, is not so fundamental an interest as to warrant a broad intrusion into otherwise free expression.[113]

The decision was upheld on appeal, with Judge Frank H. Easterbrook of the Court of Appeals for the Seventh Circuit articulating a strong endorsement of free speech:

> A power to limit speech on the ground that truth has not yet prevailed and is not likely to prevail implies the power to declare truth. At some point the government must be able to say (as Indianapolis has said): "We know what truth is, yet a free exchange of speech has not driven out falsity, so that we must now prohibit falsity." If the government may declare the truth, why wait for the failure of speech? Under the First Amendment, however, there is no such thing as a false idea ... so the government may not restrict speech on the ground that in a free exchange truth is not yet dominant.[114]

The district court, incidentally, was again called on to hear a further attempt by the Indianapolis City-County Council to regulate the content of public entertainment. In 2000 an ordinance was passed to limit the access of minors to video games depicting violence. Hamilton initially ruled for the city, impressed by the tightly drawn language of the ordinance and by two empirical studies that concluded that playing violent video games made young people more aggressive. But the ruling was reversed on appeal when Circuit Judge Richard A. Posner of the Seventh Circuit held that such visual and interactive games were better seen as children's adventure stories, "continuous with an age-old children's literature of violent themes," and as such were protected speech.[115]

Modern Crime

Police-blotter cases remained a staple of local reporting and assured that a number of the individuals charged with federal crimes in the southern district attained public notice and notoriety. One such person was the so-called "Speedway Bomber," Brett Kimberlin. In the early 1980s several bombs exploded in Speedway, the town adjacent to the Indianapolis Motor Speedway. One bomb, concealed in a gym bag near the entrance to the Speedway High School athletic field, severely injured a man who picked it up as people were leaving the field after a football game. The trail of evidence first began to point to Kimberlin because another bomb was detonated near the home of a family who were then witnesses in a murder trial in which he was involved—and because he was in possession of blasting caps that he had ostensibly purchased to help construct a survivalist home in Jackson County. The son of a prominent local family, Kimberlin appeared before Steckler and Noland in a series of lengthy trials that eventually resulted in his convictions for "manufacturing destructive devices" and "committing malicious damage by means of explosives, and with injuries."[116] Steckler rejected a challenge brought by Kimberlin, alleging one juror had said "They ought to hang him now, so that we can all go home," because no allegation of prejudice was made.[117]

Nationally, four overlapping areas of violations drove the criminal dockets of the modern federal courts: immigration, firearms, fraud, and drugs. The southern district, far from America's borders, has seen relatively few crimes involving immigration. The most widely publicized and unusual case occurred in 1984 when a seventy-one-year-old man, John Wolf, was charged under the Mann Act with luring three immigrant refugee women from southeast Asia to Indiana and then using them as sex slaves. While Wolf was convicted after a five-day trial in New Albany, his conviction was subsequently reversed by a divided panel of the Court of Appeals for the Seventh Circuit.[118]

A widely publicized firearms case in 1984 illustrates the manner in which many criminal matters come before the magistrates and magistrate judges. Two Indiana University graduate students involved in a gunrunning case appeared before Chief Magistrate Faulconer. The students, Salua Safady and Helena Freire, were Brazilian nationals living in Bloomington. They were accused by the U.S. Customs Service of purchasing high-quality handguns and ammunition in Indianapolis and illegally shipping them to Brazil and Paraguay in boxes labeled "beauty products."[119] When the forty-eight-year-old Safady pleaded indigence in her successful request to Faulconer for a court-appointed lawyer, the magistrate expressed displeasure at her answers to questions about her tax-supported scholarships at the university. And when the forty-three-year-old Freire, candidate for a performance music doctorate, asked for a piano to practice upon for her final recital, Faulconer wryly observed, "I just don't know what we can do about the piano."[120]

Firearms cases often appeared before the district court because federal law was very strict—often more so than state law—regarding possession of a weapon by an individual convicted of another crime. In a case of first impression in 2002, Tinder ruled on the legality of the weapons possessed by the marshal of the small Indiana town of Hymeria. The marshal had been jailed previously for a misdemeanor domestic violence conviction in an Indiana state court. Subsequently he had been arrested for firearms possession under the terms of the 1996 Lautenberg Amendment to the 1968 Gun Control Act. The prosecution argued that the marshal's former incarceration now made it a crime for him to possess a firearm. As the trial developed, it was shown that a clause in the text of the amendment lifted the firearms ban if an individual's civil rights had later been restored. Evidence showed that Indiana law does not routinely deprive misdemeanants of their civil rights after a sentence has been served. Thus the intent of the amendment was at variance with its plain language. In what he described as a "clear, but somewhat surprising result," Tinder found for the defendant. "The court is well aware that dismissal of the defendant's charges conflicts with the laudable congressional purposes behind this legislation. However, the court is obliged to apply the law as it is written."[121]

Fraud cases appeared frequently. In 2000 several executives of Heartland Financial Services and other related companies were charged by the Securities and Exchange Commission (SEC) with mail fraud and money laundering for running a Ponzi scheme. This criminal scheme attracted much attention for the large dollar amounts of investor losses and for the arrest of the principal figure, Kenneth R. Payne, in Mexico, where he had fled to avoid trial. The following year, during his trial in district court, Payne confessed to his crimes.[122]

Fraud sometimes appeared in connection with tax evasion cases. In 1997 a district court jury in Evansville convicted Joe Holland of thirty-four criminal counts of fraud and tax evasion. Holland was accused of using a private California bank, fake money orders, and other illegal devices to hide thousands of dollars in income, portions of which he used to fund militia and antitax groups that he had founded.[123]

Drug cases came in increasing numbers and complexity. Many of the cases represented highly organized "rings" of manufacturers and distributors operating across state boundaries. Widespread drug abuse, which knew few social or economic boundaries, created an enlarged market for the criminal enterprises and an abundance of victims from either addiction or the crime it spawned. New drugs, notably methamphetamine, joined the list of highly addictive and socially destructive substances under attack. New production techniques and high prices ($50,000 for a pound of "meth" by the mid-1980s) expanded drug-related crimes in both rural and urban areas. The government responded within the context of the 1970 Organized Crime Control Act, which defined many government enforcement responses, including task forces of specialists and using comparatively new tools such as court-approved wiretaps alongside traditional methods such as paid informants. The profits of the enterprises, as well as their products, became legitimate targets of government scrutiny. Tough mandatory sentencing guidelines for drug-related crimes were widely perceived by elected public officials as a tool of enforcement.[124]

International Ownership of Stolen Art: The Kanakaria Mosaics
No twentieth-century trial before the southern district engendered more publicity than the 1989 proceedings that decided the ownership of four early Christian mosaics taken from the apse of the Church of Panayia Kanakaria on the Mediterranean island of Cyprus.[125] Crafted in about 530 CE, they were among the very few extant examples of early Byzantine tesserae, portraits crafted in tiny pieces of marble, stone, glass, and precious metal.[126] The case reached the Indianapolis courtroom of Judge Noland because the mosaics were in the possession of Peg Goldberg, a Carmel, Indiana, art dealer, but were claimed by the Republic of Cyprus and by the Autocephalous Greek-Orthodox Church of Cyprus to have been clumsily removed by art thieves.[127] Michel van Rijn, a Dutch art broker who had admitted to Goldberg that he had encountered legal problems in some past business transactions, had alerted Goldberg to the existence of the sixth-century por-

traits. The works were in the physical possession of Aydin Dikmen, a Turkish national who lived in Munich, Germany, and who claimed to have been the official archaeologist serving the Turkish officials administering northern Cyprus. The inspection and purchase of the mosaics took place at the duty-free area of the airport in Geneva, Switzerland. Goldberg paid more than a million dollars in cash transferred from a loan made by an Indianapolis bank. Cypriot authorities became aware the art was in the United States when an officer of the world-renowned Getty Museum was offered the mosaics for $20 million and, suspicious that they were stolen, notified the government of Cyprus. These circumstances, added to the failure of the sellers to explain how the mosaics had been removed from the church or had come from Cyprus to Germany, caused many reporters to color the transaction with a sense of international intrigue.[128]

The district court, however, had specific legal issues to resolve.[129] First, Noland had to decide if either of the two governments that emerged from a 1974 war on the island of Cyprus, the Republic of Cyprus and the Turkish Republic of Northern Cyprus, had standing before the court. Second, the judge had to determine if the law of Switzerland, where the purchase was made, or the law of Indiana, where the art resided, governed the sale. Third, the judge had to decide if each claimant in the case had practiced due diligence in pursuing his or her claim to ownership: Goldberg, in determining that clear title existed, and the Republic of Cyprus and Greek Orthodox Church in widely and promptly publicizing the theft. Finally, the judge had to decide what future guidelines, if any, he should recommend be used by buyers of an international artwork subject to American law.

The first decision came quickly. Cyprus had been divided since 1974, when Turkish forces had used the excuse of a Greek-sponsored coup

Mosaic of a young Jesus Christ

against the island's government to intervene in support of the ethnic Turkish minority. Although the legitimate government withstood the coup, Turkish forces proceeded to occupy the northern portion of the island and established a separate Turkish administration. A spokesman of that administration, which called itself the Turkish Republic of Northern Cyprus, asked to become a party to the suit at the start of the trial, but Noland ruled against him. Only governments recognized by the president of the United States, Noland observed, had standing to sue in American courts—and no government of the world except Turkey recognized the breakaway entity.[130]

The second part of the decision took more time. Goldberg presented no documents to explain the journey of the icons from Cyprus to Munich; the Cypriot government, of course, asserted that they were stolen. Goldberg argued that Swiss law governed the sale, law that allowed even stolen items to be purchased if five years had passed since the theft and if the purchaser had acted in good faith. The plaintiffs argued that state law (which federal courts apply in such cases of diversity) was applicable and that a court could not award title if goods were stolen. Noland eventually ruled that Indiana law applied, dismissing the Swiss connection as transient. But he also ruled that even if Swiss law had applied, the sale was unacceptable unless the title could be shown to have been obtained in good faith.[131]

The third part of the decision, which decided that issue of title, was thus critical to the case. Goldberg had argued that she had made a variety of telephone calls to determine the status of the mosaics. Goldberg stressed the fact that the Greek Cypriot authorities had not contacted a key register of stolen art, the International Foundation for Art Research. The Autocephalous Greek Orthodox Church responded that Goldberg's telephone calls were focused on questions of import duties and not on earlier ownership. They noted that important agencies, particularly the two governments on Cyprus, had not been contacted. They also attacked the inability of Dikmen, despite his claim to Goldberg that he was an "official archaeologist" of the Turkish Cypriot government, to provide documentation for the mosaics' transfer to Germany. Such information, the plaintiffs argued, was enough to cause a prudent person to doubt seriously the legality of the title. A critical moment in testimony may have been the point when Goldberg, who had asserted that she first became aware of the definitive Megaw and Hawkins study of the mosaics only after the sale, acknowledged on cross-examination that she had referred to the book in her application for her bank loan.[132]

Noland again agreed with the plaintiffs. He noted that Goldberg offered almost no written documentation of her phone calls during the brief sales period. He accepted the Greek Cypriot testimony that they had widely publicized the art thefts in other venues. Most important, the judge agreed that Goldberg had ample evidence available to her to question the legality of Dikmen's title. In his decision, Noland quoted a witness, Gary Vikan, "All the red flags are up, all the red lights are flashing, all the sirens are blaring."[133]

Finally, Noland's decision suggested acts of prudence and due diligence that Goldberg should have pursued. She could, his decision noted, have sought the opinion of disinterested art experts, especially given the cultural significance of the items. She could have taken a more serious look at the sellers. Third, Goldberg could have looked at the vast disparity between the $20 million she believed they were worth and the $1.08 million she paid (after bargaining the price down from $3 million). Finally, she could have questioned the speed of the transaction itself. The court ordered the mosaics returned to the Orthodox Church.[134]

Goldberg promptly appealed to the Seventh Circuit while the mosaics waited in a basement bank vault in Indianapolis. Her appeal developed questions of jurisdiction and title but ultimately failed to impress the three-judge panel that heard the appeal. The decision, written by Chief Judge William J. Bauer, began by quoting lines from Lord Byron mourning the loss of ancient monuments, and included a particularly sharp attack upon art thieves.[135]

> As Byron's poem laments, war can reduce our grandest and most sacred temples to mere "fragments of stone." Only the lowest of scoundrels attempt to reap personal gain from this collective loss. Those who plundered the churches and monuments of war-torn Cyprus, hoarded their relics away, and are now smuggling and selling them for large sums are just such blackguards. The Republic of Cyprus, with diligent effort and the help of friends . . . has been able to locate several of these stolen antiquities. . . . Among such finds are the pieces of the Kanakaria mosaic at issue in this case. Unfortunately, when these mosaics surfaced they were in the hands not of the most guilty parties, but of Peg Goldberg and her gallery. Correctly applying Indiana law, the district court determined that Goldberg must return the mosaics to their rightful owner: the Church of Cyprus.

Delivered in an era when an international market in stolen art and antiquities was flourishing, and when possessors of stolen objects were seeking shelters that would permit them to avoid troubling questions of title, Noland's decision was widely applauded and continues to be recognized as a significant contribution to international law.[136] At the judge's suggestion, the plaintiffs allowed the mosaics to be displayed at the Indianapolis Museum of Art prior to their return to Cyprus.[137]

The Court in Its Third Century

The District Court for the Southern District of Indiana has moved two centuries from its origins in the Northwest and Indiana Territories. In some ways, it has changed very little. The 1816 boundaries of Indiana, and the physical geographic features within those bounds, are essentially the same. The 1787 Federal Constitution that the court was sworn to uphold, amended just fifteen times since 1816, is otherwise the same written text that Benjamin Parke knew when he became the first district judge. As Indiana Chief Justice Randall Shepard observed at the installation of District Judge Young,

> I was almost always reminded [during a day on the bench] that there was a connection between figures like James Madison and all of us who in the modern age are privileged to speak words that they wrote 200 years ago and to remind ourselves and our fellow citizens of things which are . . . truly sacred to Americans.[138]

In other ways, of course, the changes over time have been profound. Indiana's population has grown from sixty thousand to six million. Indiana has passed through one economic transformation after another: agricultural, commercial, heavy and light industrial, and service. The range of statutory and case law that conferred jurisdiction upon the court, and that constituted the body of law upon which the court was called to interpret and enforce, has vastly expanded. The volume of cases has, if anything, expanded even faster.

The most important feature of the court is its enduring involvement in the life, especially the legal life, of Indiana as it merges these elements of continuity and change. Sometimes in landmark decisions such as *Ex parte Milligan*, sometimes in significant lawsuits with national or international implications, and sometimes in cases involving the day-to-day interpretation and application of civil or criminal law, the district court has remained an important part of the fabric of Indiana life. It has been, as it will undoubtedly remain, an institution and a family that defines and reflects the Hoosier spirit.

Notes

Chapter 1

1. W. H. Hamelle, *A Standard History of White County, Indiana: An Authentic Narrative of the Past, with an Extended Survey of Modern Developments in the Progress of the Town and County*, 2 vols. (Chicago: Lewis Publishing Company, 1915), chapter seven, "The County in Law," quoted at http://www.brookston.lib.in.us/WhiteCo/chvii.htm.

2. Many excellent histories exist of the constitutional convention. The Commission on the Bicentennial of the United States Constitution, chaired by Warren Burger, often referred students to Catherine Drinker Bowen, *Miracle at Philadelphia: The Story of the Constitutional Convention, May to September, 1787* (Boston: Little, Brown, 1966), see pages 62–66 on judicial power.

3. Ibid., 168–84.

4. Ibid., 173–74; Robert M. Taylor Jr., "The Vote and the Voters," in Robert M. Taylor Jr., ed., *The Northwest Ordinance, 1787: A Bicentennial Handbook* (Indianapolis: Indiana Historical Society, 1987), 24–29.

5. Taylor, ed., *Northwest Ordinance*, xv–xxiii, provides a detailed chronology of important events in territorial history. The ordinance was again reaffirmed in statute in 1791.

6. Ibid., 31–77, provides an annotated text.

7. Ibid., 36.

8. Ibid.

9. Ibid., 59–60.

10. Brief biographical summaries of the territorial judges can be found in *Judges of the United States* (Washington, DC: The Bicentennial Committee of the Judicial Conference of the United States, 1978), 74, 147, 157, 285, 305–8, 326, 350–51, 380, 384, 399, 403, 404.

11. Most modern studies of the territorial courts draw upon Leander J. Monks, Logan Esarey, and Ernest Shockley, eds., *Courts and Lawyers of Indiana*, 3 vols. (Indianapolis: Federal Publishing Company, 1916), 1:1–46. Monks was a chief justice of the Indiana Supreme Court, and Esarey was a central figure in defining the shape and issues of Indiana historical study. Their early chapters draw heavily upon Daniel Wait Howe, *The Laws and Courts of Northwest and Indiana Territories* (Indianapolis: Bowen-Merrill Company, 1886).

12. Monks, Esarey, and Shockley, eds., *Courts and Lawyers of Indiana*, 1:6–8.

13. Ibid., 1:5; R. Douglas Hurt, *The Ohio Frontier: Crucible of the Old Northwest, 1720–1830* (Bloomington: Indiana University Press, 1996), 273–74.

14. Monks, Esarey, and Shockley, eds., *Courts and Lawyers of Indiana*, 1:19.

15. A good example of this changed emphasis can be found in Mary K. Bonsteel Tachau, *Federal Courts in the Early Republic, Kentucky, 1789–1816* (Princeton, NJ: Princeton University Press, 1978). The extent of criminal activity in the Indiana Territory is thoughtfully evaluated in Francis Philbrick, *The Laws of Indiana Territory, 1801–1809* (Springfield: Illinois State Historical Library, 1930; reprint with supplementary Indiana material, Indianapolis: Historical Bureau of the Indiana Library and Historical Department, 1931), clxxi–clxxxv.

16. Philbrick, *The Laws of Indiana Territory, 1801–1809*, pp. 8, 15–16, 77–82; James W. Ely Jr. and Theodore Brown Jr., eds., *Legal Papers of Andrew Jackson* (Knoxville: University of Tennessee Press, 1987), xxxii–xxxiv; William Baskerville Hamilton, *Anglo-American Law on the Frontier: Thomas Rodney & His Territorial Cases* (Durham, NC: Duke University Press, 1953), 95–115.

17. Monks, Esarey, and Shockley, eds., *Courts and Lawyers of Indiana*, 1:6–7.

18. Andrew R. L. Cayton, *Frontier Indiana* (Bloomington: Indiana University Press, 1996), 45–69, offers an excellent view of the French settlements.

19. George W. Geib, "Jefferson, Harrison, and the West: An Essay on Territorial Slavery," in Darrel E. Bigham, ed., *The Indiana Territory, 1800–2000: A Bicentennial Perspective* (Indianapolis: Indiana Historical Society, 2001), 106–8, 111, 112.

20. Monks, Esarey, and Shockley, eds., *Courts and Lawyers of Indiana*, 1:10–14.

21. Taylor, ed., *Northwest Ordinance*, offers a set of maps, provided between pp. 78 and 79, that illustrate the changing boundaries of the subsequent Indiana Territory.

22. Cayton, *Frontier Indiana*, 167–95.

23. Monks, Esarey, and Shockley, eds., *Courts and Lawyers of Indiana*, 1:10, 20, 39, 2:403–4; Tachau, *Federal Courts in the Early Republic, Kentucky, 1789–1816*, pp. 72–73, 105–17.

24. Monks, Esarey, and Shockley, eds., *Courts and Lawyers of Indiana*, 1:18, 20, 24, 35, 41, 2:404; Cayton, *Frontier Indiana*, 231. Alternate spellings of his name, reflecting the phonetic emphasis of some writers, exist: VanderBurgh and Vanderburg. His obituary appears in the *Vincennes Western Sun*, April 25, 1812, and stresses his "benevolent and just" public behavior, as well as his Masonic connections.

25. Philbrick, *Laws of Indiana Territory, 1801–1809*, lxv–xcviii. The most serious disputes were in the French Bottom lands of the future state of Illinois.

26. John D. Barnhart and Dorothy Riker, *Indiana to 1816: The Colonial Period* (Indianapolis: Indiana Historical Bureau and Indiana Historical Society, 1971), 314–411, treats this era.

27. Geib, "Jefferson, Harrison, and the West," 102–5.

28. Isidor Loeb, "The Beginnings of Missouri Legislation," *Missouri Historical Review* 92 (January 1998): 222–37. The article is a reprint of the original 1906 essay.

29. Taylor, ed., *Northwest Ordinance*, 72.

30. This discussion, and its historiographical context, are the subject of Geib, "Jefferson, Harrison, and the West," 99–124.

31. Monks, Esarey, and Shockley, eds., *Courts and Lawyers of Indiana*, 1:99.

32. Ibid., 1:47, 51–52, 185–86.

33. Ibid., 1:45, 48, 51, 2:404.

34. Cayton, *Frontier Indiana*, 236.

35. Monks, Esarey, and Shockley, eds., *Courts and Lawyers of Indiana*, 1:20–46; Philbrick, *Laws of Indiana Territory, 1801–1809*, cxliii–cli.

36. Philbrick, *Laws of Indiana Territory, 1801–1809*, clxiii; Hamilton, *Anglo-American Law on the Frontier*, 98–99.

37. Philbrick, *Laws of Indiana Territory, 1801–1809*, clix–clx; Monks, Esarey, and Shockley, eds., *Courts and Lawyers of Indiana*, 1:36–41.

38. Philbrick, *Laws of Indiana Territory, 1801–1809*, cxliii–cxlv; Monks, Esarey, and Shockley, eds., *Courts and Lawyers of Indiana*, 1:26–27.

39. Monks, Esarey, and Shockley, eds., *Courts and Lawyers of Indiana*, 1:41–46.

40. *Vincennes Indiana Gazette*, October 16, 1804. For a detailed treatment of Governor Harrison's involvement in another Indiana murder case that ended up being tried in Kentucky, see Tachau, *Federal Courts in the Early Republic, Kentucky, 1789–1816*, pp. 128–33.

41. "Parke, Benjamin," Federal Judicial Center biography, http://www.fjc.gov/servlet/tGetInfo?jid=1832. Each judicial biography carries its unique identification number at the end of its http address.

42. Order Book of the U.S. District Court for the District of Indiana, 1817–1833, pp. 1 (May 5, 1817), 3 (November 3, 1817). This is one of the original records still in the possession of the Clerk of the Court in the Indianapolis Federal Courthouse (hereafter cited as Order Book).

43. Cayton, *Frontier Indiana*, 242.

44. William Wesley Woollen, *Biographical and Historical Sketches of Early Indiana* (Indianapolis: Hammond and Company, 1883), 360–65, 385–86.

45. Charles Dewey, *An Eulogium upon the Life and Character of the Hon. Benjamin Parke* (Indianapolis: Bolton and Livingston Printers, 1836), 14–15.

46. Order Book, p. 5 (November 3, 1817).

47. Monks, Esarey, and Shockley, eds., *Courts and Lawyers of Indiana*, 2:406.

48. Order Book, p. 5 (November 3, 1817).

49. Ibid., p. 4 (November 3, 1817).

50. Monks, Esarey, and Shockley, eds., *Courts and Lawyers of Indiana*, 3:1139–40, 1145.

51. The state's political history is told in remarkable detail in Donald F. Carmony, *Indiana, 1816–1850: The Pioneer Era* (Indianapolis: Indiana Historical Bureau and Indiana Historical Society, 1998).

52. Monks, Esarey, and Shockley, eds., *Courts and Lawyers of Indiana*, 2:414–15.

53. Ibid., 2:415. Included is a list of appointees from 1813 to 1916.

54. William R. Holloway, *Indianapolis: A Historical and Statistical Sketch of the Railroad City* (Indianapolis: Indianapolis Journal Print, 1870), 263.

55. Monks, Esarey, and Shockley, eds., *Courts and Lawyers of Indiana*, 2:405–6.

56. Allen Sharp, "The U.S. Supreme Court on Circuit in Indiana, 1837–1891," in David J. Bodenhamer and Randall T. Shepard, eds., *The History of Indiana Law* (Athens, OH: Ohio University Press, 2006).

57. Jesse Lynch Holman to his son, May 29, 1837, Huntington Manuscript Collection, Lilly Library, Indiana University.

58. Elisha Mills Huntington to Louisa Rudd, November 30, 1843, ibid.

59. O. H. Smith, *Early Indiana Trials and Sketches* (Cincinnati: Moore, Wilstach, Keys and Company, 1858), 47. The entry is dated July 21, 1857.

60. Ibid., 38. Entry dated July 17, 1857.

61. There is, however, an excellent study available of criminal justice in the early state courts, especially in Marion County. See David J. Bodenhamer, *The Pursuit of Justice: Crime and Law in Antebellum Indiana* (New York: Garland Publishing, 1986).

62. Monks, Esarey, and Shockley, eds., *Courts and Lawyers of Indiana*, 2:406–7.

63. Woollen, *Biographical and Historical Sketches of Early Indiana*, 385; Thomas James de la Hunt, "Judge Elisha M. Huntington," *Indiana Magazine of History* 23 (June 1927): 118.

64. Monks, Esarey, and Shockley, eds., *Courts and Lawyers of Indiana*, 2:407.

65. Lawrence Friedman, *A History of American Law* (New York: Simon and Schuster, 1973), 238–39. This useful summary does not appear in the current edition of the book.

66. "Memorial Address by Mr. Zenor," in *Memorial Addresses of the Life and Character of William S. Holman* (Washington, DC: Government Printing Office, 1898), 15.

67. *United States v. Martin*, 26 F. Cas. 1183.

68. Ibid., 5.

69. Letter to unknown recipient, dated Verestau, October 5, 1835, Holman MSS, Lilly Library, Indiana University.

70. "Seeking a Federal Judgeship under Jackson," *Indiana Magazine of History* 35 (September 1939): 311–25.

71. Amos Lane to Holman, December 19, 1835, ibid., 316.

72. Holman to Allen Hamilton, February 10, 1836, ibid., 321–23.

73. Don Fehrenbacher, *The Slaveholding Republic: An Account of the United States Government's Relation to Slavery* (New York: Oxford University Press, 2001), 205–30.

74. William Hendricks to Holman, March 29, 1836, in "Seeking a Federal Judgeship under Jackson," 324.

75. Sandra Boyd Williams, "The Indiana Supreme Court and the Struggle against Slavery," *Indiana Law Review* 30 (1997): 307–9.

76. Ibid., 308.

77. Cayton, *Frontier Indiana*, 226–60.

78. See, for example, Carolyn M. Buan, ed., *The First Duty: A History of the U.S. District Court for Oregon* (Portland, OR: U.S. District Court of Oregon Historical Society, 1993); Patricia E. Brake, *Justice in the Valley: A Bicentennial Perspective of the United States District Court for the Eastern District of Tennessee* (Franklin, TN: Hillsboro Press, 1998); and Richard Cahan, *A Court That Shaped America: Chicago's Federal District Court from Abe Lincoln to Abbie Hoffman* (Evanston, IL: Northwestern University Press, 2002).

79. The parameters of this debate owe much to two defining works of scholarship: Alice Felt Tyler, *Freedom's Ferment: Phases of American Social History to 1860* (Minneapolis: University of Minnesota Press, 1944; New York: Harper and Row, 1962) and Daniel Boorstin, *The Americans: The National Experience* (New York: Random House, 1965).

80. A very detailed Holman obituary appears in the *Indianapolis Sentinel*, August 31, 1842.

81. William Cathcart, *The Baptist Encyclopedia* (Philadelphia: Louis H. Everts, 1883), 535–36.

82. Woollen, *Biographical and Historical Sketches of Early Indiana*, 384–90.

83. Dewey, *Eulogium upon the Life and Character of the Hon. Benjamin Parke*, 15.

84. Ibid.

85. Woollen, *Biographical and Historical Sketches of Early Indiana*, 389.

86. A useful Parke obituary appears in the *Vincennes Western Sun and General Advertiser*, August 1, 1835. See also Woollen, *Biographical and Historical Sketches of Early Indiana*, 385–86, 390.

87. *In re Susan*, 23 F. Cas. 444, 2 Wheeler Cr. Cas 594 (Cir.Ct., D.Ind. 1818).

88. Monks, Esarey, and Shockley, eds., *Courts and Lawyers of Indiana*, 1:199; Emily Field Van Tassel, *Why Judges Resign: Influences on Federal Judicial Service, 1789 to 1992* (Washington, DC: Federal Judicial Center, 1993), 13; (biographical account), 3, 5, Huntington Manuscript Collection.

89. "Huntington, Elisha Mills," Federal Judicial Center biography, http://www.fjc.gov/servlet/tGetInfo?=1131.

90. "Proceedings in the United States Court in Memory of the late Judge Huntington," *Indianapolis Sentinel*, May 10, 1863; White and Cravens's Letter to the Judiciary Committee, April 28, 1842; *Nomination File for Elisha Mills Huntington* (Records of the United States Senate, Record Group 46, Sen 27B-A5[4]); *Indianapolis Sentinel*, May 10, 1842.

91. Huntington to his son, August 2, 1858, Huntington Manuscript Collection.

92. Letters of August 2, 1858, and September 9, 1862, ibid. (bound letters volume).

93. Huntington to [?] Smith, February 7, 1847, ibid.

94. *Indianapolis Sentinel*, May 24, 1842 (capitalization and emphasis in original).

95. Huntington to Louisa Rudd, November 30, 1843, Huntington Manuscript Collection.

96. Huntington to his "dearest son," "Court Room Saturday Evening," December 1858, ibid.

97. Huntington to Mrs. Anna Rudd of Cannelton, November 25, 1857, ibid.

98. *Indianapolis Sentinel*, May 10, 1863.

99. *Lawrenceburg Independent Press*, November 29, 1850.

100. Dean Kotlowski, "'The Jordan Is a Hard Road to Travel': Hoosier Responses to Fugitive Slave Cases, 1850–1860," *International Social Science Reader* (Fall–Winter 2003): 71–89.

101. Ibid., 74–76.

102. *Indianapolis Sentinel*, December 22, 1854.

103. Ibid.

104. David M. Billikopf, *The Exercise of Judicial Power, 1789–1864* (New York: Vantage Press, 1973), 126–28.

105. *Indianapolis Daily Journal*, October 31, 1862; *Terre Haute Wabash Daily Express*, November 3, 1862.

Chapter 2

1. Willard King, *Lincoln's Manager: David Davis* (Cambridge, MA: Harvard University Press, 1960), 137–63.

2. Ibid., 204.

3. Smith's obituary appears in the *Indianapolis Daily Journal*, January 9, 1864.

4. Smith to Lincoln, November 12, 1862, Library of Congress Presidential Documents Collection, Microfilm Reel No. 43, N. 19514.

5. Richard Thomas, "Lisping Cale Smith: Whig Orator on the Stump," *Cincinnati Historical Society Bulletin* (Spring 1972): 21–41; "Smith, Caleb Blood," Federal Judicial Center biography, http://www.fjc.gov/servlet/tGetInfo?jid=2212.

6. An entertaining Web page, "Caleb Smith (1808–1864)" may be found at http://www.mrlincolnswhitehouse.org/. Julian's quotation is found in George W. Julian, *Political Recollections, 1840–1872* (Chicago: Jansen, McClurg and Company, 1884), 170.

7. William Wesley Woollen, *Biographical and Historical Sketches of Early Indiana* (Indianapolis: Hammond and Company, 1883), 204–10; "White, Albert Smith," Federal Judicial Center biography, http://www.fjc.gov/servlet/tGetInfo?jid=2565.

8. Woollen, *Biographical and Historical Sketches of Early Indiana*, 210.

9. See obituaries in *Indianapolis Gazette*, September 5, 1864; *Indianapolis Journal*, September 6, 1864.

10. A useful review of White's life appears in "Albert Smith White," *The Hoosier Packet* (September 2003): 2–7.

11. David Turpie, *Sketches of My Own Time* (Indianapolis: Bobbs-Merrill, 1903), 207.

12. David McDonald, *A Treatise on the Law Relating to the Powers and Duties of Justices of the Peace and Constables in the State of Indiana, with Practical Forms and Essays on Various Titles of the Common Law* (Cincinnati: H. W. Derby and Company, 1856). Commonly called *McDonald's Treatise*, it went through at least nine editions from 1856 until 1936. In the judge's lifetime it was reprinted by H. W. Derby in 1857 and by Robert Clark and Company of Cincinnati in 1860, and then issued in a revised edition coedited by Edwin Augustine Davis "to conform to the statutes in force January 1, 1863." This latter edition was copyrighted 1864 and issued by Robert Clarke [sic] and Co. in 1867 and again in 1871.

13. "McDonald, David," Federal Judicial Center biography, http://www.fjc.gov/servlet/tGetInfo?jid=1543.

14. "Documents: Diaries of Judge David McDonald," *Indiana Magazine of History* 28 (December 1932): 300, 303.

15. Donald O. Dewey, ed., "Hoosier Justice: The Journal of David McDonald, 1864–1868," *Indiana Magazine of History* 62 (September 1966): 194.

16. Flora McDonald Ketcham, "David McDonald," *Indiana Magazine of History* 28 (September 1932): 186–87.

17. *Indianapolis Journal*, January 9, 1864.

18. Ibid., January 27, 1863.

19. Dewey, ed., "Hoosier Justice," 176.

20. *Richmond Palladium*, August 31, 1869.

21. *Indianapolis Journal*, August 31, 1869.

22. Ibid., February 28, March 2, 1863.

23. Ibid., June 2, 1864.

24. Ibid., September 9, 1864.

25. Ibid., March 16, 1864.

26. Ibid., March 26, 28, 1864. The context of the Confiscation Acts is discussed in Silvana Siddali, *From Property to Person: Slavery and the Confiscation Acts, 1861–1862* (Baton Rouge: Louisiana State University Press, 2005), 4, 6, 12, 130, 140, 213–14, 246–47, 252, 257; and Daniel Hamilton, "A New Right

to Property: Civil War Confiscation in the Reconstruction Supreme Court," *Journal of Supreme Court History* 29 (2004): 254–85. Siddali, *From Property to Person*, 114, notes Caleb Smith's very cautious treatment of the legal issues while a member of the Lincoln cabinet.

27. *Indianapolis Journal*, March 28, 1864.

28. Those interested in the context of these issues should enjoy Mark E. Neely Jr., *The Fate of Liberty: Abraham Lincoln and Civil Liberties* (New York: Oxford University Press, 1991).

29. G. R. Tredway, *Democratic Opposition to the Lincoln Administration in Indiana* (Indianapolis: Indiana Historical Bureau, 1973), 224–25.

30. W. H. H. Terrell, *Indiana in the War of the Rebellion: Report of the Adjutant General* (Indianapolis: Indiana Historical Society, 1960), 288–368. This reprint of volume one of the 1869 *Report of the Adjutant General* sets forth the government case with much of the passion of the war intact. For a modern academic alternative, see Kenneth Stampp, *Indiana Politics during the Civil War* (Indianapolis: Indiana Historical Bureau, 1949), 230–52.

31. William H. Rehnquist, *All the Laws but One: Civil Liberties in Wartime* (New York: Alfred A. Knopf, 1998), 100–101.

32. Ibid., 225–48.

33. Ibid., 249–64.

34. Dewey, ed., "Hoosier Justice," 190.

35. Ibid., 193.

36. King, *Lincoln's Manager*, 260.

37. Dewey, ed., "Hoosier Justice," 203.

38. Ibid.

39. Leander J. Monks, Logan Esarey, and Ernest Shockley, eds., *Courts and Lawyers of Indiana*, 3 vols. (Indianapolis: Federal Publishing Company, 1916), 2:412; Matilda Gresham, *Life of Walter Quintin Gresham: 1832–1895*, 2 vols. (Chicago: Rand McNally and Company, 1919), 1:302–12; Charles Calhoun, *Gilded Age Cato: The Life of Walter Q. Gresham* (Lexington: University of Kentucky Press, 1987), 41; "Gresham, Walter Quintin," Federal Judicial Center biography, http://www.fjc.gov/servlet/tGetInfo?jid=915.

40. Quoted, with editorial contempt, in the *Indianapolis Sentinel*, September 10, 1869. The practice of wearing robes in court, if more than a metaphor, went out of practice in the early twentieth century.

41. *New Albany Daily Ledger*, August 26, 1869; Gresham, *Life of Walter Quintin Gresham*, 1:350.

42. *In Memory of General Walter Q. Gresham* (Indianapolis: Indiana Job Print, 1895), 15–16. The memorial service was held on May 31, 1895. A copy is in the Noble C. Butler Collection, M35, box 54, folder 6, William Henry Smith Memorial Library, Indiana Historical Society, Indianapolis.

43. Calhoun, *Gilded Age Cato*, 41.

44. *Indianapolis News*, May 28, 1895.

45. *Thompson v. Hawks*, 11 Biss. 440, 14 F. 902 (C.C.D. Ind. 1883).

46. Jacob Piatt Dunn Jr., *Greater Indianapolis: The History, the Industries, the Institutions, and the People of a City of Homes*, 2 vols. (Chicago: Lewis Publishing Company, 1910), 1:561.

47. A brief, lucid, and attractively illustrated introduction to the issue can be found in Thomas Kingsley, "Tax Paid Revenue Stamps and the Infamous St. Louis Whiskey Ring," *American Philatelist* (June 2005): 522–28.

48. Calhoun, *Gilded Age Cato*, 44–45.

49. Harry J. Sievers, *Benjamin Harrison, Hoosier Statesman* (New York: University Publishers, 1959), 87–92, details the Hiram Brownlee defense.

50. Ibid., 44–45.

51. *Fort Wayne News-Sentinel*, March 22, 1930.

52. W. R. Holloway, *Indianapolis: A Historical and Statistical Sketch of the Railroad City* (Indianapolis: Indianapolis Journal Print, 1870).

53. An excellent study of the context of the strike, and of the place of Judge Gresham within it, is Robert Bruce, *1877: Year of Violence* (Indianapolis: Bobbs-Merrill, 1959), 287–90, 308–9, 317–20.

54. Quoted in Calhoun, *Gilded Age Cato*, 53 (who notes spelling and punctuation have been corrected).

55. Lawrence Friedman, *A History of American Law*, 3rd ed. (New York: Simon and Schuster, 2005), 416–17, discusses the context of bankruptcy law in this period.

56. Calhoun, *Gilded Age Cato*, 53–55.

57. Ibid., 52–54. Drummond had been elevated to the circuit from District Judge for Northern Illinois. For his background see Richard Cahan, *A Court That Shaped America: Chicago's Federal District Court from Abe Lincoln to Abbie Hoffman* (Evanston, IL: Northwestern University Press, 2002), 12–29, 32–36.

58. Friedman, *History of American Law*, 421.

59. Otto Gresham, *The Greenbacks* (Chicago: The Book Press, 1927), 40–41.

60. *Streit v. Lauter*, 11 F. 309 (C. Ct. D. Ind. 1882) at 313.

61. *Gottfried v. Crescent Brewing Co.*, 9 F. 762-66 (C. C. D. Ind. 1881).

62. *Crescent Brewing Co. v. Gottfried*, 128 U.S. 158, 166, 168-170, 9 S. Ct. 83, 32 L.Ed. 390 (1888).

63. Ibid.

64. *Royer v. King*, 36 F. 899, 900 (C. C. D. Ind. 1888).

65. *New York Times*, June 16, 1895.

66. An excellent survey of Benjamin Harrison's role in law and politics may be found in Allen Sharp, "Benjamin Harrison, High-Priced Counsel," in Norman Gross, ed., *America's Lawyer-Presidents: From Law Office to Oval Office* (Evanston, IL: Northwestern University Press, 2004), 194–205.

67. *New York Times*, June 16, 1895.

68. Ibid.

69. Ibid.

70. *Indianapolis News*, April 17, 1883.

71. Monks, Esarey, and Shockley, eds., *Courts and Lawyers of Indiana*, 2:418–23; Rayman L. Solomon, *History of the Seventh Circuit, 1891–1941* (Washington, DC: The Bicentennial Committee of the Judicial Conference of the United States, 1981), 1–21.

72. Erwin C. Surrency, *History of the Federal Courts* (New York: Oceana Publishers, 1987), 111–43.

73. Monks, Esarey, and Shockley, eds. *Courts and Lawyers of Indiana*, 2:418–23; Solomon, *History of the Seventh Circuit*, 28–29, 59–60.

74. Monks, Esarey, and Shockley, eds., *Courts and Lawyers of Indiana*, 2:414–15; Solomon, *History of the Seventh District*, 28–29, 59–60.

75. Monks, Esarey, and Shockley, eds., *Courts and Lawyers of Indiana*, 415–16.

76. *Ex parte Perkins*, 29 F.900, 1–2, 8.

77. Andrew R. Seeger, *Federal Court Facilities in the Southern District of Indiana: A Working Bibliography* (Indianapolis: Architecture and Art Subcommittee, Court History Committee, United States District Court for the Southern District of Indiana, 1999–2003), excerpts for Evansville, Terre Haute, and New Albany, 1–15.

78. *New Albany Daily Ledger*, July 23, 26, 1887.

79. Raymond E. Gnat, comp., and Lawrence Connor, ed., *The Indianapolis Literary Club, Summarized Record 1976–2003* (Indianapolis: Indianapolis Literary Club Foundation, 2004), 2–4.

80. *Indianapolis News*, January 7, 1905.

81. Charles Evans, "Looking Backward," in Gnat, comp., and Connor, ed., *Indianapolis Literary Club*, 114–15.

82. *Outline of the Office of United States Marshals* (Washington, DC: Executive Office for United States Marshals, 1960).

83. Burton J. Bledstein, *The Culture of Professionalism: The Middle Class and the Development of Higher Education in America* (New York: Norton, 1976).

84. Ibid., 80–128.

85. "Articles of Association," quoted in Monks, Esarey, and Shockley, eds., *Courts and Lawyers of Indiana*, 2:457.

86. Ibid., 2:462–63.

87. Ibid., 2:472–86.

88. Ibid., 2:488.

89. Ibid., 2:489.

90. John Howland and Lucian Barbour, *A Manual for Executors, Administrators and Guardians* (Indianapolis: Merrill, 1862). A revised edition, in which Barbour was replaced as coeditor by Ferdinand Winter, was published in Indianapolis by Merrill, Hubbard in 1879.

91. James Frazer, John Stotsenburg, and David Turpie, *The Revised Statutes of Indiana* (Chicago: E. B. Myers, 1881).

92. *Centennial Dinner Program* (Indianapolis: Historical Society of the United States District Court for the Southern District of Indiana, 2003), 13, 17.

93. See Clifton Phillips, *Indiana in Transition: The Emergence of an Industrial Commonwealth, 1880–1920* (Indianapolis: Indiana Historical Bureau and Indiana Historical Society, 1968), chapter one, 1–49, for a discussion of the political context.

94. "Woods, William Allen," Federal Judicial Center biography, http://www.fjc.gov/servlet/tGetInfo?jid=2649.

95. *Goshen Independent*, May 12, 1883.

96. Ibid., May 19, 1883.

97. *Unpublished Memoirs of Alice (Woods) Ullman*, 60–62 (published with the permission of the judge's great-granddaughter, Martha Ullman West, Seattle, Washington).

98. "Baker, John Harris," Federal Judicial Center biography, http://www.fjc.gov/servlet/tGetInfo?jid=80.

99. *Indianapolis News*, March 18, 1892.

100. *Goshen News*, April 22, 1892.

101. *Goshen News-Times*, October 21, 1915.

102. "Woods, William Allen" and "Baker, John Harris," Federal Judicial Center biographies.

103. Harold Chase, Samuel Krislov, Keith Boyum, and Jerry Clark, *Biographical Dictionary of the Federal Judiciary* (Detroit: Gale Research Company, 1976), 12, 308.

104. *Indianapolis News*, July 1, 1901.

105. Ibid., May 20, 1889.

106. *Testimony Pertaining to the Nomination of Judge William A. Woods to the Seventh Circuit Court of Appeals*, Fifty-Second Congress, *United States Congressional Hearing Supplement* (January 29, 1892) (SJ 52-A) at 53 of 172 pages.

107. *W. B. Conkey Co. v. Russell*, 111 F. 417 (C.C.D. Ind. 1901).

108. Dunn, *Greater Indianapolis*, 1:562; *Jennings v. Menaugh*, 118 F. 612 (C.C.D. Ind. 1902).

109. *Indianapolis News*, February 17, 1925, contains the text of a talk on the history of the U.S. District Court given to the Indianapolis Bar Association by Henry H. Hornbrook on February 14, 1925.

110. Ibid., November 29, 1899.

111. *The Morning Star*, 4 Biss 62, 17 F. Cas. 773 (D. Ind. 1866).

112. *The Lewellen*, 4 Biss. 167, 15 F. Cas. 448 (D. Ind. 1868).

113. *In re Southwestern Car Co.*, 9 Biss. 76, 22 F. Cas. 833 (D. Ind. 1879).

114. *Wau-pe-man-que v. Aldrich*, 28 F. 489 (C.C.D. Ind. 1886).

115. *Turner v. Turner*, 108 F. 785 (D. Ind. 1901).

116. Dunn, *Greater Indianapolis*, 1:292–96.

117. Ibid., 296–97; *Ex parte Perkins*, 29 F. 900 (C.C.D. Ind. 1887).

118. Dunn, *Greater Indianapolis*, 1:296–98.

119. Solomon, *History of the Seventh Circuit*, 29.

120. Ibid., 59.

121. Ibid., quoting Claude Bowers, *Beveridge and the Progressive Era* (Cambridge, MA: Houghton Mifflin Company, 1932), 86.

122. Solomon, *History of the Seventh District*, 28–29, 58–60.

123. Dunn, *Greater Indianapolis*, 1:562.

Chapter 3

1. James W. Noel, "Remarks on the Occasion of the Death of C. C. Shirley," *Memorials for Members of the Indianapolis Bar Association*, vol. 7 (Indianapolis: Indianapolis Bar Association, 1928), 80.

2. *Indianapolis News*, April 28, 1928.

3. The Department of Justice files for 1902 contain a voluminous correspondence documenting the recommendation process. For the early favorites, see Harry Sheridan to Theodore Roosevelt, May 17, 1902, Howard Maxwell to Theodore Roosevelt, May 17, 1902, and James Bingham to Theodore Roosevelt, June 7, 1902. For the shift to Anderson, see Schuyler Colfax to Theodore Roosevelt, May 16, 1902, Joseph M. Johns to Theodore Roosevelt, October 31, 1902, and James E. Piety to Theodore Roosevelt, November 7, 1902.

4. *Baker and Daniels, Founded 1863* (Indianapolis: Baker & Daniels, n.d.) is a biographically focused history of the firm.

5. Edward Daniels to Theodore Roosevelt, October 31, 1902, Department of Justice files.

6. Albert Baker to Theodore Roosevelt, October 31, 1902, ibid. The two men were married to sisters.

7. Justice James H. Jordan to Theodore Roosevelt, November 25, 1902, ibid.

8. A. A. Hargrave to Theodore Roosevelt, October 31, 1902, ibid.

9. *Indianapolis Star*, April 28, 1938.

10. *United States v. Smith*, 173 F. 227 (D. Ind. 1909).

11. Ibid., at 232.

12. Ibid.

13. Theodore Roosevelt to *Collier's Weekly* Associate Editor Mark Sullivan, May 1, 1907, *The Letters of Theodore Roosevelt*, 8 vols. (Cambridge, MA: Harvard University Press, 1951–54), 5:667.

14. *Indianapolis News*, October 24, 1910.

15. *United States v. Aczel*, 219 F. 917, 923–924 (D. Ind. 1915).

16. Ibid. at 921.

17. Ibid. at 925–938.

18. Clifton Phillips, *Indiana in Transition: The Emergence of an Industrial Commonwealth, 1880–1920* (Indianapolis: Indiana Historical Bureau and Indiana Historical Society, 1968), 384.

19. *Aczel v. United States*, 232 F. 652 (C.C.D. Ind. 1916).

20. John Lewis Niblack, *The Life and Times of a Hoosier Judge* (Indianapolis: privately printed, 1973), 173. Niblack may be speaking metaphorically about the black robes, because other sources, notably Judge William Steckler, assert that the practice was not introduced until after 1950.

21. Ibid., 173–85; James H. Madison, *Indiana through Tradition and Change: A History of the Hoosier State and Its People, 1920–1945* (Indianapolis: Indiana Historical Society, 1982), 50; *Indianapolis News*, April 29, 30, 1924. McCray was later pardoned by President Herbert Hoover.

22. *The Conveyor*, 147 F. 586 (D. Ind. 1906).

23. *Baltimore & O. R. Co. v. Railroad Commission of Indiana*, 196 F. 690 (C.C.D. Ind. 1912).

24. Lawrence Meir Friedman, *American Law in the Twentieth Century* (New Haven, CT: Yale University Press, 2002), 352–55.

25. Martin Tuohy, "Interurban Railroaders and Changing Work Conditions on the South Shore Line, 1908–1937," 1–38, http://www.indianahistory.org/ihs_press/web_publications/railroad/tuohy.pdf.

26. Ibid., 10.

27. Kevin Tierney, *Darrow: A Biography* (New York: Thomas Crowell, 1979), 236–51.

28. *Ryan v. United States*, 216 F. 13 (7th Cir. 1914).

29. Ibid. at 29. Nitroglycerine is the active ingredient in dynamite.

30. Tierney, *Darrow*, 252–75.

31. *Indianapolis News*, December 6, 12, 16, 1912.

32. *Ryan v. United States, supra*, 216 F. at 43–58.

33. *Indianapolis News*, December 6, 16, 1912.

34. *Ryan v. United States, supra*, 216 F. at 19–20.

35. Ibid. at 57–58.

36. *Indianapolis News*, December 28, 1912.

37. Melvyn Dubofsky and Warren Van Tine, *John L. Lewis, A Biography* (New York: Quadrangle, 1977), 20–42.

38. Ibid., 43–58.

39. Ibid., 43–66.

40. *Borderland Coal Corporation v. International Organization of United Mine Workers of America et al.*, 275 F. 871, 872–873 (D. Ind. 1921), *decree modified by Gasaway v. Borderline Coal Corp.*, 278 F. 56 (C.C.A. 7 [Ind.] 1921).

41. Cecil Carnes, *John L. Lewis: Leader of Labor* (New York: Robert Speller, 1936), 58–59, 76, captures Lewis's combative political style.

42. Rayman Solomon, *History of the Seventh Circuit, 1891–1941* (Washington, DC: The Bicentennial Committee of the Judicial Conference of the United States, 1981), 109.

43. Merlo John Pusey, *Charles Evans Hughes*, 2 vols. (New York: Macmillan, 1951), 1:388.

44. David J. Danelski and Joseph S. Tulchin, eds., *The Autobiographical Notes of Charles Evans Hughes* (Cambridge, MA: Harvard University Press, 1973), 194n.

45. Lawrence Meir Friedman, *Crime and Punishment in American History* (New York: Basic Books, 1993), 261–76, 285–90, 325–28, 355; Friedman, *American Law in the Twentieth Century*, 102–8, 420–24.

46. Niblack, *Life and Times of a Hoosier Judge*, 176.

47. Solomon, *History of the Seventh Circuit*, 108.

48. *Turner v. Turner*, 108 F. 785 (D. Ind. 1901).

49. Harry T. Ice, *History of a Hoosier Law Firm: Ice Miller Donadio & Ryan and Its Predecessors, 1910–1980* (Indianapolis: privately printed by the author, 1980), xv.

50. *Visitors' Guide to the United States Court House, Indianapolis, Indiana, and the United States District Court for the Southern District of Indiana* (Indianapolis: Historical Society of the United States District Court for the Southern District of Indiana and the General Services Administration, 2003), 2–10, 23–26.

51. Ibid., 6–12.

52. Ibid., 10–26.

53. "Script for Building Tours" (Indianapolis: Historical Society of the United States District Court for the Southern District of Indiana, manuscript revised August 17, 2004), 3.

54. Ice, *History of a Hoosier Law Firm*, 42.

55. Friedman, *American Law in the Twentieth Century*, 251–56.

56. Lawrence H. Larsen, *Federal Justice in Western Missouri: The Judges, the Cases, the Times* (Columbia: University of Missouri Press, 1994), 96–97.

57. *Indianapolis Star*, October 8, 1933; *Noble Butler (1704–1799) of Bristol, England, Philadelphia and Chester County, Pennsylvania, His Ancestors and Descendants* (West Chester, PA: The Butler Family Association, 1982), 267–69.

58. *Indianapolis Star*, November 27, 1927.

59. I. Scott Messinger, *Order in the Courts: A History of the Federal Court Clerk's Office* (Washington, DC: Federal Judicial Center), 35–41.

60. *Indianapolis Men of Affairs, 1923* (Indianapolis: American Biographic Society, 1923), 13.

61. Solomon, *History of the Seventh Circuit*, 110.

62. *Indianapolis News*, November 25, 1924.

63. *South Bend Tribune*, January 21, 1925. A map of the districts is included.

64. *Princeton Democrat*, January 15, 1925.

65. Attorney General Harlan F. Stone to President Calvin Coolidge, February 5, 1925, Library of Congress Presidential Documents Collection, microfilm reel no. 101, no. 208N.

66. *In the Matter of the Memorial Service for the Honorable Thomas W. Slick, First Judge of the United States District Court for the Northern District of Indiana*, Record of Proceedings before the Hon. Robert A. Grant, and the Hon. Luther M. Swygert, United States District Judges at South Bend and Hammond, Indiana, January 30, 1959.

67. *Indianapolis Times*, February 19, 1925; *Indianapolis Star*, June 12, 1925.

68. *South Bend Tribune*, September 18, 1927.

69. Ibid., November 1, 1927.

70. *Indianapolis Star*, April 24, 1928. An excellent color map of the four divisions that make up the modern southern district may be found at the U.S. Attorney's Office, Southern District of Indiana, http://www.usdoj.gov/usao/ins/overvw.htm. See *Terre Haute Tribune*, October 4, 1925, for the first session of the new divisional court in that city.

71. *In re Lowman*, 8 F. Supp. 886, 887 (Ind. 1934).

72. *South Bend Tribune*, July 10, October 4, 10, November 8, 1927, February 18, March 1, 1929; the Klan cases are both *Stephenson v. Daly, Warden*, and are cited 21 F.2d 625 (D. Ind. 1927), and 1 F. Supp. 865 (N.D. Ind. 1932).

73. *South Bend Tribune*, February 18, 1929.

74. Ibid., December 27, 1933.

75. *In the Matter of the Memorial Service for the Honorable Thomas W. Slick*, 22–23.

76. Louis La Coss, "Who Is This Man Baltzell?" *Saint Louis Globe Democrat Magazine*, March 7, 1926, pp. 5, 21.

77. *Princeton Democrat*, January 15, 1925; La Coss, "Who Is This Man Baltzell?" 5, 21; Carnes, *John L. Lewis*, 123; *Baltzell, Robt C of Indiana, Papers Pertaining to Above Nomination*, Committee on the Judiciary, United States Senate, January 12, 1925; *Rockport Journal*, March 28, 1924; *Franklin Evening Star*, January 1, 1925; *Indianapolis Star*, February 15, 1925.

78. *Indianapolis News*, March 25, 1925.

79. *Indianapolis Times*, January 19, 1940, contains an excellent summary of Baltzell's career.

80. Ibid. The Jack Daniels story is told in enthusiastic detail in Albert Rosenberg and Cindy Armstrong, *The American Gladiators: Taft Versus Remus* (Hemet, CA: Aimwell Press, 1995), 51–57.

81. *Indianapolis Times*, January 19, 1940.

82. Ibid.

83 *Indianapolis Star*, August 14, 1949.

84. Judge William Steckler, videotape interview conduced by Harry Huffman and Charles Sims, June 30, 1994, Indianapolis Bar Association. The authors are not aware of any transcript of this interview, which contains fascinating materials not included in the official oral interview with the judge.

85. Friedman, *Crime and Punishment in American History*, 264–67, 290–93.

86. *Barrett v. United States*, 82 F.2d 528 (C.C.A. 7 [Ind.] 1936).

87. See Robert K. Kyle's retrospective in the *Indianapolis News*, February 13, 1977.

88. Ibid.; "Executions of Federal Prisoners (since 1927)," Federal Bureau of Prisons Chart, http://www.bop.gov/about/history/execchart.jsp. The chart mistakenly identifies Barrett's method of execution as electrocution.

89. Baltzell's scrapbooks, covering the years from 1904 to 1936, are located in the Indiana State Library, Indianapolis.

90. Steckler videotape interview.

91. Collins Fitzpatrick and William Steckler, "The Oral History of Judge William Steckler, November 24–25, 1987," transcript (Indianapolis: United States District Court for the Southern District of Indiana, 1987), tape two, 12.

92. Ice, *History of a Hoosier Law Firm*, 15–17, 98–100. He cites the Supreme Court ruling in *George Van Camp & Sons Co. v. American Can Company*, 278 U.S. 245 (1929). The key Indiana case was *American Can Company v. Ladoga Canning Company*, 44 F.2d 763 (C.C.A. 7 [Ind.] 1930), cert. den. 282 U.S. 899, 51 S. Ct. 183, 75 L.Ed.2d 792 (1931).

93. Ice, *History of a Hoosier Law Firm*, 16.

94. Friedman, *American Law in the Twentieth Century*, 251–56.

95. Ibid., 252–54.

96. "Minton, Sherman," Federal Judicial Center biography, http://fjc.gov/servlet/GetInfo?jid=1658.

97. Linda C. Gugin and James E. St. Clair, *Sherman Minton: New Deal Senator, Cold War Justice* (Indianapolis: Indiana Historical Society, 1997); William Franklin Radcliff, *Sherman Minton: Indiana's Supreme Court Justice* (Indianapolis: Guild Press of Indiana, 1996).

98. "Constructing Justice: the Architecture of Federal Courthouses," Federal Judicial Center Web site, http://www.fjc.gov/history/home.nsf/page/courthouses-bdy; Andrew R. Seager, *Federal Court Facilities in the Southern District of Indiana: A Working Bibliography* (Indianapolis: For the Architecture and Art Subcommittee, Court History Committee, United States District Court for the Southern District of Indiana, revised September 25, 2003), 9, 12–13.

99. *Indianapolis Times*, August 2, 1949.

100. The Bureau of Prisons maintains a Web site for Terre Haute penitentiary at http://www.bop.gov/locations/institutions/thp/index.jsp.

101. "Script for Building Tours," 3–4, 14–17; *Visitors' Guide to the United States Court House, Indianapolis*, 8, 24–27.

102. *Indianapolis Star*, October 19, 1950.

103. *Princeton Democrat*, January 31, 1925.

104. Ibid.

105. Russell R. Wheeler, *Origins of the Elements of Federal Court Governance* (Washington, DC: Federal Judicial Center, 1992), 11–15.

106. Messinger, *Order in the Courts*, 46–61.

107. *South Bend Tribune*, February 18, 1929.

108. *Indianapolis Star*, October 19, 1950.

109. "A Brief History of Locke Reynolds" (manuscript, n. p., n. d.), 5.

110. *Hack v. American Surety Co. of New York*, 96 F.2d 939 (C.C.A. 7 [Ind.] 1938), *cert. den.* 305 U.S. 631, 59 S. Ct. 95, 83 L.Ed. 405 (1938); *Prairie Farmer Pub. Co. et al. v. Indiana Farmer's Guide Pub. Co.*, 299 U.S. 156, 57 S. Ct. 135, 81 L.Ed. 93 (1936).

111. *Indianapolis Star*, October 19, 1950; *Turner v. Glass Corporation v. Hartford-Empire Co.*, 173 F.2d 49 (7th Cir. 1949), *cert. den.* 338 U.S. 830, 70 S. Ct. 57, 94 L.Ed. 505 (1949).

112. *Historic Area Preservation Plan, Lockefield Gardens* (Indianapolis: Indianapolis Historic Preservation Commission, 1985), H-1 to H-6.

113. *United States v. Holt*, 108 F.2d 365 (C.C.A. 7 [Ind.] 1939), *cert. den.* 309 U.S. 672, 60 S. Ct. 616, 84 L.Ed. 1018 (1940).

114. *United States v. Kortepeter*, 114 F.2d 124 (C.C.A. 7 [Ind.] 1940), *cert. den.* 311 U.S. 711, 61 S. Ct. 392, 85 L.Ed. 462 (1940).

115. *Rosen v. Lutz*, 7 F. Supp. 755 (N.D. Ind. 1934); *Premier-Pabst Sales Co. v. McNutt, Governor*, 17 F. Supp. 708 (S.D. Ind. 1935); *Kiefer-Stewart Co. v. Joseph E. Seagram & Sons, Inc.*, 340 U.S. 211, 71 S. Ct. 259, 95 L.Ed. 219 (1951).

116. *United States v. Lewis* (two cases), 110 F.2d. 460 (C.C.A. 7 [Ind.] 1940), *cert. den.* 310 U.S. 634, 60 S. Ct. 1077, 84 L.Ed. 1404 (1940).

117. *Indianapolis Star*, October 30, 1949.

118. *United States v. Pelly*, 132 F.2d 170, 179-180, 182 (Ind. 1942), *cert. den.* 318 U.S. 764, 63 S. Ct. 665, 87 L.Ed. 1135 (1943).

119. Steckler videotape interview.

Chapter 4

1. The Federal Judicial Center Web site offers a legislative history of the District Courts of Indiana, with statutory citations, at http://www.fjc.gov/history/home.nsf/page/usdc_in_leg. The statutes governing the Southern District of Indiana are 68 Stat. 8 (February 10, 1954), 75 Stat. 80 (May 19, 1961), 80 Stat. 75 (March 18, 1966), and 91 Stat. 1629 (October 20, 1978).

2. Collins Fitzpatrick and William Steckler, "The Oral History of Judge William Steckler, November 24–25, 1987," transcript (Indianapolis: United States District Court for the Southern District of Indiana, 1987), tape three, 27 (hereafter cited as Steckler interview).

3. "Steckler, William Elwood," Federal Judicial Center biography, http://www.fjc.gov./servlet/tGetInfo?jid=2279; Steckler interview, tape two, 15–29; *Indianapolis Times*, February 11, 1950; *Indianapolis Star*, February 12, 1950. A binder containing a photo, a biographical sketch, and letters of recommendation to President Harry Truman are in the possession of the judge's son, David Steckler. Steckler joined the ranks of published members of the court family with: Edwin Steers and William Steckler, comps., *Election Laws of Indiana and 1947 Town Political Calendar Governing Town Elections, Instructions to Voters and Election Officers for Election, November, 1947* (Indianapolis: State Election Board, 1947), and *Election Laws of Indiana and 1948 Political Calendar: Governing Town Elections, Instructions to Voters and Election Officers* (Indianapolis: Indiana Election Board, 1948).

4. Tinder was the father of John Daniel Tinder, who was appointed in the ensuing generation to the court. The elder Tinder wrote at the time as Indiana Commander of the Veterans of Foreign Wars, and not in his capacity as Marion County Prosecutor.

5. Steckler interview, tape two, 23–24.

6. Howard F. Burns to Honorable Pat McCarran, March 1, 1950, Telford B. Orbison to Honorable Pat McCarran, February 16, 1950, and summary minutes of hearing, April 1, 1950, United States Senate Committee on the Judiciary file.

7. *Recognition Dinner for the Presentation of Portrait of the Honorable William E. Steckler*, Indianapolis: Indianapolis Chapter, Federal Association, September 29, 1982, 563 F. Supp., lxxix.

8. "Holder, Cale James," Federal Judicial Center biography, http://www.fjc.gov/servlet/tGetInfo?jid=1071; *Indianapolis Star*, July 21, 1974.

9. Steckler interview, tape six, 26.

10. Russell Pulliam, *Publisher Gene Pulliam, Last of the Newspaper Titans* (Ottawa, IL: Jameson Books, 1984), 155–66, 177–81. Pages 179 and 180 quote two of the vitriolic telegrams that the publisher wrote to Eisenhower's chief of staff, Sherman Adams.

11. U.S. Department of Justice, Cale J. Holder Recommendation File. (A copy containing the judge's biography and his recommendation letters is in the possession of the Holder family and was graciously provided to the authors for their review.)

12. Hugh E. Reynolds Sr. to Herbert Brownell, May 24, 1954, and Theodore Locke to Herbert Brownell, May 25, 1954, Holder Recommendation File.

13. Wray H. Fleming to Herbert Brownell, June 3, 1954, ibid.

14. Walter Leckrone to Herbert Brownell, June 4, 1954, ibid.

15. *Indianapolis Star*, May 25, 27, 29, July 12, August 22, 1954; *Indianapolis Times*, July 16, 1954; William E. Jenner Jr., interview with Donald B. Kite Sr., November 2, 1994.

16. *Indianapolis Star*, August 22, 1954.

17. "Dillin, Samuel Hugh," Federal Judicial Center biography, http://www.fjc.gov/servlet/tGetInfo?jid=620.

18. Collins Fitzpatrick and S. Hugh Dillin, "The Oral History of Judge S. Hugh Dillin, July 19, 1994," transcript (Indianapolis: United States District Court for the Southern District of Indiana, 1994) (hereafter cited as Dillin interview).

19. Dillin interview, tape three, side B, 11–12. Anecdotal comments to the authors also spoke of Judge Dillin providing useful support to Governor Matthew Welch in the Indiana State Senate.

20. William Potter, II, and James Noland, "The Oral History of the Honorable James E. Noland, March 27, 1990," transcript (Indianapolis: United States District Court for the Southern District of Indiana, 1990), esp. 2–4, 8–9, 16–19, 22–24, 38–41, 46 (hereafter cited as Noland interview). Identified as a "rough draft," it has not subsequently been edited. The interview's contents conclude with Noland's election to Congress in 1948.

21. "Noland, James Ellsworth," Federal Judicial Center biography, http://www.fjc.gov/servlet/tGetInfo?jid=1774. Noland joined the ranks of court family authors with: Edwin Steers Sr. and James E. Noland, comps., *Town Laws of Indiana and 1959 Town Political Calendar, Governing Town Elections, Instructions to Voters and Election Officers for Election, Nov. 3, 1959* (Indianapolis: Indiana Election Board, 1959).

22. Noland interview, 34.

23. *Memorial Service and Courtroom Dedication for the Honorable James E. Noland* (Indianapolis: United States District Court, Southern District of Indiana, Indianapolis Division, December 11, 1992), 21.

24. "Brooks, Gene Edward," Federal Judicial Center biography, http://www.fjc.gov/sedrvlet/tGetInfo?jnd=274; Gene Brooks and Collins Fitzpatrick, "The Oral History of Retired Judge Gene E. Brooks," transcript (Chicago: United States Court of Appeals for the Seventh Circuit, 2000), 1, 4–5, 8–10, 13, 15–16 (hereafter cited as Brooks interview). In the opinion of the authors, this oral history should be taken with a grain of salt. Prepared four years after Brooks retired from the bench to reenter private practice, it makes several assertions on topics such as court administration that are clearly exaggerations for dramatic effect, or expressions of his biting style of humor. The judge's recollections allow him some self-serving assessments of situations that other participants have recalled in a different light.

25. Brooks interview, 17–19.

26. Ibid., 17–20.

27. Ibid., 23–24.

28. Ibid., 24.

29. Ibid., 26–27.

30. Ibid., 27.

31. Ibid., 24–26.

32. Lawrence Meir Friedman, *American Law in the Twentieth Century* (New Haven, CT: Yale University Press, 2002), 388.

33. Brooks interview, 33–34.

34. Steckler interview, tape three, 20.

35. Ibid.

36. The three related cases are *Chavis v. Whitcomb & Ruckelshaus, Central Christian Leadership Conference v. Whitcomb,* and *Dortch v. Lugar,* 305 F. Supp 1359 (S.D. Ind. 1969), *order rescinded by* 397 U.S. 984, 90 S. Ct. 1112, 25 L.Ed.2d 392 (1970).

37. *Chavis v. Whitcomb,* 305 F. Supp 1364 (S.D. Ind. 1969), *order rescinded by* 397 U.S. 979, 90 S. Ct. 1103, 25 L.Ed.2d 390 (1970), *and reversed by* 403 U.S. 124, 91 S. Ct. 1858, 29 L.Ed.2d 363 (1971); *Chavis v. Whitcomb,* 307 F. Supp 1362 (S.D. Ind. 1969), *order rescinded by* 397 U.S. 984, 90 S. Ct. 1112, 25 L.Ed.2d 392 (1970); *Chavis v. Whitcomb,* 57 F.R.D. 32 (S.D. Ind. 1972), *order rescinded by* 397 U.S. 984, *supra; Cantwell v. Hudnut,* 419 F. Supp 1302 (S.D. Ind. 1976), *aff'd in part, rev'd in part* 566 F.2d 30 (7th Cir. 1977), *cert. den.* 439 U.S. 1114, 99 S. Ct. 1015, 59 L.Ed.2d 71 (1979).

38. *Vance Hartke v. Richard L. Roudebush et al.,* 321 F. Supp. 1370 (S.D. Ind. 1970), *rev'd* 405 U.S. 15, 92 S. Ct. 804, 31 L.Ed.2d 1 (1972).

39. *Roudebush v. Hartke,* and *Sendak v. Hartke,* 405 U.S. 15, 92 S. Ct. 804, 31 L.Ed.2d 1 (1972).

40. Dillin interview, tape four, 7–8.

41. Judge William Steckler, videotape interview conducted by Harry Huffman and Charles Sims, June 30, 1994, Indianapolis Bar Association. Anecdotal comments to the authors suggest that Steckler was concerned about projecting an image of "gravitas" that would counter any criticism of his comparative youth.

42. Ibid.

43. Ibid.

44. Ibid. The work of the Judicial Conference committees upon which Steckler participated resulted, among other achievements, in *Handbook of Recommended Procedures for the Trial of Protracted Cases* (Washington, DC:

The Judicial Conference, 1960; St. Paul: West Publishing, 1960). This was later revised as *Manual of Suggested Procedures for Pretrial and Trial of Complex and Multi-District Litigation* (Washington, DC: The Judicial Conference, 1969), which was issued in at least five editions by various publishers and with various supplements until 1985 when it was supplanted by *Manual for Complex Litigation, Second* (St. Paul: West Publishing, 1985). In his oral interviews Steckler references this latter volume. His suggestion for a newsletter, *The Third Branch*, is noted in *Recognition Dinner for the Presentation of Portrait of the Honorable William Steckler*, lxxxiv. Current copies of the newsletter may be found at http://www.uscourts.gov/ttb/.

45. *Recognition Dinner for the Presentation of Portrait of the Honorable William Steckler*, lxxiii–lxxxiv.

46. Steckler interview, tape two, 20.

47. "Barker, Sarah Evans," Federal Judicial Center biography, http://www.fjc.gov/sedrvlet/tGetInfo?jid=94; see chapter five for a discussion of Barker's biography.

48. Useful short biographies may be found at Martindale-Hubbell's reference site, http://lawyers.martindale.com/ and at her current law firm, Landman & Beatty, http://www.landlaw.ws/lawyer.html/#virginia.

49. *Eli Lilly & Co v. Staats*, 574 F.2d 904.

50. Perry Secrest, "Commissioners, Magistrates, & Magistrate Judges Serving the Southern District of Indiana," unpublished staff study, 1997. Cody had been the law partner of Supreme Court Justice Sherman Minton.

51. 82 Stat. 1107.

52. "Magistrate Judgeships," Federal Judicial Center article, http://www.fjc.gov/history/home.nsf/page/magistrate_judges. The title of magistrate judge was not created by law until 1990.

53. *Reports of the Proceedings of the Judicial Conference of the United States*, March 16–17, 1970, p. 43; October 29–30, 1970, p. 69; October 26–27, 1972, p. 65; September 1–20, 1974, p. 85; March 9–10, 1978, p. 20; September 21–22, 1978, p. 63.

54. Secrest, "Commissioners, Magistrates, & Magistrate Judges Serving in

the Southern District of Indiana," 1–3; *Indianapolis Star*, March 3, 1971.

55. See his son's book, Tom Faulconer, *In the Eyes of the Law: The True Story of Love, Betrayal, Murder, Fame and Justice in 1950's America* (Bloomington, IN: First Books, 2000), 15–32, 104–12, 249–50. The authors express thanks to the Faulconer family for meeting with the authors and for sharing the judge's clipping file.

56. *Indianapolis Star*, October 27, 1985.

57. "Magistrate Judgeships." The relevant acts are 90 Stat. 2729 and 93 Stat. 643.

58. *Indianapolis Star*, October 27, 1985; *Harrison Post*, September 9, 1977; "Indiana's First Federal Magistrate Dies," *Indiana Lawyer*, January 26–February 8, 2005, p. 26.

59. *Visitors' Guide to the United States Court House, Indianapolis, Indiana, and the United States District Court for the Southern District of Indiana* (Indianapolis: Historical Society of the United States District Court for the Southern District of Indiana and the General Services Administration, 2003), 9; "Script for Building Tours" (Indianapolis: Historical Society of the United States District Court for the Southern District of Indiana, manuscript revised August 17, 2004), 5, 11.

60. Steckler interview, tape seven, 10–11. The actual inscription reads "United States Court House and Post Office"—and a later inscription on the north side in the 1930s addition reads the reverse: "United States Post Office and Court House."

61. Dillin interview, tape four, 19–20. The desk in question is now in the conference room of Judge John D. Tinder's chambers in Indianapolis.

62. Andrew R. Seager, *Federal Court Facilities in the Southern District of Indiana: A Working Bibliography* (Indianapolis: For the Architecture and Art Subcommittee, Court History Committee, United States District Court for the Southern District of Indiana, revised September 25, 2003), 2, 8, 16.

63. I. Scott Messinger, *Order in the Courts: A History of the Federal Court Clerk's Office* (Washington, DC: Federal Judicial Center), 52–61; *Recognition Dinner for the Presentation of Portrait of the Honorable William Steckler*, lxxxiv.

64. *Rules* [Effective January 1, 1957] (Indianapolis: United States District Court, Southern District of Indiana, 1956); *Rules of the United States District Court, Southern District of Indiana: Effective October 1, 1970* (Indianapolis: The Court, 1970).

65. The holdings of the Chicago branch are described on the National Archives and Records Administration (NARA) Web site, http://www.archives.gov/great-lakes/chicago/.

66. Dillin interview, tape three, side B, 13–14.

67. Ibid.

68. Judge Sarah Evans Barker, interview with the authors, July 7, 2005.

69. James Strain, moderator, "Court History Symposium," transcript (Indianapolis: Historical Society of the United States District Court for the Southern District of Indiana, 2003), 1–37.

70. Ibid., 19.

71. Ibid., 34–35.

72. Ibid., 7.

73. Ibid., 12.

74. Ibid., 10.

75. Ibid., 5–6.

76. Ibid., 10.

77. Ibid., 22.

78. Ibid., 25.

79. *Memorial Service for the Honorable Cale James Holder* (Indianapolis: United States District Court, Southern District of Indiana, Indiana Division, October 7, 1983), 28–30.

80. William F. Welch to A. Scott Chinn, October 2, 2003. A copy was provided to the authors.

81. Strain, "Court History Symposium," 7.

82. Ibid., 13.

83. Ibid., 29.

84. Welch to Chinn.

85. Strain, "Court History Symposium," 9.

86. Ibid., 16.

87. Ibid., 23–24.

88. Ibid., 23.

89. *Memorial Service and Courtroom Dedication for the Honorable James Noland*, 14.

90. Ibid., 23.

91. Strain, "Court History Symposium," 9.

92. *Recognition Dinner for the Presentation of Portrait of the Honorable William E. Steckler*, lxxxii.

93. Steven Harmon Wilson, *The Rise and Fall of Judicial Management in the U.S. District Court, Southern District of Texas, 1955–2000* (Athens: University of Georgia Press, 2002), 119; Lawrence Meir Friedman, *Crime and Punishment in American History* (New York: Basic Books, 1993), 411.

94. Dillin interview, tape 3, side B, 23.

95. Steckler interview, tape four, 9–12 (quotation on page 9).

96. Emma Lou Thornbrough, *Indiana Blacks in the Twentieth Century* (Bloomington: Indiana University Press, 2000) discusses this background in detail in chapters one through five.

97. Steckler interview, tape six, 16–17; Thornbrough, *Indiana Blacks in the Twentieth Century*, 35.

98. Several recent district court histories develop the southern precedents. See, for example, Wilson, *Rise of Judicial Management in the U.S. District Court, Southern District of Texas*, 11–49; Patricia Brake, *Justice in the Valley: A Bicentennial Perspective of the United States District Court for the Eastern District of Tennessee* (Franklin, TN: Hillsboro Press, 1998), 101–25; or Tony Allan Freyer, *Democracy and Judicial Independence: A History of the Federal Courts of Alabama, 1820–1994* (Brooklyn: Carlson Publishing, 1995), 135–214.

99. Thornbrough, *Indiana Blacks in the Twentieth Century*, 154–60; Colin Karn, "A Question of Consolidation" (master's thesis, Butler University, 2002), 14–17.

100. Thornbrough, *Indiana Blacks in the Twentieth Century*, 154–56.

101. Dillin interview, tape three, side B, 17–18.

102. Ibid., 19–20.

103. Thornbrough, *Indiana Blacks in the Twentieth Century*, 156–59; Karn, "Question of Consolidation," 27–31.

104. Thornbrough, *Indiana Blacks in the Twentieth Century*, 157–60.

105. Ibid.

106. *Recognition Dinner for the Presentation of Portrait of the Honorable William E. Steckler*, lxxxv.

107. Thornbrough, *Indiana Blacks in the Twentieth Century*, 160.

108. Ibid., 150.

109. *Indianapolis News*, August 25, 1983.

110. *Perry v. Columbia Broadcasting System, Inc.*, 499 F.2d 797 (7th Cir.), cert. den. 419 U.S. 883, 95 S. Ct. 150, 42 L.Ed.2d 123 (1974).

111. *Jennings v. Markley*, 186 F. Supp 611 (S.D. Ind. 1960), aff'd 290 F.2d 892 (7th Cir. 1961).

112. *International Society for Krishna Consciousness Inc. v. Bowen*, 456 F. Supp. 437 (S.D. Ind. 1978), aff'd 600 F.2d 667 (7th Cir. 1979), cert. den. 444 U.S. 963, 100 S. Ct. 448, 62 L.Ed.2d 375 (1979).

113. *Sandidge v. Rogers*, 167 F. Supp. 553 (S.D. Ind. 1958).

114. Lawrence H. Larsen, *Federal Justice in Western Missouri: The Judges, the Cases, the Times* (Columbia: University of Missouri Press, 1994), 225–26; *United States v. Paramount*, 334 U.S. 131, 68 S. Ct. 915, 92 L.Ed. 1260 (1948).

115. Steckler interview, tape four, 29–30, tape five, 1–2.

116. Ibid., tape five, 1.

117. *Allied Theatre Owners of Indiana Inc. v. Volpe*, 426 F.2d 1002 (7th Cir. 1970), cert. den. 400 U.S. 941, 91 S. Ct. 238, 27 L.Ed.2d 245 (1970).

118. Steckler interview, tape 7, 21–23.

119. Ibid., 22–23; *STP Corporation v. United States Auto Club, Inc.*, 286 F. Supp. 146 (S.D. Ind. 1968).

120. Steckler interview, tape four, 5–8; *Eli Lilly & Co. v. Schenley Laboratories Inc.*, 112 F. Supp. 296.

121. Steckler interview, tape three, side one, 24–25.

122. Barker interview, July 6, 2005.

Chapter 5

1. At the present time none of the currently serving judges has prepared an oral history of their service.

2. See Federal Judicial Center biographies, http://www.fjc.gov/.

3. "Barker, Sarah Evans," Federal Judicial Center biography, http://www.fjc.gov/servlet/tGetInfo?jid=94.

4. "McKinney, Larry J.," Federal Judicial Center biography, http://www.fjc.gov/servlet/tGetInfo?jid=1573.

5. "Tinder, John Daniel," Federal Judicial Center biography, http://www.fjc.gov/servlet/tGetInfojid=2392.

6. "Hamilton, David F.," Federal Judicial Center biography, http://www.fjc.gov/servlet/tGetInfo?jid=957.

7. "Young, Richard L.," Federal Judicial Center biography, http://www.fjc.gov/servlet/tGetInfo?jid=2754.

8. See FJC biographies.

9. Ibid.

10. Many additional examples of public service could be added to those listed in this short paragraph. Barker was a legal assistant in the U.S. House and Senate. McKinney was an Indiana Deputy Attorney General. Tinder was the Marion County Chief Trial Deputy Prosecutor, trying four death penalty cases. Young was a staff assistant to U.S. Congressman Philip H. Hayes from 1975 to 1976.

11. This section on appointment, and many of the other features of this chapter, relies heavily on interviews with various court and legal staff. The authors are indebted to them for their assistance on this project and are particularly grateful to the district judges who took time to meet with them: S. Hugh Dillin (June 18, 2004), Sarah Evans Barker (January 26, 2005), Larry J. McKinney (December 29, 2004), John D. Tinder (January 19, 2004), David F. Hamilton (October 5, 2004), and Richard L. Young (November 24, 2004 and July 25, 2005). They also express thanks to Magistrate Judge V. Sue Shields (August 3, 2005), attorney Terry Albright (July 14, 2005), and bankruptcy clerk John O'Neal (February 23, 2005). Their meetings with, and debts to,

clerk of the court Laura Briggs and law clerk Perry Secrest are too numerous to mention.

12. For examples of press coverage of the appointment process for these individuals, see the *Indianapolis Star*, October 1, 26, 1983 (Barker); *Indianapolis Star*, January 3, 1987, *Indianapolis News*, August 13, November 24, 1986 (McKinney and Tinder); *Indianapolis Star*, October 9, 1994 (Hamilton); and *Evansville Press*, March 3, April 22, 1998, and *Evansville Courier*, April 22, 1998 (Young).

13. *Indianapolis State Employees Ass'n v. Indiana Republican State Cent. Committee*, 630 F. Supp. 1194 (S.D. Ind. 1986).

14. *Plainfield Hendricks County Flyer*, February 22–28, 1994; *Terre Haute Tribune-Star*, July 18, 19, 20, 21, 1994, January 19, 1995; *Indianapolis Star*, July 20, 1990; *Indiana Legislative Insight*, June 8, 1992; *Louisville Courier-Journal*, June 4, 1992; *Indianapolis News*, June 4, 1992.

15. *Americanos v. Carter*, No. 1P94-C-0040 M/S (S.D. Ind.), 74 F.3d 138 (7th Cir. 1996), *cert. denied* 517 U.S. 1222, 116 S. Ct. 1853, 134 L.Ed.2d 953 (1996).

16. *United States v. Gutman*, 725 F.2d 417 (7th Cir. 1984), *cert. denied* 469 U.S. 880, 105 S. Ct. 244, 83 L.Ed.2d 183 (1984).

17. *United States v. Dugan*, 902 F.2d 585 (7th Cir. 1990), and *Dugan v. United States*, 18 F.3d 460 (7th Cir. 1994) (denying post-conviction relief).

18. IP 89-50-CR, Government's Sentencing Memorandum, June 21, 1989, pp. 3–5. Judge Sufana retired from the bench on October 1, 1987. IP 89-50-CR, Presentence Memorandum of Defendant, 13.

19. This company received the majority of liquidation and appraisal business dictated by the Bankruptcy Court in the Southern District of Indiana.

20. IP 89-50-CR, Government's Sentencing Memorandum, June 21, 1989, pp. 3–5.

21. IP 89-50-CR, Judgment in a Criminal Case, June 22, 1989.

22. 104 Stat. 5089.

23. The statistical tables are found at http://www.uscourts.gov/judbus2002/contents.html. The criminal figures are drawn from Tables

Notes 307

M-2 through M-5 that deal with cases handled by magistrate judges in the administrative year ending September 30, 2002. Table M-2 covers "Petty Offense Defendants Disposed of," M-3 "Felony Preliminary Proceedings Handled," M-4 "Criminal Pretrial Matters Handled," and M-5 Civil Consent Cases Terminated."

24. The assignments and salaries of this office are traced in detail in the *Report of the Proceedings of the Judicial Conference of the United States Held in Washington, D.C.,* September 19–20, 1979, p. 85; March 12–13, 1981, p. 32; September 24–25, 1981, p. 84; September 21–22, 1983, p. 75; March 8–9, 1984, p. 24; March 12–13, 1986, p. 25; March 17, 1987, p. 35; September 14, 1988, p. 97; and September 20, 1989, p. 76.

25. Staff study prepared by Perry Secrest, February 29, 1997, with subsequent information taken from court directory available at the court's Web site, http://www.insd.uscourts.gov.

26. Federal Judicial Center "Bankruptcy Judgeships." It references *Northern Pipeline Construction Co. v. Marathon Pipeline Co.*, 458 U.S. 50, 102 S.Ct. 2858, 73 L.Ed.2d 598 (1982), and 98 Stat.333 for the 1984 Act.

27. "U. S. Bankruptcy Courts, Business and Nonbusiness Bankruptcy Cases Commenced," Table F-2 of the Administrative Office Web site's statistical reports. The reporting period ends September 30, 2003.

28. For more on Judge Sufana, see pp. 7–8.

29. *Indianapolis Star*, April 19, 1987.

30. The fourteen articles, and accompanying supporting stories, appeared in the *Indianapolis Star* consecutively from April 19 to May 2, 1987.

31. *Indianapolis Star*, April 19, 1987.

32. Fitzpatrick/Brooks interview transcript, 26.

33. See the United States Bankruptcy Court Web site: http://www.insb.uscourts.gov.

34. *Press Release, United States District Court, October 18, 2005*, available on the court Web site, http://www.insd.uscourts.gov/Public/default.htm; *Indiana Lawyer*, September 21–October 4, 2005, pp. 3, 24.

35. The quotation is from District Judge Douglas Woodlock of Massachusetts in "The Renaissance of the Federal Courthouse," *The Third*

Branch, vol. 34, no. 12, December 2002, p. 7. Judge William Steckler was one of the individuals responsible for initiating this useful newsletter.

36. Building Tour script, 5, 8–11.

37. Memorial Service and Courtroom Dedication for the Honorable James E. Noland, December 11, 1992, pp. 24–25.

38. "The Renaissance of the Federal Courthouse," *The Third Branch,* vol. 34, no. 12, December 2002, pp. 1–7, which may also be viewed at the Administrative Office of the U.S. Courts Web site: http://www.uscourts.gov/newsroom/renaissance.htm.

39. "Renaissance" stresses the importance of the Administrative Office's 1991 *U.S. Courts Design Guide* in this process.

40. *Rules of the United States District Court Southern District of Indiana: Effective January 1, 1983* (Indianapolis: The Court, 1983); *Local Rules of the United States District Court for the Southern District of Indiana* (Indianapolis: The Court, 1992); *Attorney's Handbook* (Indianapolis: United States District Court, Southern District of Indiana, 1995).

41. *Inside Federal Court* video recording (Indianapolis: United States Attorney's Office, Southern District of Indiana and Office for Victims of Crime, Office of Justice Programs, U. S. Department of Justice, 1990–96).

42. Larry J. McKinney, David E. Bennett, and Theodore Lockyear, *Federal Civil Procedure before Trial—7th Circuit* (St. Paul, MN: West Group, 1998–).

43. http://icreport.loc.gov/cgi-bin/query/F?r102:1:./temp/~r102Vo4mv8:e0:

44. http://www.insd.uscourts.gov/Judges/bio_SEB.htm; author interview with Judge Barker, January 26, 2005.

45. http://www.insp.uscourts.gov/ThomasGahl.htm.

46. *Indianapolis News,* September 21, 1994, citing the *New York Times* wire service.

47. *Indiana Lawyer,* November 7–20, 2001, pp. 16–17.

48. The court's Web site, with many links, including a discussion of e-filing resources, is found at http://www.insd.uscourts.gov/. Computer management in the courts is discussed in L. Scott Messinger, *Order in the Courts: A History*

of the Federal Court Clerk's Office (Washington, DC: Federal Judicial Center, 2002), 71–73.

49. "U. S. District Court—Judicial Caseload Profile, Indiana Southern" located at http://www.uscourts.gov. Figures are tabulated for "*12-month period ending September 30.*"

50. James Strain, transcript, Court History Symposium, Luncheon and Panel Discussion: Reflections and Reminiscences on the Practice of Law in the Southern District 3, October 17, 2003, p. 15. See also Suzanne Buchko, "Three Bank Tellers Is Enough: Personal Reminiscences of Legal Practice by Members of the Bench and Bar," Courthouse Centennial Celebration and History Symposium, *Indiana Law Review*, 37 Ind. L. Rev. 699, 6.

51. Buchko, "Three Bank Tellers Is Enough," 15.

52. Fitzpatrick/Brooks interview, 39–40. See also *U. S. v. Bruscino*, 662 F.2d 450 (7th Cir. 1981) *aff'd en banc*, 687 F2d 938 (7th Cir. 1982) *cert denied*, 459 U.S. 1211, 103 S.Ct. 1205, 75 L.Ed.2d 446 (1983), and 459 U.S. 1228, 103 S.Ct. 1228, 75 L.Ed.2d 468 (1983).

53. *Reuther v. Southern Cross Club, Inc.*, 785 F.Supp. 1339 (S.D.Ind. 1992).

54. These, and a wealth of other revealing statistics, are available at the Administrative Office of the U.S. Courts Web site, http://www.uscourts.gov.

55. *Indianapolis Star*, December 8, 1992.

56. Interview with the authors, July 7, 2005.

57. Fitzpatrick/Dillin history, tape four transcript, 8.

58. *Craig v. Christ*, No. IP 96-1570-C-H/G, 1999 WL 1059704, (S.D.Ind. Sept. 10, 1999).

59. Ibid.

60. Emma Lou Thornbrough, *Indiana Blacks in the Twentieth Century* (Bloomington: Indiana University Press, 2000), 159–60; No. IP 68-C-225, Memorandum of Opinion, (S.D.Ind, Feb. 27, 1977), and Judgment (June 25, 1998); *United States v. Board of School Commissioners of the City of Indianapolis*, 128 F.3d 507 (7th Cir. 1997).

61. Lawrence Meir Friedman, *American Law in the 20th Century* (New Haven, CT: Yale University Press, 2002), 300–306.

62. *Eckles v. Consolidated Rail Corporation*, 890 F.Supp. 1391 (S.D.Ind. 1995), 94 F.3d 1041 (7th Cir. 1996), *cert. denied*, 520 U.S. 1146, 117 S.Ct. 1318, 137 L.Ed. 480 (1997).

63. *Hodgkins ex rel. Hodgkins v. Goldsmith*, 2000 WL 892964, 1 (S.D.Ind. July 3, 2000), *Bedford Herald-Times*, July 9, 12, 2000; *Indianapolis Star*, July 6, 2000.

64. *Hodgkins ex rel. Hodgkins v. Goldsmith*, 2000 WL 892964 (S.D.Ind. July 3, 2000), *amended* 2000 WL 1201599 (S.D.Ind. July 20, 2000); *Hodgkins v. Peterson*, 175 F.Supp.2d 1132 (S.D.Ind. 2001), *rev'd and remanded* 355 F.3d 1048 (7th Cir. 2004); *Evansville Courier & Press*, November 7, 2001.

65. The tests applied by the court are found in *Lee v. Weisman*, 505 U.S. 112 S.Ct. 2649, 120 L.Ed.2d 467 (1992) and *Lemon v. Kurtzman*, 403 U.S. 602, 91 S.Ct. 2105, 29 L.Ed.2d 745 (1971).

66. *Tanford v. Brand*, 932 F.Supp. 1139, 1143 (S.D.Ind. 1996).

67. Ibid., *Tanford v. Brand*, *aff'd* 104 F.3d 982 (7th Cir. 1997), *cert. denied*, 522 U.S. 814, 118 S.Ct. 60, 139 L.Ed.2d 23 (1997).

68. *Indiana Civil Liberties Union v. O'Bannon*, 110 F.Supp.2d 842 (S.D.Ind. 2000), *aff'd* 259 F.3d 766 (7th Cir. 2001), *cert. denied*, 534 U.S. 1162, 122 S.Ct. 1173, 152 L.Ed.2d 117 (2002); *Kimbley v. Lawrence County Indiana*, 119 F.Supp.2d 856 (S.D.Ind. 2000).

69. *United States v. Indianapolis Baptist Temple*, 61 F.Supp.2d 831 (S.D.Ind. 1999) and 61 F.Supp.2d 836 (S.D.Ind. 1999), *both aff'd at* 224 F.3d 627 (7th Cir. 2000), *cert. denied*, 531 U.S. 112, 121 S.Ct. 857, 148 L.Ed.2d 771 (2001).

70. *United States v. Indianapolis Baptist Temple*, 2001 WL 522416 (S.D.Ind. April 6, 2001).

71. Friedman, *American Law in the 20th Century*, 196–99.

72. *Government Suppliers v. Bayh*, No. IP 90-303-C (S.D.Ind); *Waste Tech News*, April 9, 1990, p. 1; *Indianapolis News*, June 26, September 10, December 27, 28, 1990; *Indianapolis Star*, April 8, June 29, July 3, 31, August 5, December 28, 31, 1990; *Miami Herald*, December 28, 1990; *Atlanta Constitution*, December 29, 1990.

73. *Government Suppliers Consolidating Services, Inc. v. Bayh*, 975 F.2d 1267 (7th Cir. 1992), *cert. denied*, 506 U.S. 1053, 113 S.Ct. 977, 122 L.Ed.2d 131 (1993).

74. *Indianapolis Star*, April 16, 1995.

75. *United States v. Seymour Recycling Corp.*, 554 F.Supp 1334 (S.D.Ind. 1982).

76. Ibid., 618 F.Supp. 1 (S.D.Ind. 1984).

77. Many studies review the changing American economy. For a good popular account, based heavily upon government data, see Theodore Caplow, et al., *The First Measured Century* (Washington, DC: American Enterprise Institute, 2001). Chapter nine, pp. 160–79, summarizes family income data; chapter seven, pp. 120–33, reviews leisure trends.

78. *Mays v. Trump Indiana, Incorporated*, 255 F.3d 351 (7th Cir. 2001). The decision is rich in humorous invective directed toward the perceived greed of the plaintiffs.

79. Fitzpatrick/Steckler interview transcript, tape five, 2–3; *Indianapolis Colts v. Mayor and City Council of Baltimore*, 741 F.2d 954 (7th Cir. 1984), *cert. denied*, 470 U.S. 1052, 105 S.Ct. 1753, 84 L.Ed.2d 817 (1985).

80. *Fazekas v. Crain Consumer Group Div. of Crain Communications, Inc.*, 583 F.Supp. 110 (S.D.Ind. 1984).

81. Fitzpatrick/Steckler interview transcript, tape six, 11–13.

82. *Harris v. Mutual of Omaha Companies*, 1992 WL 421489 (S.D.Ind. August 26, 1992), *aff'd* 992 F.2d 706 (7th Cir. 1993).

83. *Indianapolis Star*, April 15, 2005 ("Maker of Generic Drugs to Appeal").

84. *Eli Lilly and Co. v. Zenith Goldline Pharmaceuticals*, 364 F.Supp.2d 820, 829-830 (S.D.Ind. 2005).

85. *Indianapolis Star*, April 15, 2005 ("Lilly Wins Round 1 of Zyprexa Battle: Appeal Is Certain and Likely Will Take a Year or Longer").

86. *Eli Lilly, supra*, 364 F.Supp.2d at 830.

87. *Indianapolis Star*, April 15, 2005 ("Lilly Wins Round 1 of Zyprexa Battle: Appeal Is Certain and Likely Will Take a Year or Longer").

88. See, for example, *Eli Lilly, supra*, 364 F.Supp.2d at 830–836, 852–869, 896–897.

89. *Indianapolis Star*, April 15, 2005 ("Maker of Generic Drugs to Appeal"). The appeal, docketed under docket number 05-1396, was filed on May 13, 2005, and was pending at the time of publication.

90. Fitzpatrick/Dillin history, tape four transcript, 8–9.

91. Bureau of Prisons Web site, *Executions of Federal Prisoners (since 1927)*, 3; the other executions were Juan Raul Garze in 2001 and Louis Jones in 2003: www.bop.gov//about/history/execchart.jsp.

92. Interview with Larry J. McKinney, December 29, 2004.

93. *Watkins v. Miller*, 92 F.Supp.2d 824 (S.D.Ind. 2000).

94. Ibid. at 826.

95. Ibid. at 828.

96. Ibid. at 827.

97. Ibid. at 838.

98. Ibid. at 840.

99. Ibid. at 857.

100. *Watkins v. Miller*, 2000 WL 680421 (S.D.Ind., May 15, 2000).

101. Those interested in Judge Hamilton's approach to questions involving strong public and private feelings should also see his decision in *A Woman's Choice Eastside Women's Clinic v. Newman*, 132 F.Supp.2d 1150 (S.D.Ind. 2001), *rev'd*, 305 F.3d 684 (7th Cir. 2002), *cert. denied*, 537 U.S. 1192, 123 S.Ct. 1273, 154 L.Ed.2d 1026 (2003).

102. *Entertainment Network Inc. v. Lappin, Harley*, No. TH 01-C-76-T/H; *Indianapolis Star*, April 19, 2001.

103. *French v. Owens*, 538 F.Supp. 910 (S.D.Ind. 1982), *aff'd in part, rev'd in part* 777 F.2d 1250 (7th Cir. 1985), *cert. denied*, 479 U.S. 817, 107 S.Ct. 77, 93 L.Ed.2d 32 (1986).

104. *Jones v. Kelley*, No. IP 90-C-1448-M/F; *Indianapolis News*, March 31, 1993; *Indianapolis Star*, April 1, 1993.

105. *Marion County Jail Inmates v. Cottey*, 2002 WL 1042167 (S.D.Ind. April 29, 2002); *Marion County Jail Inmates v. Anderson*, 270 F.Supp.2d 1034 (S.D.Ind. 2003).

106. *Schaefer v. Newton*, 868 F. Supp. 246 (S.D.Ind. 1994), *aff'd*, 57 F.3d 1073 (7th Cir. 1995). The quotation from the book is on page 298 of Michael Newton, *Hunting Humans: The Encyclopedia of Serial Killers* (Port Townsend, WA: Loompanics Unlimited, 1990), reprinted as a mass market paperback by Avon Books in 1992 and 1993. The book is referenced by this title in the

court records, and in Worldcat, but appears only by its subtitle in some other bibliographic listings.

107. *Sanders v. City of Indianapolis*, 837 F.Supp 959, 960 (S.D. Ind. 1992). See also: http://www2.indystar.com/library/factfiles/crime/law_enforcement/line_of_duty/deaths.html.

108. *Sanders v. City of Indianapolis*, 837 F.Supp. 959 (S.D.Ind. 1992).

109. *American Booksellers Association, Inc., v. William H. Hudnut, III, Mayor of the City of Indianapolis*, 598 F.Supp. 1316 (S.D.Ind. 1984), *aff'd*, 771 F.2d 323 (7th Cir. 1985), *aff'd*, 475 U.S. 1001, 106 S.Ct. 1172, 89 L.Ed.2d 291 (1986).

110. *American Booksellers Association, Inc., v. William H. Hudnut, III, Mayor of the City of Indianapolis*, 598 F.Supp. 1332.

111. Ibid., 1327.

112. Ibid., 1337-1339.

113. Ibid., 1336.

114. *American Booksellers Association, Inc., v. William H. Hudnut, III, Mayor of the City of Indianapolis, supra*, 771 F.2d 323, 330-331 (7th Cir. 1985).

115. *American Amusement Machine Association v. Kendrick*, 115 F.Supp.2d 943 (S.D.Ind. 2000), *rev'd*, 244 F.3d 572 (7th Cir.), *cert. denied*, 534 U.S. 994, 122 S.Ct. 462, 151 L.Ed.2d 379 (2001).

116. Fitzpatrick/Steckler interview transcript, tape four, 16–21.

117. *United States v. Kimberlin*, 527 F.Supp. 1010 (S.D.Ind. 1981), *aff'd*, 805 F.2d 210 (7th Cir. 1986), *cert. denied*, 483 U.S. 1023, 107 S.Ct. 3270, 97 L.Ed.2d 368 (1987).

118. *United States v. Wolf*, 787 F.2d 1094 (7th Cir. 1986). The Court of Appeals for the Seventh Circuit held that "(1) instruction which permitted jury to convict defendant under Mann Act if it found that he was harboring immoral design when he took women across state lines, even if those designs played no causal role in the transportation, was plain error, and (2) prosecutor's improper cross-examination of defendant and defense counsel's ineffectiveness denied defendant fair trial." See also *Indianapolis News*, November 30, December 7, 1984; *Indianapolis Star*, December 3, 7, 8, 1984.

119. *Indianapolis Star*, October 11, 12, 13, 1984.

120. No. IP 84-91-CR02; *Indianapolis News*, October 12, 1984.

121. *United States v. Michael Brown*, No. TH 02-19-CR-01 T/L; *Indiana Lawyer*, November 20–December 3, 2002, pp. 3, 11.

122. *United States v. Payne*, No. IP00-CR-0129-01-T/F; *Indianapolis Star*, August 20, September 14, 2000, January 31, 2001; *Indianapolis Monthly*, February, 2001, pp. 112–17, 216–24 contains a detailed review of the story.

123. *United States v. Francis Joe Holland*, No. EV 96-14-CR-01-T/H; *Evansville Press*, April 23, 30, 1997; *Evansville Courier*, May 3, 1997.

124. See the *Indianapolis Star*, June 30, 1985, feature article on drug task forces for a particularly good summary of local efforts. The context within which the federal courts operate is nicely summarized in Carol Hoffecker, *Federal Justice in the First State: A History of the United States District Court for Delaware* (Wilmington: The Historical Society for the United States District Court for the District of Delaware, 1992), 191–93.

125. The decision and its context have been widely discussed and evaluated. For press summaries reflecting the opinions of observers and commentators see: Constance Lowenthal, "Custody Battle Over Byzantine Mosaics," *The Wall Street Journal*, July 28, 1989; Jess Birnbaum, "Romancing the Stones," *Time* (International Edition), July 31, 1989, pp. 28–29; R. Joseph Gelarden, "Mosaics Belong in Cyprus, Court Says," *Indianapolis Star*, August 4, 1989; John Dorsey, "Case Alters Rules for Art Transactions," *The Philadelphia Enquirer*, August 15, 1989; Steve Mannheimer, "Litigators of the Lost Art," *The Saturday Evening Post*, October, 1989, pp. 63–68; Stanley Meisler, "Art and Avarice," *Los Angeles Times Magazine*, November 12, 1989, pp. 8–17. For examples of journal articles and opinions see: Charles Palmer, "Stolen Art and the Struggle for Good Title," *The Entertainment and Sports Lawyer*, vol. 7, no. 4 (Winter, 1990): 1, 8–17; Christopher Chippindale, "Editorial," *Antiquity*, vol. 63, no. 241 (December, 1989): 651–54; Demetrios Michaelides, "The Early Christian Mosaics of Cyprus," *Biblical Archaeologist*, vol. 52, no. 4, (December, 1989): 192–202.

126. The definitive modern history of the church and its art is: A. H. S. Megaw & Ernest Hawkins, *The Church of the Panagia Kanakaria at Lythrankomi in Cyrus: Its Mosaics and Frescoes* (Washington, DC: Dumbarton Oaks Center for Byzantine Studies, 1977).

127. *Autocephalous Greek-Orthodox Church of Cyprus v. Goldberg & Feldman Fine Arts, Inc.*, 717 F. Supp. 1394, 1378 (S.D.Ind. 1989). The mosaics were stolen in August 1976 and October 1979, during the occupation of northern Cyprus by Turkish forces.

128. The case was extensively covered in the national and world press. For examples of coverage incorporating the theme of international intrigue, see *Boston Globe*, May 13, 1989; *New York Times*, May 17, 1989; *International Herald-Tribune*, May 20–21, 1989; and *Los Angeles Times*, May 30, 1989.

129. *Autocephalous Greek-Orthodox Church of Cyprus v. Goldberg & Feldman Fine Arts, Inc.*, 717 F. Supp. 1394, 1377 (S.D.Ind. 1989), *aff'd*, 917 F.2d 278 (7th Cir. 1990). No case before the modern court has a lengthier bibliography. This section of chapter five is based primarily upon the texts of the decisions rendered in the district and circuit courts, cited above.

130. *Autocephalous Greek-Orthodox Church of Cyprus v. Goldberg & Feldman Fine Arts, Inc.*, 717 F. Supp. 1394, 1377, 1378 (S.D.Ind. 1989).

131. Ibid., 1394.

132. Ibid., 1303–1304.

133. Ibid., 1402.

134. Ibid., 1404. Judge Noland's decision was the subject of a number of generally favorable editorials. See as examples: "Let the Art Buyer Beware," *Los Angeles Times*, August 7, 1989; "Caveat, Art Dealers," *Atlanta Constitution*, August 7, 1989; "Return to Sender," *Washington Post*, August 10, 1989; "The Cyprus Mosaics," *Indianapolis Star*, August 13, 1989.

135. *Autocephalous Greek-Orthodox Church, supra*, 917 F.2d 293.

136. Keith Highet and George Kahale III, "Autocephalous Greek-Orthodox Church of Cyprus v. Goldberg & Feldman Fine Arts, Inc.," *American Journal of International Law*, vol. 86, no. 1 (January 1992): 128–33.

137. *Louisville Courier Journal*, June 2, 1991; *Huntington Herald Press*, June 2, 1991; *Indianapolis Star*, June 3, 1991.

138. *Investiture of Richard L. Young, United States District Judge* (Evansville: United States District Court for the Southern District of Indiana, Evansville Division, April 21, 1998), 21.

Glossary of Legal Terms

certiorari (writ of) Latin, "to be informed," (abbreviated *cert.*). Technically, a writ or order issued by an appellate court directing a lower court to deliver a certified record of a case for review. The term commonly refers to the process by which the United States Supreme Court selects the appeals that it will hear. Virtually all of the appeals heard by the Supreme Court today are discretionary and it grants only about 1 percent of the petitions for certiorari that it receives. If a petition is granted, the certified record is now merely requested from the lower court; the actual writ is rarely issued.

de facto Latin, "in point of fact." Actual; existing in fact, not as a matter of law.

de jure   Latin, "as a matter of law." Existing by right or according to law.

demurrer   French, "to wait or stay." An older pleading stating that, while the facts in a complaint might be true, they do not sufficiently state a cause of action. In current federal practice, the function of the demurrer has been replaced by the motion to dismiss.

diversity jurisdiction   A federal court's power or authority to hear cases based on state law between parties from different states that also involves a minimum amount in controversy (currently $75,000).

federal question jurisdiction   A federal court's authority to hear cases arising under federal law or treaties.

grand jury   A group of citizens impanelled by a court to investigate and/or determine whether probable cause exists to file felony criminal charges against a person. A grand jury does not determine guilt or innocence, only whether probable cause exists to initiate criminal proceedings against a person. Prosecutors also utilize a grand jury to issue subpoenas, investigate, and gather the evidence necessary to make a probable-cause case. While the grand jury just determines the issue of whether probable cause exists, it is still up to prosecutorial discretion whether to go ahead and file the charges.

habeas corpus   Latin, "you have the body." The traditional means by which a detained person obtains independent court review of the legality of his confinement. Technically, it refers to the ancient writ or order issued by a court to a detainee's custodian to bring the detainee before the court for further proceedings.

injunction   A court order that an action be taken or not taken.

petit jury   A group of citizens impanelled by a court to determine the facts and render a verdict in a trial.

pro se   Latin, "for self." The term applied to someone who acts as his or her own attorney in a court proceeding.

receiver   A person appointed by a court to protect, collect, or manage property that is the subject of litigation.

recuse   An act by which a judge removes himself or herself from hearing a case. Either party in a case may move for recusal of a judge, or the judge may recuse himself or herself on his or her own initiative.

summary judgment   A ruling by a judge on a claim or defense without trial where there is no genuine issue of material fact and judgment is entered as a matter of law.

voir dire   French, "to speak the truth." Part of the jury selection process, by which a potential juror is questioned by the judge or the lawyers to determine whether the person is qualified and suitable to serve on a jury.

Index

Abolition, 34
Adams, John, 13
Administrative Office of the United States Courts, 189, 222, 229, 235
Admiralty law cases, 101, 117
Air Quality Act (1967), 244
Altes, Peggy Sue, 253, 254, 255
American Bridge Company, 119
American Can Company, 148
American Federation of Labor, 119
American Judicature Society, 230
Americanos, Peter, 219
Americans with Disabilities Act (ADA), 240, 241
Anderson, Albert Barnes, 99, 108–118, 121, 122–24, 125, 126, 135–36, 142, 151; (illus.), 109

Anderson, Frank, 231, 244
Annakin, Joseph Woody, 185
Antitrust cases, 154, 155, 248
Appeals, 19–20
Appellate court, 131, 132; jurisdiction, 19
Armstrong, John, 7, 8
Arnold, Walter, 140
Arthur, Chester, 84, 85, 93, 94, 95
Articles of Confederation, 5
Aspinwall v. County Commissioners, 49
Attorney's Handbook, 230
Auto racing, 206–7, 247
Auto Week (magazine), 248
Autocephalous Greek-Orthodox Church, 265, 266, 268–69, 270

Badollet, John, 19
Baker, Albert, 108–9
Baker, Conrad, 83, 94
Baker, Francis, 104
Baker, John Harris, 93, 96–97, 98–99, 100–101, 102, 104, 105, 108; (illus.), 94
Baker, Tim A., 223; (illus.), 234
Baker & Daniels (law firm), 93
Baltimore, 248
Baltzell, Robert, 136, 142–48, 151–52, 153, 154, 155–56, 157–58, 161, 162, 181, 182; (illus.), 141
Bankruptcy, 76, 77; courts, 31, 221–23; cases, 154, 175–76, 220, 223–26
Bankruptcy Act (1841), 30–31
Bankruptcy Act (1867), 77
Baptist Encyclopedia, 39
Barker, Sarah Evans, 184, 191, 192, 193, 194, 195, 196, 209, 212, 213, 214, 215, 216, 220, 229, 230, 231, 235, 242, 256, 257–61; (illus.), 175, 213, 259
Barnes, Hickum, Pantzer and Boyd (law firm), 181
Barnes & Thornburg (law firm), 181
Barrett, George, 146–47
Bartholomew, Pliny Webster, 72
Barton, William, 7
Bassett, Horace, 25
Bauer, William J., 270
Bayh, Birch E., 173, 174, 175, 178, 225, 227
Bayh, Evan, 195, 215
Bayt, Philip, 187
Bayt, Robert L., 225, 226
Beatty, James, 173

Belknap, Jerry, 181
Bell, Mifflin, 88
Bell, William, 29
Beveridge, Albert, 104, 108
Bickham, Harold, 231
Bingham, Fred, 138
Bingham, Gordon, 74
Bingham, John, 74
"Black History: Lost, Stolen, or Strayed," 203
Blackstone, William, 23
Blaine, James G., 84
Blake, Thomas, 25
Blatchford, Samuel, 81
"Block of five" case, 103–4
Blue Cross and Blue Shield, 249
Bombings, 118–20, 262
Bradley, Bill, 244
Brady v. Maryland, 253
Bridgestone/Firestone case, 233
Briggs, Laura A. (illus.), 259
Bright, Jesse, 26
Bristow, Benjamin, 75
Brooks, Gene Edward, 173–78, 212, 226–27, 234–35; (illus.), 175
Brown, Jack C., 167
Brown v. Board of Education, 199–200, 201
Browne, Thomas, 87
Brownell, Herbert, Jr., 167
Bryan, William Jennings, 98–99, 151
Burnett, Henry, 64
Burns, Howard, 164
Busing, 237
Butler, John H., 134
Butler, Nobel Chase, 90, 94, 117, 133–35, 154; (illus.), 133

Cain, John, 44
Callahan, William, 143
Camp Atterbury, 157
Capehart, Homer E., 163, 166
Capital Improvement Board, 248
Carter, Jimmy, 173, 184
Carter, Pamela, 219
Carter, Solon, 148
Caseloads, 181–84, 189, 209, 219–20, 232, 235–37
Cathcart, William, 39
Caven, John, 76
Cayton, Andrew, 17
Central Christian Leadership Conference, 179
Central Competitive Field, 122
Chambers, Smiley, 96
Chancery jurisdiction, 18, 19
Chase, Salmon P., 134
Chavis, Patrick, 179
Christian, Grant, 153
Church of Panayia Kanakaria, 265
Circuit courts, 26, 85, 87; judges of, 26–27; jurisdiction, 27
Civil Justice Reform Act (1990), 236
Civil Legal Assistance Panel, 232
Civil liberties, 204
Civil Rights Act (1964), 199
Civil rights cases, 159–60, 198–204, 209, 239–41
Civil War, 51, 53, 61–62, 72
Clark, Charles, 149
Clark, Mary, 36
Clark, William, 1, 13
Clay, Henry, 33, 38
Clayton Antitrust Act (1914), 125, 148, 205

Clean Air Act, 246
Clerks, 25, 90, 189–90, 232–33
Cleveland, Grover, 85
Clinton, Bill, 212, 215; (illus.), 216
Coachys, James K., 226; (illus.), 224
Coal, 244; mining, 122
Cobourn, Henry, 24
Cody, John, Jr., 184, 185, 223
Coke, Edward, 23
Columbia Broadcasting System (CBS), 203, 204
Columbian Exposition (1893), 128
Commissioners, 184, 185, 208
Common law, 10, 14, 18
Compagnoitte, Charles, 2
Comprehensive Drug Abuse Prevention and Control Act (1970), 196–97
Compromise of 1850, p. 44
Confederation Congress (New York), 2, 5, 7
Conference of Senior Circuit Judges. *See* Judicial Conference of the United States
Confiscation Acts (1861, 1862), 62
Confiscation cases, 62, 63
Conformity Act, 148
Congressional Land Law (1800), 13
Conrail, 240
Constitutional Convention (Philadelphia), 2, 4
Conveyor (ship), 117
Cooley, _____ (judge), 112
Coolidge, Calvin, 137, 139, 142, 143
Corruption cases, 217–19
Corydon, 21, 22
Cosby, Bill, 204
Court reporting, 191–92

Courts and Lawyers of Indiana, 8
Cowgill, Margaret Lung, 140, 155
Coy, Simeon, 103
Craig, Richard, 238
Crane Naval Depot, 157
Cravens, James Harrison, 42
Crescent City (tow boat), 101
Criminal cases, 25, 26, 29, 196–98, 262–65
Crispus Attucks High School, 201
Cudahy, Richard, 215
Curfew law, 241
"Custom of the country," 10, 14

Daniels, Edward, 108
Darrow, Clarence, 119, 120
Davis, David, 46, 54, 68–69, 70, 90–91; (illus.), 68
Davis, Thomas Terry, 13, 16, 19
Daylight saving time, 206
Death penalty cases, 252–53
Defamation cases, 203–4
Desegregation, 179, 199, 200–203, 239–40
Devens, Charles, 78
Dewey, Charles, 23, 24, 30, 40, 42
Dikmen, Aydin, 266, 269
Dillin, S. Hugh, 169–71, 180, 183, 188, 190, 191, 194, 195, 196, 197, 200–202, 205, 212, 228, 237, 238–39, 252, 255; (illus.), 170, 175
Discretionary funds, 246
District attorneys, 25, 26, 86
District courts, 26, 27, 85, 86–87, 131, 132
DNA tests, 253, 254, 255
Dodd, Harrison, 65, 66

Douglas, Stephen A., 44
"Downtown Police Brawl," 238
Draft laws, 64
Drug cases, 264–65
Drummond, Thomas, 78, 84, 85
Drummond, William, 73
Dudley, William W., 83, 84, 91, 104
Duffy, Robert, 184
Dugan, Michael T., II, 220
Dunlap, William, 91
Dunn, Jacob Piatt, 74
Dyer Act (1919), 145

Easterbrook, Frank H., 261
Eckles, Terry, 240–41
Eighteenth Amendment, 126
Eighth Amendment, 256
Eisenhower, Dwight D., 164, 166, 168
Election fraud, 82–83, 87, 91, 102–4, 113–14
Election recounts, 179–80
Eli Lilly and Company, 184, 207, 208, 250–52
Eli Lilly and Company v. Zenith Goldline Pharmaceuticals, 250
Emancipation Proclamation, 62
Enabling Act, 149
Endsley, J. Patrick, 223
English, Elisha, 91
Entertainment Network Inc., 255
Environmental cases, 244–46
Esarey, Logan, 8
Eschbach, Jesse, 171
Establishment Clause. *See* First Amendment
Evans, Charles, 90
Evansville, 87, 88; courthouse, 189

Evansville Housing Authority, 199
Ex parte Milligan, 53, 63–70
Excise tax, 197–98
Executions, 146, 252–53

Faber, Matt John, 256
Fairbanks, Charles Warren, 98, 104
Faulconer, Thomas J., 186–87, 223, 263; (illus.), 186
Fazekas, Dale, 248–49
Federal Bureau of Investigation (FBI), 130, 217, 221
Federal Judges Association, 230
Federal Judicial Center, 182, 185
Federal Magistrates Act of 1968, p. 185
Feller, Albert, 118
Fetchit, Stepin. *See* Perry, Lincoln Theodore
Fielding, Henry, 23
Fifth Amendment, 99
Fillmore, Millard, 46
Firearms cases, 262–64
First Amendment, 242, 258, 260, 261
Fishback, William Pinkney, 90
Fleming, Wray H., 167
Food and Drug Administration (FDA), 208
Foreign Intelligence Surveillance Court, 230
Fort Wayne Treaty (1809), 20
Foster, John, 84
Foster, Kennard P., 223; (illus.), 234
Fourth Amendment, 241
Franklin, Benjamin, 2
Fraud cases, 262–64
Freire, Helena, 263
Friedman, Lawrence, 78, 177

Frische, Mike, 232
Fugitive Slave Act (1793), 35, 41
Fugitive Slave Act (1850), 47, 48, 49
Fugitive slave cases, 36–37, 41–42, 46, 47, 48–49

Gabbert, D. Joe, 185
Gahl, Thomas E., 230
Galilean Magazine, 157
Gallatin, Albert, 19
Galvin, Timothy, 140
Gambling, 113, 247
Gates, Ralph F., 167
Geddes, Robert, 185
General Services Administration (GSA), 228–29
Geneva (Switzerland), 266
Getty Museum, 266
Gilliam, Arthur L., 138
Gilligan's Island, 235
Gilman, Joseph, 7
Godich, John Paul, 223; (illus.), 234
Goldberg, Peg, 265, 266, 268, 269, 270
Gompers, Samuel, 119, 121
Goodloe, Charles, 195, 233, 234
Goshen News, 96
Gottfried v. Crescent Brewing Co., 79–81, 82
Government Suppliers Consolidating Services Inc., 245
Granatelli, Andy, 206–7
Grand jury, 1–2, 20, 27, 103
Grant, Ulysses S., 70, 72, 73
Great Depression, 151, 152, 155
Greater Indianapolis Amusements Inc., 205
Gresham, Otto, 78

Gresham, Walter Q., 70–85, 93, 94, 95, 101, 103, 134; (illus.), 71
Griffin, John, 1, 13, 16
Gun Control Act (1968), 263
Gutman, Philip E., 219–20

Hack v. American Surety, 155
Hall, Arvin, 174, 175
Hamilton, David F., 212, 213, 215, 241, 253–55, 260; (illus.), 175, 218
Hammond, 87
Handley, Harold W., 167
Hanna, Mark, 104
Hanna, Robert, 26
Harbin, John, 20
Harbin, Joshua, 20
Hare Krishna, 204
Hargrave, A. A., 110
Harlan, John Marshall, 103
Harris, Judith, 249–50
Harrison, Benjamin, 75, 83, 84, 85, 93, 94, 95, 96, 103, 104
Harrison, Bertha, 192
Harrison, William Henry, 1, 13, 14, 15, 16, 20, 25, 26, 44
Harrison Marching Society, 112
Harrison Narcotics Drug Act (1914), 126
Hartke, Vance, 169, 170, 171, 174, 179–80, 181
Hawkins, Edward, 91
Hayes, Rutherford B., 76, 77
Hays, Will, 142
Health care, 249–52
Heartland Financial Services, 264
Hendricks, Thomas, 66, 83

Hendricks, William, 26
Hendry, W. J., 116
Henegar, Thomas, 137
Herbal remedies, 208
Hickam, Hubert, 181
Hickey, Andrew, 137, 138
Hilton, Andrew, 29
Hines, Cyrus, 94
Historic Landmarks Foundation of Indiana, 134
Historical Society of the United States District Court for the Southern District of Indiana, 227
Hobbs, Barnabas, 41
Hogate, E. G., 108
Holder, Cale J., 164–69, 176–77, 190, 191, 192–94, 203, 205, 212, 233; (illus.), 165
Holland, Joe, 264
Holloway, W. R., 76
Holman, Jesse Lynch, 25, 27, 31, 32–36, 38, 41, 72; (illus.), 32
Holstein, Charles, 94
Horse Thieves Protective Association, 99
Housing Division of the Federal Emergency Administration of Public Works, 156
Howard, Tilghman, 26
Howland, John D., 72, 90, 91, 92
Hudnut, William, 201
Hughes, Charles Evans, 124, 125
Hunting Humans: The Encyclopedia of Serial Killers, 256
Huntington, Elisha Mills, 28, 30, 42–50, 52, 53; (illus.), 43
Hurst, Henry, 21, 25

Hussman, William G., Jr., 223; (illus.), 234
Hynes, T. A., 138

Ice, Harry T., 132, 148
Ice Miller Donadio & Ryan (law firm), 132
Immigration, 262
In re Clark, 36, 38, 41
In re Susan, 41
Income tax, 125, 126
Indentured servants, 35, 36
Indiana Civil Liberties Union (ICLU), 241
Indiana Constitution (1816): and slavery, 35, 36
Indiana Constitution (1851), 243, 247
Indiana Constitutional Convention (1816), 16
Indiana Constitutional Convention (1850), 43
Indiana Court of Appeals, 254
Indiana General Assembly, 202
Indiana General Court, 18, 19
Indiana Historical Society, 41, 134
Indiana Railroad Association, 220
Indiana Railroad Commission, 117
Indiana Reformatory, 255
Indiana Republican State Central Committee, 217
Indiana State Bar Association, 91–92
Indiana State Employees Association, 217
Indiana State Library, 92
Indiana State Press Association Inc., 167–68

Indiana Supreme Court, 36
Indiana Territory, 1, 10, 271; court of, 11–20
Indiana University (Bloomington), 241–42
Indianapolis: railroad strike in, 76–77; district court offices in, 87
Indianapolis, Bloomington and Western Railroad, 77
Indianapolis Baptist Temple (IBT), 243
Indianapolis City-County Council, 261
Indianapolis Colts, 248
Indianapolis Courthouse. *See* U.S. Courthouse and Post Office Building (Indianapolis)
Indianapolis 500 Mile Race, 206
Indianapolis Housing Authority, 239, 240
Indianapolis Journal, 60, 61
Indianapolis Museum of Art, 271
Indianapolis News, 84, 96, 98, 100, 111, 166
Indianapolis Police Department, 238, 241
Indianapolis Public Schools (IPS), 200, 201, 202, 239
Indianapolis Sentinel, 45
Indianapolis Star, 144, 154, 166, 169, 187, 225, 236
Indianapolis Times, 144, 152, 168
Injunctions, 77–78, 180
Inside Federal Court (video), 230
Intellectual property cases. *See* Patent law
Internal Revenue Service (IRS), 144, 243

International Association of Bridge and Structural Iron Workers, 119
International Foundation for Art Research, 268
Interstate Commerce Clause, 245, 246
Irsay, Robert, 248

Jack Castenova Inc., 245
Jackson, Andrew, 33, 34, 35, 38
Jacobs, Andrew, Jr., 173, 229
Jefferson, Thomas, 13, 16
Jenkins, James, 85
Jenner, William, 163, 164, 166, 167, 190
Jennings, Jonathan, 16, 37, 40
Jennings, Wyatt, 204
Johnson, Lyndon B., 171, 173
Johnston, General Washington, 36
Jones, Acquilla Q., 93
Jones, Clyde A., 137
Jones, David M., 256
Jordan, James, 110
Judicial Advisory Committee, 230
Judicial appointment, 161–78
Judicial Code of 1911, p. 133
Judicial Conference of the United States, 154, 161
Judicial Improvement Act, 222
Judicial Panel on Multidistrict Litigation, 233
Judicial power, 3, 4, 6, 7, 10, 19
Judicial tenure, 3, 7
Julian, George W., 48, 55
Jurisdiction, 3, 4, 6, 18, 19, 27, 87, 107, 132, 148, 155, 187, 270
Justices of the peace, 14, 18

Kanakaria mosaics, 265-71; (illus.), 267
Kappes, William, 154
Kastenmeier, Robert, 231
Kautzman, John, 194
Kearns, Michael H., 225
Kellogg, Thomas, 128
Kennedy, Bobby, 171
Kennedy, John F., 169
Kercheval, _____ (marshal), 100
Kiley, David, 170
Kimberlin, Brett, 223, 262
King, John, 63
Klein, Nelson, 146
Knights of the Golden Circle, 61, 64
Krieg DeVault LLP (law firm), 93
Krum, Chester, 120
Ku Klux Klan, 99, 140

Labor violence, 118–22
Ladoga Canning, 148
Land cessions, 29–30
Landfills, 244–46
Landis, Charles B., 108
Lane, Amos, 34
Languedoc, Fr., 2
Lautenberg Amendment (1996), 263
Law schools, 92
Lawrence, William T., 223, 234; (illus.), 234
Lawrence County Courthouse (Bedford), 242
Leckrone, Walter, 168
Lee test, 242
Legal codes, 8, 14, 15, 85
Legal professionalism, 92–93, 183–84
Lemon test, 242, 243

Index 329

Lever Act, 124
Lewellen (boat), 101
Lewis, Irving, 156
Lewis, John L., 122, 125, 143
Lewis, Jordan D., 223; (illus.), 234
Lewis, Rose, 156
Libel suits, 111–12, 248, 256
Lilly, Eli, 134
Limestone industry, 205
Lincoln, Abraham, 44, 54, 55, 56, 58, 64, 66, 68, 69, 72
Lindbergh Act (1932), 145
Lipsey, Charles, 251
Liveontheweb.com, 255
Local Rules, 230
Locke, Theodore L., 167
Locke Reynolds (law firm), 155
Lockefield Gardens, 156
Lorch, Basil H., III, 226; (illus.), 224
Lord Byron, 270
Los Angeles Times, 118
Louisiana, 14, 15
Louisiana Purchase, 14
Lugar, Richard G., 203, 215, 217

Madison, James, 2, 4, 271
Madison County Jail, 256
Magistrates, 25, 87, 184–87, 209, 222–23
Mail fraud, 114–15
Mann Act, 125, 156, 262
A Manual for Executors, Administrators, and Guardians, with Forms Adapted to the Statutes of Indiana, 93
Marion County Jail, 256
Marshall, Thurgood, 199

Marshals, 24, 26, 91
Martin, William, 31
Master in chancery, 90
Maxwell's Code, 8
McCarty, Virginia Dill, 184, 231
McCray, Warren T., 114, 115; (illus.), 115
McDonald, David, 51, 54, 57–59, 60–61, 63, 66–68, 70, 72, 101; (illus.), 52
McGuire and Shook (architects), 153
McHale, Frank, 163
McKinley, William, 104, 118
McKinney, Frank, 163, 164
McKinney, Larry J., 212, 214, 215, 219, 230, 245, 253; (illus.), 175, 214
McLean, John, 27, 58, 68, 69
McManigal, Ortie, 118, 119
McNamara, James, 118–19
McNamara, John, 118–19
McNutt, John, 92
McVeigh, Timothy, 252, 255
Meat Inspection Act (1906), 125
Meek, Brazil, 30
Meigs, Return Jonathan, 7, 8
Merit Selection Committee, 217
Methamphetamine, 264–65
Metz, Anthony J., III, 226; (illus.), 224
MGM, 205
Midwest Liquidators, 221
Migratory Bird Treaty Act (1918), 125
Military tribunals, 53, 63, 64–65, 66, 70
Miller, David, 223
Miller, Warren Drake, 152
Milligan, Lambdin P., 65, 69, 70; (illus.), 67

Minton, Sherman, 150–51, 188; (illus.), 150
Minton-Capehart Federal Building, 188
Monks, Leander, 8, 16, 24
Monroe, James, 22
Montplaiseur, Andrew, 2
Moore, Harbin, 24
Moore, Joseph M., 45
Morning Star (passenger steamer), 101
Morris-Butler House, 134
Motley, Constance Baker, 199
Motor Vehicle Air Pollution Control Act (1965), 244
Munich (Germany), 266, 268
Mural: Knox County Courthouse, 1
Murder cases, 187

National Association for the Advancement of Colored People (NAACP), 198, 199, 200, 203, 217
National Conference of Bankruptcy Judges, 177
National Environmental Policy Act (1970), 244
National Firearms Act of 1934, p. 145
National Motor Vehicle Act of 1919. *See* Dyer Act (1919)
National Stolen Property Act of 1934, p. 145
Naturalization, 153
Naville, Michael G., 223, 234; (illus.), 234
New, Henry, 113
New Albany, 87, 88; courthouse, 88–89, 188; federal building, 189
New Albany Commercial, 72
New Deal, 145, 149, 150, 152, 244

Newton, Michael, 256
Niblack, John, 114, 126
Nicholas, Connie, 187
Nixon, Richard M., 160, 171
Noel, James, 108
Noland, James E., 171–73, 176, 185, 191, 194–95, 196, 212, 219, 228–29, 230, 262, 264, 265, 266, 267, 268; (illus.), 172
Northwest Ordinance, 2, 5–6, 10, 11, 102; and courts, 6–7; and slavery, 15, 35
Northwest Territory, 268; division of, 1, 10, 11; court of, 7–10

O'Bannon, Frank, 215
Oare, Lenn J., 138
Ochitree, Tom, 98
Ohio, 11
Ohio Company, 8
Opium Exclusion Act (1909), 125–26
Orbison, Telford, 164
Organized Crime Control Act (1970), 265
Orr, Robert D., 218
Otte, Frank J., 226; (illus.), 224
Owen, Robert Dale, 43

Panama Canal: and libel suit, 111–12
Panics, 30, 75
Pantzer, Kurt, 166, 181
Pardons, 20
Parke, Benjamin, 16, 17, 21, 22, 23, 24, 25, 30, 33, 39–41, 92, 271; (illus.), 17
Parsons, Samuel Holden, 7, 8
Patent law, 78–82, 207, 250–52
Patronage cases, 217–19

Index 331

Pattie, Cyrus E., 138
Payne, Kenneth R., 264
Pelley, William Dudley, 157
Penicillin, 207
Perry, Lincoln Theodore, 203–4
Personal injury cases, 117–18
Petit jury, 27
Pettit, John, 26
Pharmaceuticals, 207–8
Pleadings: styles of, 130–31
Pollution, 244
Ponzi scheme, 264
Pornography ordinance, 258–61
Posner, Richard A., 261
Potter, William, 88
Prisoner cases, 252–58
Pro bono program, 232
Probation, 154
Progressive Era, 244
Prohibition, 125, 143, 145, 151, 155, 156
Prozac, 251
Pulliam, Eugene C., 163, 166–67, 168, 169
Pure Food and Drug Act (1906), 125
Putnam, Rufus, 7, 8

Quayle, Dan, 215

Rabb, Albert L., 110
Racine family, 13
Rankin, John Hall, 128
Rea, John, 90
Reagan, Ronald, 212, 215
Record storage and retrieval, 190
Redman, Eli, 113, 114
Reed, Sam, 223

Reform issues, 31, 37, 38–39, 43–44, 47, 49, 59–61, 75
Rehnquist, William, 65, 231
Remus, George, 144
Republic of Cyprus, 265–70
Republican National Committee, 103
Reynolds, Hugh E., Sr., 167
Rhind, John Massey, 129
Rhodehamel, Harley W., Jr., 208
Richardson, Henry, 199
Richmond Palladium, 60
Roberts, John G., Jr., 151
Robinson, Arthur, 139
Robinson, John, 48
Rockville Republican, 110
Roosevelt, Franklin D., 145, 151, 169
Roosevelt, Theodore, 104, 108, 110, 111, 112–13, 118
Rose, David, 91
Ross, James, 132, 147, 148
Roudebush, Richard, 179–80
Rudd, Louisa, 28
Rust Belt, 247

Safady, Salua, 263
Sanders, Fred C., 256–57
Sandidge, Mary Lucille, 205
Scanlon, Tom, 181
Schaefer, Gerald, 256
Schricker, Henry F., 163
Scott, James, 16
Secret societies, 61, 64, 66, 70
Securities and Exchange Act of 1934, p. 145
Securities and Exchange Commission (SEC), 264
Selective Service, 157

Sentencing guidelines, 197, 265
Service industries, 247, 248
Seventh Circuit Court. *See* U.S. Court of Appeals, Seventh Circuit
Shake, Gilbert, 184
Shawnee Prophet, 20
Shepard, Randall, 271
Sherman, Roger, 2
Sherman Antitrust Act (1890), 125
Shields, V. Sue, 223, 231; (illus.), 234, 259
Shirley, Cassius Clay, 108
Shockley, Ernest, 8
Silver Shirts, 157
Sixteenth Amendment, 126, 127
Slaughter, Robert, 20
Slavery, 15–16, 35, 36, 37, 47, 48, 55, 56
Slaymaker, Locke & Reynolds (law firm), 167
Slick, Thomas W., 137–42
Smith, Caleb Blood, 54–55, 59, 60, 61, 62; (illus.), 53
Smith, Oliver H., 28–29
Smith, Watt, 90
Smollette, Tobias George, 23
Sogmeier, Albert C. "Soggy," 154
"Sons of Liberty," 66, 70
South Bend Tribune, 139, 140
South Shore Line, 118
South Street Post Office, 188
Southwestern Car Company, 102
"Speedway Bomber," 262
Spooner, Benjamin, 77
Sports Car Club of America, 248
St. Clair, Arthur, 8
State Capitol Building (Indianapolis), 242–43

Steckler, William, 145, 147, 158, 160, 162–64, 166, 174–75, 176, 178–79, 180, 181–82, 183, 188, 190, 191, 192, 196, 197, 199, 203, 205, 207, 208, 212, 227–28, 248, 249, 262; (illus.), 162, 175
Steers, Edwin K., 167
Stephenson, D. C., 140
Stipher, Karl, 193
Stone, Harlan F., 137, 143
STP Corporation, 206
Strain, James, 192, 194
Strange, Mike, 221
Streit v. Lauter, 79
Strikes, 75–78, 123
Studebaker Corporation, 206
Sufana, Nicholas W., 220–21, 225
Sun Belt, 247
Symmes, John Cleves, 7, 8, 13
Syndicate Theaters, 205

Taft, Robert, 166
Taft, William Howard, 111, 119
Tally Sheet Forgery Cases (1886), 102–3
Tarsney Act (1892), 128
Tax cases, 29
Tax evasion, 264
Tax exemptions, 243–44
Taylor, E. W., 138
Taylor, Waller, 16, 19
Tecumseh, 20
Teel, Forrest, 187
Terre Haute, 87, 88, 251; federal building, 88, 152, 227
The Third Branch, 182
Thomas, Benjamin, 26

Thompson, William P., 24
Time zones, 206
Tinder, John D., 212, 213, 214–15, 232, 241, 243, 249–50, 255, 256, 263, 264; (illus.), 175, 219
Tinder, John G., 163
Tippecanoe, battle of, 20, 25
Tipton, John, 33
Treason, 65, 66
Treasury Relief Art Project (TRAP), 153
Treat, Samuel, 49
Truman, Harry, 151, 162, 163, 164
Trump, Donald, 247–48
Trusler, Nelson, 83
Tuohy, Martin, 118
Turkish Republic of Northern Cyprus, 266
Turner, George, 7, 8, 11
Turner Glass Company, 155
Turpie, David, 57, 86, 92
Turpin, François, 2
Twenty-first Amendment, 145, 156
Tyler, John, 26, 42, 44
Typographical Union, 99

Ullman, Alice Woods, 95
Uniform Time Act, 206
Unigov, 179, 202–3
Unions, 119–20, 122–24
United Mine Workers, 122–24
United States Auto Club (USAC), 206, 207
United States v. Paramount, 205
U.S. Bankruptcy Court, 177
U.S. Commissioners, 87
U.S. Congress, 1, 14, 18, 21, 26, 64, 85, 160, 187, 206, 223, 236

U.S. Constitution, 2, 7, 10, 35, 62, 99, 161, 180, 224, 236, 271; article 3, pp. 3–4, 65; and the judiciary, 3–5; bicentennial of, 37, 229; Sixth Amendment, 111; Seventeenth Amendment, 114; Eighteenth Amendment, 126; Sixteenth Amendment, 126, 127; Twenty-first Amendment, 145, 155; Fourteenth Amendment, 199; First Amendment, 204, 242, 258, 260, 261; Fourth Amendment, 241; and Interstate Commerce Clause, 245; Eighth Amendment, 255
U.S. Court of Appeals, Seventh Circuit, 124, 131, 134, 135, 151, 154, 157, 192, 202, 203, 217–18, 227, 232, 239, 240, 241, 243, 246, 247, 258, 260, 261
U.S. Courthouse and Post Office Building (Indianapolis), 128–31; renovation of, 225–27; (illus.), 127, 128, 129, 130, 131, 188, 228
U.S. Customs Service, 263
U.S. District Court for the District of Indiana: organization of, 21–24; and commercial law, 24; and business, 24, 30–31, 51, 77, 101–2, 117; structure and personnel of, 24–28, 90, 91; and federal crimes, 29; and Native Americans, 29–30, 102; and reform issues, 31, 37, 38–39, 43–44, 47, 49, 59–61, 75, 107, 125–26; and Civil War, 51, 52–70; drawn into political factionalism, 51, 82–85, 93–101, 102–5, 111, 113, 114; and strikes, 76–78, 98–99, 123; and injunctions,

77–78, 123; and patent law, 78–82; and election fraud, 82–84, 91, 102–4; federal building program for, 88, 126–30; and legal professionalism, 92–93; and vigilantism, 99; and admiralty law cases, 101, 117; and libel suits, 111–12; and mail fraud, 114–15; and worker liability cases, 117–18; and labor violence, 118–22; change and continuity in functions of, 130–34; division of, 134–41, 160; procedural changes in, 148; and claims limits, 155. *See also* U.S. District Court for the Southern District of Indiana

U.S. District Court for the Southern District of Indiana: and salaries, 134; creation of, 134–41, 160; fees structure and personnel of, 139, 153–54, 160–61, 176, 177, 184–87, 189–91, 208, 222–27; reform issues, 142, 149, 156; and Prohibition cases, 143–44, 151–52, 154; federal statutes provide cases for, 144–45; and murder cases, 145–47, 187; and antitrust cases, 147–48, 154, 155, 205, 249; and federal building projects for, 151–53; and naturalization, 153; and probation, 153; and bankruptcy cases, 154, 175–76, 223–25; and jurisdiction, 155, 187; and wholesale liquor distribution, 155–56; World War II cases, 156–57; and caseloads, 161, 175, 181, 189, 209, 222–23, 235–37; appointment of, 161–78, 212–17; and political questions, 178–81; and injunctions, 180; internal advisory group for, 181–82; changes in practices and procedures, 181–84, 189, 205, 209, 232; and legal professionalism, 183–84; and changes in facilities, 186–89, 227–29; and record retrieval and storage, 190; and skills of judges, 191–96; and criminal cases, 196; and civil rights, 198–204, 239–41; and desegregation, 200–3, 239–40; and civil liberties, 204; and time zones, 206; and auto racing cases, 207, 248–49; and patent law, 207–8, 250–52; and patronage cases, 217–20; and corruption cases, 219–21; and bankruptcy judgeships, 223–26; and changes in divisions, 226–27; bicentennial of, 227, 228; publications of, 230; and televised trials, 231; and pro bono program, 232; and "Downtown Police Brawl," 238; and curfew law, 241; and church and state issues, 241–44; and environmental cases, 244–46; and gambling cases, 247–48; and Colts lawsuit, 248; and libel suits, 248–49, 256; and health-care cases, 249–50; and death penalty cases, 252–53; and prisoner cases, 252–58; and pornography ordinance, 258–61; and video games, 261; and bombings, 262; and firearms cases, 263–64; and fraud cases, 264; and sentencing guidelines, 265; and Kanakaria mosaics, 265–71. *See also* U.S. District Court for the District of Indiana

U.S. Federal Building (Indianapolis), 87

U.S. Judicial Conference, 182, 185, 230, 231

U.S. Justice Department, 215, 223
U.S. Probation Office, 231
U.S. Senate Judiciary Committee, 215
U.S. Supreme Court, 18, 26, 27, 53, 63, 66, 68, 69, 70, 81, 85, 148, 149–51, 155, 202, 205, 215, 221, 242, 245, 253, 255, 260

Van Buren, Martin, 26, 33, 38
Van Camp Packing, 148
Van Rijn, Michel, 265
Vanderburg, Henry, 1, 13–14, 15, 16
Vandivier, Richard W., 225
Varnum, James Mitchell, 7, 8
Vawter, John, 24
Video games, 261
Vigilantism, 99
Vikan, Gary, 269
Vincennes, 1, 10, 15, 22
Volstead Act (1919), 126
Voorhees, Daniel, 26
Voyles, James, 191, 192, 193, 195

W. B. Conkey Co., 98, 99
Wabash Valley Ordnance Plant, 157
Walker, Applegate, Oakes and Ritz (architects), 189
Washington, George, 7
Waterhouse, Benjamin, 48
Watkins v. Miller, 253–55
Watkins, Jerry E., 253–55
Watson, James E., 136, 137, 143
Wayne, Anthony, 13
We Fight for This Republic Only, 157
Webster, Humphrey, 24

Welch, William, 194
Western Reserve, 11
Whiskey Ring, 74, 75
White Caps, 99
White Slave Traffic Act (1910). *See* Mann Act
White, Albert Smith, 54, 55–57, 59, 61–62, 63, 66; (illus.), 56
White, John Haxen, 138
White, Joseph L., 42
Wholesale liquor distribution, 155–56
Williams, Brian, 223
Wilson, James, 2
Wilson, Woodrow, 123, 124
Wishard, _____ (district attorney), 100
Wolf, John, 262–63
Women's Christian Temperance Union, 143
Woods, Floyd, 96
Woods, William Allen, 87, 93, 94–96, 97, 98, 102–4; (illus.), 86
Woollen, William, 41, 55
Worker liability cases, 117–18
Works Progress Administration (WPA), 156
World Wide Web, 232

Yeager, Ralph O., 152
Young, Richard L., 212, 213, 215, 250–52, 271; (illus.), 216
Young, Roseann (illus.), 216

Zenor, William Taylor, 31
Zyprexa, 250–52